Writing the Renaissance
Essays on Sixteenth-Century French Literature
in Honor of Floyd Gray

FRENCH FORUM MONOGRAPHS

77

Editors **R.C. LA CHARITÉ and V.A. LA CHARITÉ**

For complete listing, see page 232

Writing the Renaissance

Essays on Sixteenth-Century
French Literature
in Honor of Floyd Gray

Edited by
Raymond C. La Charité

FRENCH FORUM, PUBLISHERS
LEXINGTON, KENTUCKY

Copyright © 1992 by French Forum, Publishers, Incorporated, P.O.
Box 130, Nicholasville, Kentucky 40430.

Library of Congress Catalog Card Number 91-73985

ISBN 0-917058-81-X

Printed in the United States of America

Contents

PREFACE   7

TABULA GRATULATORIA   11

LIST OF THE PUBLISHED WRITINGS OF FLOYD GRAY   13

Part I
Rabelais

RAYMOND C. LA CHARITÉ
Originality and the Alimentary Design
of Rabelais's *Pantagruel*   19

TOM CONLEY
Du mot à la carte: Verbal Cartographies
of *Gargantua* (Ch. 33)   29

TERENCE CAVE
The Death of Guillaume Du Bellay:
Rabelais's Biographical Representations   43

MARCEL TETEL
Le Physetère bicéphale   57

MICHEL JEANNERET
Rabelais, les monstres, et l'interprétation
des signes (*Quart Livre* 18-42)   65

Part II
Marot, Pernette du Guillet,
Du Bellay, Ronsard

GÉRARD DEFAUX
Clément Marot: poésie, autobiographie et roman 79

ROBERT D. COTTRELL
Pernette Du Guillet and the Logic of Aggressivity 93

ROBERT GRIFFIN
Du Bellay's Wisdom: Judgment and Desire 115

GLYN P. NORTON
Du Bellay and the Emblematics of Regret 131

GREGORY DE ROCHER
Ronsard's Dildo Sonnet: The Scandal of Poissy
and Rasse des Nœux 149

Part III
Montaigne

RICHARD L. REGOSIN
Montaigne's Child of the Mind 167

LAWRENCE D. KRITZMAN
Montaigne's Fantastic Monsters
and the Construction of Gender 183

FRANÇOIS RIGOLOT
Sur des vers de Montaigne: La Boétie en Béotie 197

GISELE MATHIEU-CASTELLANI
Crise dans les *Essais* 211

ANDRÉ TOURNON
"Un langage coupé . . ." 219

Preface

No matter how one might wish to assess the field of French Renaissance studies today, Floyd Gray would appear at the very top of any list. For those of us who are fortunate enough to know him, not just as the superb scholar everyone has come to appreciate but also as the dedicated teacher and devoted friend he has been to so many, it is an honor and a rare privilege as his students, colleagues, and friends to come together in this volume to recognize his achievements and to praise his qualities and commitment to the highest professional standards.

Floyd Gray has attained the reputation and eminence he now enjoys on the basis of more than 35 years of outstanding teaching and through published writings whose power, passion and lucidity remain a model for all of us to follow.

Throughout his career, as teacher and as scholar-critic, he has remained committed to the primacy of the text, to the elucidation of the literariness of the great masterpieces of French literature. It is also of the greatest significance—and a measure of the man—that he set out on this path at a time when French Renaissance studies were mired in traditional approaches and pursuits. He was thus a pioneer in our field, in fact almost a loner in the late fifties and sixties, and he continues today upon that steady course.

His work has had a seminal effect. His approach to style, for example, as evidenced in his work on Montaigne, has been repeatedly used and praised in similar studies throughout the spectrum of French scholarship. Indeed, the impact of his incisive and fertile mind has gone far beyond the confines of the Renaissance period.

Our understanding today of Rabelais, Montaigne, Du Bellay, and La Bruyère owes a great deal to his uncanny ability to retrieve the writerly art that gives life to their works. Perhaps more than anyone else in our field, he has showcased the dynamics of the Renaissance's urge to write and to poeticize while striving intertextually to become itself through Ancient literature.

In order to judge the achievements of such a consummate professional, it does not suffice to list the number and range of publications, although many and enviable, or the number of dissertations directed, although impressive (almost 40) and therefore a significant measure of the man's appeal and impact on students at the University of Michigan. Too often we fail to recognize one basic fact in our scholarly lives: most of us owe the richness, the vibrancy, and the sense of accomplishment of our own careers to but a very select few of our colleagues. No one writing today in the field of French Renaissance literature can do so without recognizing and acknowledging Floyd Gray's steady, gentle, and guiding presence.

When told of this project, his former students reacted enthusiastically and offered their support. However, what impressed me most was that their replies contained thoughtful and unsollicited remarks about the man, the teacher, and the scholar. Their admiration and respect were overwhelming and touching, and I would be remiss if I did not include the following statement, which best exemplifies the high esteem his students, past and present, have for him: "Le Professeur Gray mérite bien l'hommage collectif qui lui est rendu, une marque aussi bien de respect que de reconnaissance. Il s'est consacré à ses tâches—dans l'enseignement, la recherche et la publication—avec un rare dévouement. Il s'est identifié avec son 'ministère' multiple comme quelqu'un qui serait entré dans les ordres.... Sa maîtrise des sujets, l'équilibre de ses cours continuellement renouvelés, sa rigueur à l'égard de soi-même et de ses étudiants, ses fréquentes allusions aux plus récentes publications pour encourager des habitudes d'érudits consciencieux, la droiture et la cohérence de ses convictions—le tout assaisonné d'un humour fin et varié, malgré un soupçon de timidité sous-jacente—sans oublier l'ouverture, la disponibilité ou l'aide discrète dans des situations difficiles: ses qualités et son exemple ont influencé des générations de disciples et donnent la vraie mesure de l'homme derrière le professeur. Je m'estime privilégié et honoré d'avoir été parmi ses étudiants" (Pietro E. Copiz).

A teacher-scholar of this calibre merits our accolade and affection, and this volume is meant to convey to Floyd Gray what he has meant and will continue to mean to his students, colleagues, and many friends throughout the profession.

Raymond C. La Charité

Tabula Gratulatoria

Arthur E. Babcock
Mary J. Baker
Cathleen M. Bauschatz
Jean S. Bidwell
Vincent and Barbara Bowen
James A. Boyse
Frieda S. Brown
Terence Cave
Tom Conley
Pietro E. Copiz
Robert D. Cottrell
Gérard Defaux
JoAnn DellaNeva
Gregory de Rocher
Diane Desrosiers-Bonin
Mia De Weer-D'Hooghe
Lance K. Donaldson-Evans
Edwin Duval
E. Thomas Ezell
†Stiles and Jane Ezell
Michèle Farrell
Gemma M. Galli
Perry J. Gethner
Hope H. Glidden
John Graham
Eugene F. Gray
Robert Griffin

Joyce M. Hanks
Patrick G. Henry
Ralph M. Hester
Hollins College
University of Hull
    Brynmor Jones Library
Michel Jeanneret
L.W. Johnson
Ellen R. Justice-Templeton
Ann Sorey Kirkland
Lynn E. Klausenburger
Charlotte Costa Kleis
Lawrence D. Kritzman
Raymond C. La Charité
Virginia A. La Charité
Ullrich Langer
Carleen LePage
Kenneth Lloyd-Jones
Deborah N. Losse
Germain Marc'hadour
Chantal A. Marechal
Nadia Margolis
Gisèle Mathieu-Castellani
Mary B. McKinley
Marianne S. Meijer
Hassan Melehy
Anna L. Miller

Nicole F. Minnick
Jerry C. Nash
Fred J. Nichols
Glyn P. Norton
Ray Ortali
Keith A. Palka
François Paré
Allan H. Pasco
Isabelle Peltier
George A. Petrossian
Dora E. Polachek
David Matthew Posner
Christine McCall Probes
University of Puget Sound
Richard L. Regosin
Regine Reynolds-Cornell
François Rigolot
Danièle Rodamar

Daniel Russell
Martine Sauret
Richard Shryock
Cynthia Skenazi
Isidore Silver
Michel Simonin
Pauline M. Smith
Marianna K. Staples
Marcel Tetel
André Tournon
Elie R. Vidal
Marcelle M. Welch
Janet S. Whatley
Colette H. Winn
Diane S. Wood
Cathy Yandell
Ruth G. Zibart

List of the Published Writings of Floyd Gray

I. Books

Le Style de Montaigne. Paris: Nizet, 1958.

Montaigne, textes d'Albert Thibaudet établis, présentés et annotés par Floyd Gray. Paris: Gallimard, 1963.

Anthologie de la poésie française du XVIe siècle. New York: Appleton-Century-Crofts, 1967.

Rabelais et l'écriture. Paris: Nizet, 1974.

La Poétique de Du Bellay. Paris: Nizet, 1978.

Textes et Intertextes: études sur le XVIe siècle pour Alfred Glauser. Edited by Floyd Gray and Marcel Tetel. Paris: Nizet, 1979.

Poétiques. Edited by Floyd Gray. *Michigan Romance Studies* 1 (1980).

La Balance de Montaigne: exagium/essai. Paris: Nizet, 1982.

La Bruyère: amateur de caractères. Paris: Nizet, 1986.

Montaigne bilingue: le latin des Essais. Paris: Champion, 1991.

II. Translations

Voltaire. *Candide and Other Writings.* Trans. Floyd Gray. New York: Modern Library, 1956.

Rabelais. *Gargantua and Pantagruel: Selections.* Translated and Edited by Floyd Gray. New York: Appleton-Century-Crofts, 1966.

III. Articles

"La Boîte de Montaigne." *Nouvelle Revue Française* 92 (1960) 385-92.

"Montaigne's Friends." *French Studies* 15 (1961) 203-21.

"Montaigne and the *Memorabilia*." *Studies in Philology* 58 (1961) 130-39.

"The Unity of Montaigne in the *Essais*." *Modern Language Quarterly* 12 (1961) 79-88.

"*Adulescens* and the Date of Rabelais's Birth." *Modern Language Notes* 76 (1961) 733-35.

"Reflexions on Charron's Debt to Montaigne." *French Review* 35 (1962) 377-82.

"Un Inédit d'Albert Thibaudet." *Le Figaro Littéraire* (13 Oct. 1962) 4.

"Structure and Meaning in the Prologue to the *Tiers Livre*." *L'Esprit Créateur* 3 (Summer 1963) 57-62.

"The 'Nouveaux Docteurs' and the Problem of Montaigne's Consistency in the *Apologie de Raymond Sebond*." *Symposium* 18 (Spring 1964) 22-34.

"Réflexions sur Charron et Montaigne." *Bulletin de la Société des Amis de Montaigne* No. 29 (1964) 41-46.

"Montaigne devant Sebond et La Boétie, une question d'ambivalence." *Mémorial du Ier Congrès International des Etudes Montaignistes. Bulletin de la Société des Amis de Montaigne*, Troisième Série, No. 29 bis (1964) 150-55.

"Ambiguity and Point of View in the Prologue to *Gargantua*." *Romanic Review* 56 (1965) 12-21.

"Variations on a Renaissance Theme: The Poetic Landscape and a *Stance* of Agrippa d'Aubigné." *Philological Quarterly* 44 (1965) 433-44.

"Ambiguity and Point of View in the Prologue to *Gargantua*." In *Rabelais*. Ed. August Buck. Darmstadt: Wissenschaftliche Buchgesellschaft, 1973. 397-410.

"Montaigne and Sebond: The Rhetoric of Paradox." *French Studies* 28 (174) 134-45.

"Du Bellay et la poétique de l'anonymat." *French Forum* 1 (1976) 14-23.

"Montaigne's Pyrrhonism." In *O un amy! Essays on Montaigne in Honor of Donald M. Frame*. Ed. Raymond C. La Charité. French Forum Monographs 5. Lexington, KY: French Forum, 1977. 119-36.

"Pragmatisme et naturalisme dans l'*Apologie de Raimond Sebond*." In *Textes et Intertextes: études sur le XVIe siècle pour Alfred Glauser*. Eds. Floyd Gray and Marcel Tetel. Paris: Nizet, 1979. 79-92.

"Rabelais." In *A Critical Bibliography of French Literature: The Sixteenth Century*. Volume II, Revised. Ed. Raymond C. La Charité. Syracuse: Syracuse UP, 1985. 182-205.

"Montaigne et La Bruyère: un phénomène intertextuel." In *Crossroads and Perspectives: French Literature of the Renaissance. Essays in Honour of Victor E. Grahm*. Eds. Catherine M. Grisé and C.D.E. Tolton. Travaux d'Humanisme et Renaissance 211. Geneva: Droz, 1986. 221-29.

"Des *Livres* (1580) aux *Trois Commerces* (1588)." In *Montaigne, regards sur les* Essais. Eds. Lane M. Heller and Felix R. Atance. Waterloo, ON: Wilfrid Laurier UP, 1986. 89-98.

"Rabelais's First Readers." In *Rabelais's Incomparable Book: Essays on His Art*. Ed. Raymond C. La Charité. French Forum Monographs 62. Lexington, KY: French Forum, 1986. 15-29.

"Eros et l'écriture: *Sur des vers de Virgile*." In *Le Parcours des* Essais: *Montaigne 1588-1988*. Eds. Marcel Tetel and G. Mallary Masters. Paris: Aux Amateurs de Livres, 1989. 263-72.

"Montaigne et le langage des animaux." In *Le Signe et le Texte: études sur l'écriture au XVIe siècle en France.* Ed. Lawrence D. Kritzman. French Forum Monographs 72. Lexington, KY: French Forum, 1990. 149-59.

"D'Aubigné et l'éros martial." In *Chemins de la connaissance. Mélanges de langue, d'histoire et de littérature française offerts à Enea Balmas.* Eds. Anna Maria Raugei et al. Paris: Klincksieck (1992) (in press).

IV. Reviews

"*Jean Santeuil*: Proust's Lost Novel." *Milwaukee Journal*, Literary Supplement, Feb. 19, 1956.

Amiel, *Journal intime de l'année 1866. French Review* 33 (1960) 115-16.

Raymond Queneau, *Zazie dans le métro. French Review* 33 (1960) 309.

Charles du Bos, *Choix de textes. French Review* 33 (1960) 522-23.

Clément Marot, *Epîtres*, ed. C.A. Mayer. *Symposium* 14 (1960) 308-10.

Manuel de Diéguez, *Rabelais par lui-même. French Review* 35 (1961) 107-08.

Henry de Montherlant, *Fils de personne*, ed. France Anders. *Modern Language Journal* 48 (Nov. 1964) 457.

Henry de Montherlant, *Le Chaos et la Nuit. French Review* 37 (1964) 496-97.

Frieda S. Brown, *Religious and Political Conservatism in the* Essais *of Montaigne. Romanic Review* 56 (1965) 64-65.

Henry de Montherlant, *Le Maître de Santiago*, ed. Lucille Becker and Alba Della Fazia. *Modern Language Journal* 50 (Feb. 1966) 113-14.

Jean Mesnard, *Pascal et les Roannez. French Review* 40 (1966) 289.

Saint-Evremond, *Œuvres en prose*, ed. René Termois. *French Review* 40 (1966) 299.

Marcel Tetel, *Le Comique de Rabelais. Symposium* 20 (1966) 89-91.

André Mage de Fiefmelin, *Images*, ed. Pierre Menanteau. *French Review* 40 (1967) 835-36.

Philip P. Hallie, *The Scar of Montaigne: An Essay in Personal Philosophy. Romanic Review* 59 (1968) 219-20.

Odette de Mourgues, *Racine: or, The Triumph of Relevance. French Review* 41 (1968) 734-35.

Raymond C. La Charité, *The Concept of Judgment in Montaigne. Bulletin de la Société des Amis de Montaigne* No. 17 (1969) 44-45.

Donald M. Frame, *Montaigne's* Essais: *A Study. L'Esprit Créateur* 10 (Summer 1970) 158-59.

Jacques Bailbé, *Agrippa d'Aubigné, poète des Tragiques. French Review* 43 (1970) 688-90.

Agrippa d'Aubigné, *Les Tragiques*, ed. I.D. McFarlane. *French Review* 45 (1971) 274-75.

Jacques Grévin, *César*, ed. Ellen S. Ginsberg. *Modern Language Journal* 56 (1972) 470.

John F. Winter, *Visual Variety and Spatial Grandeur: A Study from the Sixteenth to the Seventeenth Century in France*. *Renaissance Quarterly* 30 (1977) 55-56.

Ruth Mulhauser, *Maurice Scève*. *Modern Language Journal* 62 (1978) 135.

Richard L. Regosin, *The Matter of My Book: Montaigne's* Essais *as the Book of the Self*. *Modern Language Journal* 39 (1978) 191-93.

John C. Lapp, *The Brazen Tower: Essays on Mythological Imagery in the French Renaissance and Baroque*. *French Review* 52 (1979) 636-37.

Timothy J. Reiss, *Tragedy and Truth: Studies in the Development of a Renaissance and Neoclassical Discourse*. *Sub-stance* 29 (1981) 111-12.

Robert D. Cottrell, *Sexuality/Textuality: A Study of the Fabric of Montaigne's* Essais. *Renaissance Quarterly* 35 (1982) 306-09.

Keith Cameron, ed., *Montaigne and His Age*. *Renaissance Quarterly* 35 (1982) 306-09.

Raymond C. La Charité, *Recreation, Reflection and Re-creation: Perspectives on Rabelais's* Pantagruel. *L'Esprit Créateur* 21 (1981) 111.

Jules Brody, *Lectures de Montaigne*. *French Forum* 8 (1983) 181-82.

André Tournon, *Montaigne: la glose et l'essai*. *Renaissance Quarterly* 37 (1984) 294-96.

Barbara C. Bowen, *Words and the Man in French Renaissance Literature*. *French Review* 57 (1984) 869-70.

Joyce Main Hanks, *Ronsard and Biblical Tradition*. *French Review* 58 (1984) 282-83.

Ullrich Langer, *Rhétorique et intersubjectivité:* Les Tragiques *d'Agrippa d'Aubigné*. *French Review* 59 (1985) 886-87.

Gérard Defaux, ed., *Montaigne: Essays in Reading*. *Revue d'Histoire Littéraire de la France* 85 (1985) 76-77.

Agrippa d'Aubigné, *Histoire universelle*, ed. André Thierry. *French Review* 58 (1985) 446-47.

Gérard Defaux, *Marot, Rabelais, Montaigne: l'écriture comme présence*. *French Forum* 13 (1988) 369-70.

Henri Weber, *A travers le seizième siècle*. *Continuum* 1 (1989) 259-62.

Jean Céard and Jean-Claude Margolin, eds., *Rabelais en son demi-millénaire. Actes du colloque international de Tours*. *Renaissance Quarterly* 42 (1989) 346-47.

Edwin M. Duval, *The Design of Rabelais's* Pantagruel. *French Forum* 17 (1992) 94-96.

David Lewis Schaefer, *The Political Philosophy of Montaigne*. *Renaissance Quarterly* (in press).

Part I
Rabelais

Raymond C. La Charité

Originality
and the Alimentary Design
of Rabelais's *Pantagruel*

> N'oubliez pas l'art tout de même. Y a pas que la
> rigolade, y a aussi l'art.
> Raymond Queneau, *Zazie dans le métro*[1]

Rabelais's *Pantagruel*, the "commencement de l'Histoire horrificque" (385) of "le meilleur petit bon homme qui fust d'ici au bout d'un baston" (376), is an acclaimed masterpiece whose sense of configuration and deployment critics were slow to discern.[2] Too often its readers judged it in light of an esthetic that was not its own. Admired and praised in terms of some of its parts, *Pantagruel* was long perceived as a somewhat sloppy and hurried fiction, loosely and tenuously modeled on the heroic epic, without real compositional thrust and with little or no narrative syntax.

In the course of the last 20 years, a number of studies have shown the extent to which *Pantagruel* is indeed a coherent whole and its author much more than a fledgling apprentice in his craft.[3] Perceptive and convincing analyses have clearly delineated the book's serio-comic manipulation of the arbitrariness of signs, sophistry, and redemptive typology. Notions of order and unity, design, narrative logic, and management of structural elements no longer seem out of place in critical discussions of *Pantagruel*. It now seems possible in fact to approach the book as a finished product, one whose complex configuring systems work their way methodically and inevitably toward closure.

Rabelais's closural practice in *Pantagruel* is by no means simple nor readily discernible, but attention to its many manifestations reveals that Rabelais has crafted his mock epic with considerable care. Edwin M. Duval has shown, for example, that Pantagruel's "Messianic" mission reaches its climactic moment in chapter 29 when, in single combat and with the approval ("Fais ainsi, et tu auras victoire") and help (". . . si Dieu n'eust secouru le bon

Pantagruel . . . ," 362) of God, he defeats and slaughters the villainous Loup Garou "tout armé d'enclumes Cyclopicques" (347). As a result, Anarche's grab for power and invasion ("les Dipsodes estoyent yssus de leurs limites, et avoyent gasté un grand pays de Utopie, et tenoyent pour lors la grande ville des Amaurotes assiegée," 335) is crushed, the people of Amaurotes are liberated (ch. 31) as Pantagruel is greeted "en grande pompe triumphale, avecques une liesse divine" (374), and the overpowering and occupation of Dipsodie begin (chs. 31-32). In this way, what Gargantua foresaw at Pantagruel's birth ("voyant, en esprit de prophetie, qu'il seroit quelque jour dominateur des alterez," 231) comes to pass as Pantagruel, now "Roy des Dipsodes" (his rank and kingdom already heralded in the title), substitutes his authority and reign for that of Anarche.

The redemptive model thus actuates an overall sense of closure; the narrative movement of the work is magnetized by an end, by the sense of an ending. However, *Pantagruel* also points toward other ends—complementary to be sure. As a work of deliverance, it energizes change, transformation, and cleansing in other ways. Moreover, the book has several closural episodes, each dependent upon a different delimitation and definition of its textual boundaries. A few of these final chapters are still considered unrelated extras, but examination of their disposition in the economy of things—concocted in the book's elaborate beginning—shows that they function within that important strand of meaning strewn about the text, namely its struggle to be itself, a new form.

The seeds of closure for these complementary episodes are planted in the post-Edenic ground of chapter one in general and more specifically within the magic "mesles," a fruit whose unparalleled fictional powers conform to the fructification of the earth in Genesis: "And God said, Let the earth bring forth grass, the herb yielding seed, and the fruit tree yielding fruit after his kind, whose seed is in itself, upon the earth: and it was so" (Gn 1.11).

Rabelais's "mesles" of course do more than initiate the narrative. As a fable of desire, they also orchestrate the fictional innovator's search for form and his attempt to gain authority. They are the centerpiece of his intertwining of individual story (Pantagruel), collective history (humankind down to Pantagruel), and the struggle of the text (*Pantagruel*) to be itself as it competes with other fictional forms. It is for this reason that the whole of chapter one, "De l'origine et antiquité du grand Pantagruel," is given over to a deliberate and elaborate retelling of the story of Creation and of the central role of the "mesles" in the ancestry and emergence of the hero.[4]

By playing off Genesis, Rabelais's metaphorics of beginning actuate a totalizing perspective, one which claims textual continuity from the very beginning of time and, in the bargain, channels our reading intertextually while laying the groundwork for a reading that deals with the creative process. Moreover, by assembling various textual forms as possible models in both the prologue and chapter one, Rabelais posits fusional creation as the mainspring of his work.

If Rabelais takes the trouble to establish an origin for his fictional account by embroidering upon his especial model, Genesis or the text of creation, of beginning, it is because he understands that his fiction, if it is to be original and liberative, must lay waste the forms that propel it. Textual quest is, therefore, operative from the very beginning in Rabelais. Absorbing, scrambling, transforming, and blending anything and everything, he collapses and fuses Arabian, Berberine, Roman, Greek, biblical, medieval, and fanciful genealogies in order to extricate his hero's ancestry. As part of the process, the text feasts on an intermingling, confusion, and reversal of pertinent parts of Genesis. The result is the fable of the "grosses mesles," whose volcanic effervescence and engendering vigor stand metonymically for the metaphorics and erotics of history and narrative in *Pantagruel*. By means of the "mesles," a composite of human procreation/proliferation and textual energetics, Rabelais establishes the foundation of an alimentary epic within which Alcofribas and Pantagruel together explore the production and generation of texts.

If I refer to Pantagruel's eventual dominion over one and all as the "reign of the 'grosses mesles,'" it is because the "mesles" are the symbol of *Pantagruel* as both founding epic and innovative form. They stand at the "commencement du monde" and at the beginning of the fiction, but, whereas Genesis focuses on God and the creation of man, Rabelais's account dwells on the refashioning of man by the all-powerful "mesles." At the outset, they subvert and upend known textuality by supplanting the quest for order, measurement, and relationship that characterizes the unfolding plan of the "beginning" in Genesis. In its place, the "mesles" install themselves as the primordial element and unleash merry and beneficent upheaval, deviation, diversity, and wild growth. It cannot be otherwise since they are the product of an "espoventable" mixup; whereas in Genesis the spilling of Abel's blood leads to anathema and the promise of a nomadic and barren life, in Rabelais the earth, apparently unaccountably unproductive by other means, is so fertilized by the "sang du juste," and its bounty in "mesles" so great that the year's harvest is commemorated in the annals of man as "l'année des grosses mesles."

Naturally then, like the birth of Pantagruel later, their emergence and powers of transformation are heralded by highly unusual activity, "qui sont cas bien espoventables" (222); stars leave their normal cluster, celestial movement accelerates, the moon veers from its normal course, and the sun begins to stumble to its left. Of course, the calendar and temporality follow suit; the Romans predate the Greeks, mid-August emerges in the month of May, and "la sepmaine des troys jeudis" ushers in the nine-day week. In fact, the impossibilia are such that the narrator is barely able to recall whether it all took place "On moys de octobre . . . ou bien de septembre."

Hence, the "mesles" come into their own under the sign of confusion and conflation; they rise from collapse. But, paradoxically, their "grande vertu et puissance," hidden seductively beneath and within their beauty and flavor ("car elles estoient belles à l'œil et delicieuses au goust"), is dilation. Happy but unsuspecting eaters ("Faictes vostre compte que le monde voluntiers mangeoit desdictes mesles") begin to grow and expand in different directions; while some protrude and curve outward ("aulcuns enfloyent par le ventre," "Les aultres enfloyent par les espaules," 223) and still others increase in bodily length ("Aultres croyssoient par les jambes," 223; "Les aultres croissoyent en long du corps," 224), there are even those whose facial ("Es aultres . . . croissoit le nez. . . . Aultres croissoyent par les aureilles") and sexual parts ("Les aultres enfloyent en longueur par le membre. . . . Aultres croissoient en matiere de couilles," 223) bear the brunt—or the bragging rights—of the physical fermentation wrought by the "mesles."

Indeed, they all get more than they bargain for, but, unlike Noah, "le sainct homme (auquel tant sommes obligez et tenuz de ce qu'il nous planta la vine, dont nous vient celle nectaricque, delicieuse, precieuse, celeste, joyeuse et deïficque liqueur qu'on nomme le piot)" [222], they are not immobilized and diminished by their ingestion of "mesles." On the contrary, invigorated and inspired, they become "gens de bien et bon raillars" (223), "amateurs de purée septembrale" (224), writers ("de ceste race yssit Esopet, duquel vous avez les beaulx faictz et dictz par escript," 223; "Nason et Ovide en prindrent leur origine," 224), and capable and prolific engenderers.

At the close of the episode, Alcofribas teases his narratees. "Avés vous bien le tout entendu?" (228) he asks. Clearly, there is much more going on in this "hysterically deliberate" opening than is required for the introduction and birth of Pantagruel in chapter two.[5] In fact, what we witness in the tale of the "grosses mesles" is the birthing of Rabelaisian practice. The whole of his work is in fermentation here; the fable of the "grosses mesles" is the fable of narrative.[6]

Rabelais gets underway by toying with beginning and a search for origins. Using Genesis as the authorizing subtext of his fiction, he not only motivates his tale of adventure historically but also foregrounds creation and his creative process. While procreation is hammered out repeatedly in the extended list of engenderings, thus legitimizing Pantagruel and laying the groundwork for his role as conquering and founding hero, textual creation emerges through the fusion of the alimentary and the body, "mesles" and man. Michel Jeanneret has shown that, whenever food is in the offing in Rabelais, narrative cannot be very far away.[7] Indeed, in chapter one, it seeks to burst and bubble forth, to break out into the open. Ingestion and literary creation go hand in hand and, like Noah's "piot," the "mesles" initiate change. As the unwary bodies distend, new and different forms appear. Dilation and transformation of the human/textual body are therefore the result of admixture, of "mesles," the originating force of Rabelaisian narrative.

To be sure, everything in Rabelais is mediated by physiology, and the association of textuality with food and the body goes all the way back to Antiquity. What is truly original about Rabelais's orchestration is that, by means of the "mesles," he not only dramatizes the uncontrollable and explosive eruption of his text and its statement as form, but also positions the digestive/intestinal tract as the metaphorical conduit through which his narrator and hero will take the measure of one another and of the achievement of their fictional exploration.

Understandably, Alcofribas waxes poetic about "ce beau et gros fruict" (222), for it is the perfect embodiment of *Pantagruel* as narrative act. And it is for this reason that Rabelais chooses to call it a "mesle." While it is true that a "mesle" or medlar functions quite nicely if it is imperative to specify what remains unidentified beyond the word *fruit* in Genesis, Rabelais could have just as easily chosen to call it a *pomme* or some other fruit. However, he calls his fantastic specimen a "mesle" because of its homonymic play on the equally feminine noun *mesle* or *melle* (< *mesler*), that is *mélange*, a mixture.[8] Aptly associated as well with passion, quarrel, accumulation and confusion, the word *mesle* articulates for the magic "mesles" the very components of their textual birth and powers: transposition, hybridization, fusion. Hence, the "grosses mesles" launch a nutritional narrative whose basic recipe is mashing and mixing.

In answer to Pantagruel's prayer prior to battle (ch. 29), God promises "'*Hoc fac et vinces*'; c'est à dire: 'Fais ainsi, et tu auras victoire'" (362). The single combat between Loup Garou and Pantagruel is ferocious and bloody and, at its conclusion Loup Garou is dead, defeated, and headless, and his 300 gigantic cohorts lie lifeless as well. Victorious but exhausted, Pantagruel shows his final contempt for Loup Garou by tossing what is left of him against the walls of the city and collapses: "et tomba comme une grenoille sus ventre en la place mage de ladicte ville" (365). His "prouesses" are clearly over, his mission almost complete, and the end of the fiction is at hand.

In chapter 30, in the midst of reinvigorating "flaccons" (365), Pantagruel witnesses the resuscitation of Epistemon and hears his report of the "estrange façon" (367) in which the inhabitants of the netherworld are punished. Although dilatory in the extreme, the episode belongs where it is in the narrative of conquest; in the aftermath of war, sentencing and punishment come naturally. Decorations and rewards as well (ch. 31): Pantagruel indentures Anarche to Panurge, who, inspired by Epistemon's account of how the "gros seigneurs en ce monde icy, guaingnoyent leur pauvre meschante et paillarde vie là bas" (371), marries him off to "une vieille lanterniere" (376) and starts his training as a hawker of green sauce in order to teach him to be an "homme de bien": "Ces diables de roys icy ne sont que veaulx, et ne sçavent ny ne valent rien, sinon à faire des maulx es pauvres subjectz, et à troubler tout le monde par guerre, pour leur inique et detestable plaisir. Je le veulx mettre à mestier, et le faire crieur de saulce vert."

While the immediate battle has been won, Anarche defeated, and "la ville des Amaurotes" (Badebec's birthplace) liberated, Pantagruel, as the cautious tactician and astute politician he is, recognizes that "ce pendent que le fer est chault il le fault batre" (374). Portions of chapters 31 and 32 are naturally devoted to preparations for the invasion of Dipsodie and the quelling of resistance on the part of the Almyrodes, who confront the migrating "enfans d'Israel" (375) and advancing "bande" (377) determined to colonize and populate Dipsodie, alleviating in the process overcrowding and overpopulation among the Amaurotes. Because of the "grosse housée de pluye" (377-78) encountered by the mop-up operation and the concomitant disappearance of the narrator/chronicler within Pantagruel himself, the final skirmish is not de-scribed. However, the whole of Dipsodie greets Pantagruel as conquering hero. His destiny is now fulfilled, and the *geste* of Pantagruel ends, just as readers of the Bible and epics might expect, on the movement of population.

The story of Pantagruel's ascension to the lofty "mestier" of "Roy des Dipsodes" is clearly over, and, although there will be further adventures to relate, as Alcofribas points out in the epilogue, Pantagruel's attainment and universal acceptance function as closural confirmation. But the story of narrative and its quest is far from over. While the reign of Pantagruel has come into its own, the reign of the "grosses mesles" is not yet ready to hail itself; it lacks a final accounting.

Setting aside the epilogue (ch. 34), Guy Demerson remarks that "Les quatre chapitres de conclusion [30-31-32-33] donnent l'impression de regrouper des épisodes qui, à part l'entrée triomphale dans la ville des Amaurotes, ont été bourrés en fin de volume faute de place au cours du récit."[9] While this assessment is probably an accurate reflection of the majority view with regard to the disposition of the final chapters, it is clearly wrong; the implications of war—its triumphs, defeats, and administrative burdens—justify in and of themselves the subject matter of chapters 31 and 32; therefore, they come naturally and logically after the signal triumph of chapter 29. They belong together and in the order in which we find them; they could not appear elsewhere in the sequential progression of things. As for the combination of chapters 32 and 33, it is the only possible conclusion to the examination and absorption of fictional modes which the text has engineered. Together, these two chapters, like the two devoted to Epistemon and Anarche, settle accounts and bring about closure in their proclamation of an end to the fictional quest and Pantagruel's restoration to good health: "et par ce moyen fut guery et reduict à sa premiere convalescence" (384).

Fittingly, this final exploration takes place within Pantagruel himself. The text goes beyond the dismantling and incorporation of models and dares to plumb and assess itself. Through the use of buccal and stomachal episodes, Rabelais reverses the expected—tales of destruction by means of devouring, tales of travel to exotic and *different* lands—by focusing instead on the creative process associated with penetration and convergence of disparates. While the backdrop for these scenes (Gargantua in the *Chroniques gargantuines*, the story of Jonah, Lucian's *Verae Historiae*) stresses danger and the cavernous dimension of the swallower, Rabelais uses the extraordinary swallowings motif *en fin de texte* as an evacuant agent, an obvious closural procedure, for the creative and fictional struggle which has been at issue from the very beginning.

François Rigolot and Alfred Glauser have shown the extent to which the swallowing of Alcofribas functions as an interrogation of fiction and as a resume of the work as a whole.[10] By descending into his own creation, Alcofribas places himself at center stage as a character, while attempting to experience the effect of his own work. Conversely, the ensuing dialogue between Pantagruel and Alcofribas enables Pantagruel to comment on both the narrator and the fiction.

To be sure, the episode promotes assessment, but the fact of the matter is that there is nothing left for Alcofribas to do but to become one with his endeavor, for therein lies the ultimate struggle, as well as renewal and acceptance. Alcofribas seeks the protective enclosure of Pantagruel's mouth because he has run out of gas; both he and his fiction have exhausted the available models. As a figural embedding of the writerly process, the swallowing of Alcofribas signals that the battle of the texts has run out of steam precisely because the nutritive value of the many forms available has been depleted. Hence, Alcofribas takes refuge in the only form he has left to gauge, the one he has wrought himself.

By coming together face to face as creator and creation, Pantagruel in essence gulping down his chronicler, the text valorizes the absorption and devouring of form which the alimentary thrust of the reign has bodied forth all along. In daring to turn on itself, to feed on itself so to speak, the text comes full circle and acclaims itself as the victor in the clash of forms. Thus, the swallow scene is both a call to order and a celebration of the new fiction's strength and dynamics.

It is for this reason, pace Erich Auerbach, that the scene ends on a conversation between narrator and character and with the awarding of what amounts to scriptural Palmes, the castellany of Salmigondin.[11] In spite of Alcofribas's admission that for more than six months he has been defecating in his master's mouth ("'Voire mais, [dist il], où chioys tu?' 'En vostre gorge, Monsieur, dis je'"), Pantagruel remains very fond of him: "Ha, ha, tu es gentil compaignon, (dist il). Nous avons, avecques l'ayde de Dieu, conquesté tout le pays des Dipsodes; je te donne la chatellenie de Salmigondin." Moreover, Pantagruel does so in spite of the fact that he has had to become his own chronicler due to Alcofribas's long absence, a deficiency of which the narrator is well aware when he thanks Pantagruel, saying "Vous me faictes du bien plus que n'ay deservy envers vous" (381).

If Pantagruel now shows his affection ("tu es gentil compaignon") for Alcofribas—just as he does earlier at the conclusion of Panurge's tale of the lion-fox episode ("tu es gentil compaignon," 299)—it is because he recognizes, as he does in the case of Panurge, that he and Alcofribas are a pair, an inseparable team. Pantagruel understands that together, in their exchange on how and what Alcofribas ate and drank and where he relieved himself, they are articulating the means by which the Rabelaisian text comes into its own. Because he understands that he and Alcofribas have ground their form out of that of others, that they have been energized with innovative vigor by means of admixture, he aptly makes him castellan of Salmigondin, that is, the warden of the Rabelaisian concoction, of the marvelous mess they have invented. By his final words and act in the text, Pantagruel acknowledges Alcofribas's gifts as "meslangeur"-mixer extraordinaire and closes the circle that unites "mesles" and Salmigondin in the thematization of narration as an alimentary act, a mixing and arranging of an assortment of parts gathered hither and yon and served up, not as a mere ragoût, but as a chef's creation, a Salmigondin.[12]

Pantagruel's collapse upon defeating Loup Garou (ch. 29) is now replayed in the illness that assails him in the second of the two swallow stories, "Comment Pantagruel feut malade, et la façon comment il guerit" (ch. 33): "Peu de temps après, le bon Pantagruel tomba malade et feut tant prins de l'estomach qu'il ne pouvoit boire ny manger . . ." (382). The textual struggle is at an end, but it has taken its toll; the redemptive hero who was able to rid the world of its repressive forces is overcome by the accumulation of textual forms he and his narrator have thrown into the pot.[13] Clearly, Pantagruel's illness in the final episode of the book indicates that both he and his fictional quest are ready to exit. The alimentary narrative, so magnificently orchestrated in the opening scene of the book, comes to rest of necessity in a closing, stomachal scene. Why else should Pantagruel be ill and all the more so *at the very end*? Throughout the fiction, the textual/digestive tract has absorbed, mashed, and mixed everything in its path. In the process, it has become itself, but this operation must be memorialized through a final declaration, in a literal cleansing of the mechanism. It is for this reason that Pantagruel's illness and restoration to good health appear where they do in the organization of the fiction; they provide the fictional quest with its own final, cathartic moment. It is at this truly closural point—when Pantagruel disgorges the clean-up crew and their baskets full of "une montjoie d'ordure" (384)—that the embattled hero, "guery et reduict à sa premiere convalescence," and the reign of the "grosses mesles" emerge whole, healthy, and triumphant. With good reason, Alcofribas may now say in the epilogue "This is it!"

Far from being extraneous or flawed, Rabelais's final chapters fulfill in every respect the liberative evacuation that shapes *Pantagruel* and gives it its direction from the very beginning in the prologue. Through its vigorous search for form and joyous struggle for originality, the reign of the "grosses mesles" establishes the foundations of Rabelais's marvelous art and reminds us re-soundingly that "Y a pas que la rigolade, y a aussi l'art."

Notes

[1] Unless otherwise indicated, all references to Rabelais's *Pantagruel* are to vol. 1 of Pierre Jourda's edition of the *Œuvres complètes*, 2 vols. (Paris: Garnier, 1962) and will appear within the text (221). References to the original text (1532) of *Pantagruel* are to V.-L. Saulnier's edition, *Pantagruel* (Paris: Droz, 1965) and appear in the text under the name Saulnier.

[2] Raymond Queneau, *Zazie dans le métro*, Coll. Folio 103 (Paris: Gallimard, 1959) 167.

[3] I cite the pertinent criticism chronologically: Gerard J. Brault, "The Comic Design of Rabelais' *Pantagruel*," *Studies in Philology* 65 (1968) 140-46; Raymond C. La Charité, "The Unity of Rabelais's *Pantagruel*," *French Studies* 26 (1972) 257-65; Gérard Defaux, *Pantagruel et les Sophistes: contribution à l'histoire de l'humanisme chrétien au XVIème siècle* (The Hague: Martinus Nijhoff, 1973); Floyd F. Gray, *Rabelais et l'écriture* (Paris: Nizet, 1974); La Charité, *Recreation, Reflection and Re-Creation: Perspectives on Rabelais's* Pantagruel, French Forum Monographs 19 (Lexington, KY: French Forum, 1980); François Rigolot, "Vraisemblance et narrativité dans le *Pantagruel*," *L'Esprit Créateur* 21 (1981) 53-68; Defaux, *Le Curieux, le glorieux et la sagesse du monde dans la première moitié du XVIe siècle: l'exemple de Panurge (Ulysse, Démosthène, Empédocle)*, French Forum Monographs 34 (Lexington, KY: French Forum, 1982); and Edwin M. Duval, "Pantagruel's Genealogy and the Redemptive Design of Rabelais's *Pantagruel*," *PMLA* 99 (1984) 162-78, and *The Design of Rabelais's* Pantagruel (New Haven: Yale UP, 1991).

[4] For a fuller account of the intertextual interplay between Genesis and Pantagruel and the metaphorics of beginning, see my "Par où commencer? Histoire et récit dans le *Pantagruel* de Rabelais," in *Le Signe et le Texte: études sur l'écriture au XVIe siècle en France*, ed. Lawrence D. Kritzman, French Forum Monographs 72 (Lexington, KY: French Forum, 1990) 79-89.

[5] In his study of the problematics of beginnings, Edward W. Said, *Beginnings: Intention and Method* (New York: Basic Books, 1975) 43-44, identifies "Two obvious, wide-ranging categories of literary starting point" as the "hysterically deliberate (and hence the funnier of the two) and the solemn-dedicated, the impressive and noble."

[6] Marcel Tetel discusses chapter one and its relationship to Rabelaisian thematics in general in "Genèse d'une œuvre: le premier chapitre de *Pantagruel*," *Stanford French Review* 3 (1979) 41-52.

[7] In several articles and in his splendid *Des mets et des mots: banquets et propos de table à la Renaissance* (Paris: Corti, 1987).

[8] "*Mesle, melle* n.f. (1170, Percev.). 1. Mélange. —2. Boucle, anneau. *Mesle a mesle, mesle et mesle* (1175, Chr. de Tr.). *Mesle pesle* (1160, Ben.), pêle-mêle," A.J. Greimas, *Dictionnaire de l'ancien français jusqu'au milieu du XIVe siècle* (Paris: Larousse, 1968) 410. See also Oscar Bloch and W. von Wartburg, *Dictionnaire étymologique de la langue française*, 3rd ed. (Paris: PUF, 1932) 395: "*pêle-mêle*, XIIe (Chrétien), altération (pour éviter la répétition de *m*) de *mesle mesle*, qui se trouve dans les manuscrits du même texte, outre *melle pelle* et des formes plus altérées *brelle mesle, melle et brelle*."

[9] Guy Demerson, *Rabelais* (Paris: Balland, 1986) 171.

[10] François Rigolot, *Les Langages de Rabelais*, Etudes Rabelaisiennes 10 (Geneva: Droz, 1972) 119-22, and "Vraisemblance et narrativité dans le *Pantagruel*," 62-65; Alfred Glauser, *Fonctions du nombre chez Rabelais* (Paris: Nizet, 1982) 210-16.

[11] "Apparently the conversation with the giant, which closes the scene, serves no purpose but that of giving a comical characterization of the kind-hearted Pantagruel, who shows a lively interest in the bodily welfare of his friend, particularly in his being supplied with plenty of good drink, and who good-humoredly rewards his undaunted admission concerning his defecations with the gift of a chatelleny . . ." (234). Erich Auerbach, "The World in Pantagruel's Mouth," in *Mimesis: The Representation of Reality in Western Literature*, trans. Willard Trask (Garden City, NY: Doubleday Anchor Books, 1957) 229-49.

[12] "Salmigondis. . . . C'est proprement un terme de cuisine, désignant une sorte de ragoût." Gloss by Lazare Sainéan, *Pantagruel*, in *Œuvres complètes de François Rabelais*, ed. Abel Lefranc, 6 vols. (1912-55) 4: 336n30. Rabelais scholars traditionally annotate *Salmigondin* as *ragoût*. However, a Salmigondin or Salmigondis is anything but a humble ragoût or stew. In fact, a Salmigondin/dis is what one can create out of leftover ragoût. Specifically, it is a ragoût of *several sorts* of meat reheated. A reheated poultry ragoût, for example, is called a *capillotade*. A Salmigondin/dis is also a chef's salad, a creation consisting of whatever the chef can imagine; it consists of various kinds of meat, eggs, celery and other vegetables. There is an interesting recipe in Randle Cotgrave: "Salmigondin: m. A Hachee; or meat made ordinarily of cold flesh, cut in little pieces, and stewed or boyled on a chafing dish, with crummes of bread, wine, verjuyce, vinegar, sliced Nutmeg, and Orange pills." Randle Cotgrave, *A Dictionarie of the French and English Tongues*, London, 1611, reprinted by William S. Woods (Columbia: U of South Carolina P, 1950) s.v. *Salmigondin*. Oscar Bloch and W. von Wartburg date the appearance of Salmigondis "sous la forme *salmigondin*" as of 1552, an obvious error. *Dictionnaire de la langue française*, 3rd ed. (Paris: PUF, 1960) 562-63. As all readers of Rabelais know, the "chatellenie de Salmigondin" is given to Panurge in the *Tiers Livre*. For an extended study of "le parole alimentari" in *Pantagruel*, see Matteo Majorano, *Percorsi nelle evidenze. Valenze alimentari in "Pantagruel"* (Fasano, It.: Schena, 1988); and for its symbolic dimension, see Françoise Charpentier, "Le Symbolisme alimentaire du *Pantagruel*," in *Pratiques et discours alimentaires à la Renaissance* (Paris: Maisonneuve et Larose, 1982) 219-31.

[13] "L'expédition dirigée dans l'estomac de Pantagruel . . . est donc une autre interrogation de sa créature. . . . Le commentaire que l'on peut tirer de ce court épisode serait la remise en état du héros, après un livre d'aventures, dont il devrait être purgé pour aller au-devant de nouvelles aventures. Annexe scatologique au chapitre de la bouche de Pantagruel, et qui termine la suite des descentes aux Enfers" (Glauser 216).

Tom Conley

Du mot à la carte:
Verbal Cartographies of
Gargantua (Ch. 33)

In his many books on writers of the French Renaissance and classical age,
Floyd Gray shows how style embodies movement and passage. The masters
who fashion the French literary idiom project discourse through time and space
born in writings of total creation. They reach an almost sublime shape of
ekphrasis when, suddenly, graphic montages of writing overtake whatever
meaning had been controlling their descriptions. Style thus comes with
dazzling effects surpassing every cause and intention. All of Floyd Gray's
works therefore tell us that good literature holds no easy or direct relation with
meaning. Movement is a measure of style. For the author of *Le Style de
Montaigne,* transformation and change are so decisive to art and literature that
they can allow us to formulate what might be called *Gray's Law*: to wit, that
great works of art take fragments of recognized and accepted social forms,
overlap and reconfigure them and, through their different combinations, beget
new modes of passage and drive. As his students, in turn, we must strive to think
of the art of criticism in the same vein. The very style of Floyd Gray's analyses
impels us to engender strong forms of reading and writing, in other words, to
create new and complex shapes with materials taken from the traditions in
which we live.

Gray's studies of Rabelais, Du Bellay, and Montaigne do not reconstitute
a fabled object that falls under the rubric of *le seizième siècle*, nor are they
framed by the severe intellectual and methodological limits that *seiziémisme*
tends to impose on its century. Rather, they displace the force of early modern
style into our own world, and therefore make an abundant font of material all
the more vibrant and compelling in the field of our own lives. In a similar
relation to his discipline, early on in his last work, written in transit and passage
from Vienna to London, Freud notes in *Moses and Monotheism* that what we
call "tradition" amounts to "incomplete and blurred memories of the past." It
is only the *artist* who can transform these "gaps in memory according to the
desires of his imagination."[1] Floyd Gray treats of the French Renaissance with

the same creative vision. An artist of the kind Freud imagines, Gray takes a well known corpus—our sixteenth century "canon" inherited from post-nineteenth century literary manuals—and produces readings of enthusing and breathtaking movement. His tact and manner, a model of rhythm and force, are often the substance of analysis.

In the paragraphs that follow I would like to see how the kinds of *montage* that he discovers in Rabelais are constituted from endless flickerings of letters and vocables. Rabelais's writing everywhere articulates movement of forms that at once appear and disappear. Its art of montage derives in part from superimpositions or collages of plastic and verbal material of diverse origin. Quite often, the text appears to be creating verbal pictures that virtually change the contour of everything that inspires them. I do not want to suggest that a cinematic metaphor of montage can be applied to *Gargantua* and *Pantagruel*, but that we might do better by asking if their writing engages movement through a practice that simultaneously divides and binds tracks of verbal and visual expression. Following Gray, I would prefer to argue that the Rabelaisian style is born when inert shapes—typographical letters, nouns, toponyms—are set in motion through thrusts of expression that distort and reconfigure their relations of figure and ground. The style verbalizes common or static information and, in doing so, bends recognizable forms in order to have them move and shift before our eyes.

The tenets of montage can be tested through study of tensions that emerge from comparison of cartography and writing. In the world of Rabelais, emerging practices developing in reeditions of Ptolemy tend to reshape the art of writing. Cartographical space inflects printed material with new perspectives on description and analogy. We know that the first two books, *Pantagruel* and *Gargantua*, engender a world that goes, among many others, by the names of Lerné, Chinon, Tours, Le Gué de Vede, and Thélème. In Rabelais's universe of the 1530s, to name a place is tantamount in the same blow to discovering, surveying, and arrogating it. These acts of nomination that both produce and distort space would also be ones subjecting a common sensibility of the world's extension to pressures of writing. Such is the effect of the rapport of discourse and cartography in one of the more cosmographical moments in *Gargantua*, when "Certains gouverneurs de Picrochole, par conseil précipité, le mirent au dernier péril."[2] In that chapter a common articulation of space is extended through a verbal montage. Units demarcating space (toponyms) and cartographical coordinates are transformed into multiple movements that lead simultaneously in all cardinal directions. The book programmatically globalizes and mirrors itself in ways that had been, for the most part, initially intuited in *Pantagruel*.

In his chapter entitled "Artillerie et imprimerie," on the birth and venture of Rabelais's *écriture*, Gray shows that the enemy of the Gargantuistes,

Picrochole, is a creature not only "délaissé de Dieu" but a sad soul bereft of the good gifts of language. A human stick-figure, his schematic character hardly merits the wealth of allusion in the name that recalls Greece and classical medicine. His advisers (Duke Menuail, Count Spadassin, and Captain Merdaille) stage the beginning of an idiotic "Operation Desert Shield" that will lead two armies in a great pincers movement around the Northern and Southern parts of Europe eastward to the Holy Land. They will retrieve what the Crusades were never able to win over to the West. Conferring together, the four men reproduce a cliché of "mapping and briefing" common to military narrative. Each of their staccato volleys of place-names articulates a sequence in their imaginary conquest of the world. But Picrochole, listening to his counselors, mistakes words for real places: "Les mots deviennent pour lui des réalités, transformés, détournés de leurs possibilités signifiantes: *nommer,* c'est conquérir."[3] The three noblemen name the world for the man who does not have the slightest inkling of its extension. They set notable regions in place, map out its perimeters, and flatter their stupid monarch by setting the sum of the Europe and the East under the innocuous name of Picrochole.

The chapter is ostensibly as much a satire of a lesson in cartography as a rewriting of Lucian's *Dialogues of the Dead* held among Scipio, Minos, Hannibal, and Alexander the Great.[4] Rabelais is said to invert a classical source, in which Hannibal and Alexander outdo each other's braggadocio, turn it into a scene of ridicule, and reshape the materials into both a parable—the moral of the fable of the *pot-au-lait*—and an adventure of style. According to M. A. Screech, the chapter represents a thorny but faithful rendering of French history. Rabelais displaces current events of grand scale, negotiations between Francis I and Charles V, into the microcosm of the Touraine: "Ever since his release from captivity after the defeat of Pavia, Francis I's rivalry with Charles V took on a new dimension: Charles was convinced of French treachery; Francis was embittered by the crippling ransom imposed upon the kingdom and the obligation to send his two oldest children as hostages to the imperial court. The war in *Gargantua* contains overt allusions to these events and is partly conceived as propaganda."[5] An allegory results, in which Picrochole, personifying Charles V, is condemned for having ransomed Francis's children. The preparations laid for the conquest of the world narrated in chapter 33 would thus superimpose Lucian's text on events taking place in 1534. "Mapping" contemporary time according to a classical paradigm, Rabelais would have Charles take Tunis from the hands of the Mulley Hassan and prepare to conquer Constantinople. Screech wonders if the text indeed ridicules the Emperor *before* he wins over Barbarossa or if he satirizes events of 1535, at the very moment when the second edition of *Gargantua* is published. No matter which, for Screech the text alludes to Charles's emblem of the two columns bearing the device *plus oultre* through identity with Hercules's columns (that mark one stage of Picrochole's crusade from Chinon around Western Europe and down to Africa before heading to the Holy Lands, and that are a commonplace illustrated in Ptolemy). Thus, when he wants to conquer the world, the personification of Charles V-Alexander the Great-Picrochole figures as an invincible monarch striking fear in the hearts of the French after the defeats at Pavia (1525) and the loss of Milan (1526). The allegory would prefer to invert the ill-fortunes of France into an imaginary happy-ending where the good Gallic giants win over the pusillanimous Picrochole.

For the reconstruction of the cause or intentions behind the chapter, Screech's interpretation holds firm. But since attention to the symbolic efficacy of the allegory does not emphasize willful distortions of fact, we should ask how the rewriting of Lucian and of history works with the articulation of geographical space. Now in *Rabelais et l' écriture*, Gray notes that the relation of writing and space begins tentatively—almost timorously—when the author follows an itinerary that Pantagruel takes in the course of his education: "Vint à Poitiers . . . vint à Bourdeaulx . . . vint à Thoulouse . . . vint à Montpellier," etc. (91). The education subscribes to a list of cities and towns as displayed in an *itinerarium*. Yet it marks off a verbal extension that, later, can be transformed through more complex treatment of space and language.[6] The linear discourse inferred from the serial aspect of syntax in the early cartographical moments in *Pantagruel* is turned and folded along bending surfaces in chapter 33 of *Gargantua*. Where the initial text discovers and locates a space in a childlike nomination of place-names—in the *balbutie* of style—the later writing reprojects them through allegory, history, and the trials of writing.

The text of *Gargantua* begins from a dialogic matrix. One voice listens to or punctuates the discourse of the three others spoken in unison. Picrochole merely counterpoints [the cursive formula, "—Je (dist Picrochole) . . ." is marked ten times] the rhythm of the collective enumeration [its formula, "—Nous (dirent-ilz) . . ." and its variants printed eleven times] of place-names that come, in the first military movement, in five textual blocks. A chorographic rendering of "Gallia" in their first volley leads South to Spain and Portugal before the discourse crosses Gibraltar ("Vous passerez par l'estroict de Sibyle, et là érigerez deux colonnes plus magnificques que celles de Hercules à perpétuelle mémoire de vostre nom") and moves eastward, to Western North Africa, and Italy (98). They will procede to the Mediterranean Islands before reaching Asia Minor, cross the Caspian Sea (la mer Hircane), Armenia, and arrive at the Euphrates (99). A second army will go north, through Gallia above the Loire, and move to Germany (notably, Lubeck, a center of cartographic production), Scandinavia, Greenland, and the British Isles. It will procede through Poland, the Baltic countries, Russia, and move southward to Hungary, Bulgaria, Turkey, and Constantinople. It will reach the Holy Land in rejoining the other half of the Picrocholine expedition. The sum of the description makes up a world-map of Europe, while each of the seven-odd discursive units can be likened to the conical projections included in all editions of Ptolemy's *Geographia* known since the 1480s. Where, in *Pantagruel*, a local space is fashioned, this chapter superimposes various schemes of extension onto narrative in order to figure the greater curvature of the globe. The serial itinerary begun in the second book is now segmented according to dialogic rhythms of interlocution. Each unit conceivably recalls the arrangement of names in space following the disposition of Ptolemy's atlas, as of 1490, that had been apportioned into twenty-six regional projections following a world map. The text follows the movement (West to East) from Europe to the four sections describing Africa.[7] Each of the advisers' discourses makes up a conically projected map recalling the patterns of names and regions in the sequence of Ptolemy's atlas. The frieze of spatial verbal units that results is animated through the literary interference, on the one hand, of Lucian and, on the other, the tenor of the style coming with the montage of toponyms and their tabular disposition as they appear to be recalled from Ptolemy.

Even though coordination of the dialogue with the projections displays a double inspiration of the Greek writer and Alexandrian geographer, the poetic enumeration of names, because of the analogical and verbal force invested in them, shows that the toponyms cannot be fixed or inlaid as they are in cartographical practices.[8] The toponyms figure in a mobile network of divisible forms—letters—that scatter and mix across each dialogical unit in the chapter and through the entirety of *Gargantua* and *Pantagruel*. Nor does each "reply-projection" follow a law of center and periphery as a structuring agency common to maps and metaphors of the body and space.[9] The names acquire a verbal life of their own by virtue of resemblances seen, like other toponyms, in the letters and characters of other words.

The place-names have an elasticity and contribute to the movement and measure of the volume by virtue of graphic amphiboly. They contain opposing forces in each other and, by cancelling each other's imaginary projection—like the greed of Spadassin, Merdaille, and Menuail—work as a constructively biological form moderating the excess of what is simultaneously being put forward. They offer a counterexample to the outrageous speakers who utter them and hence bring the reader's eyes back from an abstract cosmographical scheme to a literal view of the words themselves.[10] When the conferral begins, the three lords announce obsequiously, "Cyre, aujourd'hui nous vous rendons le plus heureux plus chevalereux prince qui oncques feust depuis la mort de Alexandre Macedo" (97). By marking the western or northern end of the chapter and before recurring at the implicitly eastern or southern terminus, *cyre* serves as an organizing vector, like a windrose or a cardinal indication of latitude ("occidens" and "oriens"). In cartography since the time of the incunabulum, printers occasionally produced maps by arranging words in the form of "figure-poems" whose center is marked by a notable city and whose periphery is disgnated by *septentrio, meridies, oriens* and *occidens* on the four margins.[11] Likewise, *Cyre*, printed first as an oral sign marking hierarchy (abstract vertical extension), ends the chapter in allusion to Cyrus the Great. The recurrence implies that a horizontal course is drawn along the dialogue so as to mark the presence of a parable leading from an origin to a moral end.[12] The vocables of the incipit generate variation by marking their presence in other toponyms. These lead the text into various regions before an orientation is regained at the end. *Cyre* designates Picrochole in the fawning eyes of the three advisors, but also bleeds into their mention of *Cypre* (99), *Célicie, Lydie, Phrygie* (99), *Satalie, Samagarie* (99), *Siriace* (99), and *Surie* (101), especially when the text generates space from the common noun by analogy: "Je vous donne," utters Picrochole about how he will award future spoils to his generals, "la Carmaigne, *Surie* [Syria] et toute Palestine. —Ha! (dirent-ilz) *Cyre*, c'est du bien de vous" (101). The place is verbalized as an effect of the outrageous desire to capture what is being situated in the very *form* of the enunciation, that is, to encircle the very circle the word would ideally draw around the space it designates. Cyre is in Syrie long before Pantagruel can even dream of getting there: "A Bayonne, à Sainct-Jean-de-Luc et Fontarabie *sayzirez* toutes les naufs" (98). Here the *sire* is seized by an endless flow of language that circulates around him. The overweaning drive to reach the Holy Land or eastern region of the map is shown as a mirror-image reproducing the *cirage* of the three sycophants' words. Two cardinal points form an axis from which other figures decline. Schematically:

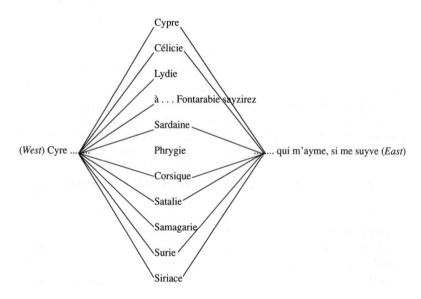

If it foretells of the *pot-au-lait* of Syria to the East, or the endpoint long before it can be reached, *Cyre* also indicates where cartographical and common forms fold over each other. In their dreams the soldiers have already reached the Euphrates: "—Voyrons-nous (dist Picrochole) Babylone et le Mont Sinay?" (99). Because, early in the volume, practice of amphiboly and anagram have been advanced, *Sinay*, a common toponym often illustrated in relief in maps of the Holy Land, can allude both to a variety of *itineraria* as well as to Picrochole himself, *niais*, whose speech avers to be *babil*. All of a sudden the cartography elides qualities, characters, and places. On the one hand, an overriding allegory tends to control the direction that verbal recombination will take, since the staging of the briefing promotes association of *babil* with *Babylone* and *niais* with *Sinay*. But on the other, the verbal process suggests that an unpredictable melding of space and language can take place when discourse and volume become coextensive, or when words are identical to pictures and descriptions of places.

The model for these virtual recombinations effectively extends and twists the borders of both the episode and the book. Two other words, *soubdain* and *transfréter*, follow a broader trajectory that develops the same patterns of textual expansion. When Picrochole loses hold of his advisors' words, he drifts from the position of an active listener to a would-be tourist daydreaming about the aura of the place-names echoing in his ears. He still wonders if he will ever behold Babylon and Sinai, two points often pictured on contemporary maps. Spadassin, Menuail, and Merdaille bring him back to the business at hand: "— Il n'est (dirent-ilz) jà besoin pour ceste heure. N'est-ce pas assez tracassé dea avoir transfrété la mer Hircane, chevauché les deux Arménies et les troys Arabies?" (99). The sites named are clearly based on the fourth and fifth projections of Asia in standard editions of Ptolemy's *Geographia*, but their predicate, *transfrété*, takes up Rabelais's particular verbal cartography, recalling, in *Pantagruel*, the Limousin student's first words that attempt to "map" the city of Paris through allusion to rectilinear city-planning: "Nous transfretons la Sequane au dilucule et crépuscule; nous déambulons par les compites et quadrivies de l'urbe . . ." (191). All of a sudden, in the words of these three advisers, space dilates through the force that vocables exercise on the space of memory obtained with familiarity of the book seen engendering its own world.

The initial meeting of Pantagruel with the Limousin in the sixth chapter of *Pantagruel*, we remember, inaugurates articulation of a global, curvilinear surface replacing the orthogonal plan of the giant's youth in the immediately preceding chapter that held analogy with the *itinerarium*. In effect, *transfréter* marks where the language of cartography, Latin, meets what the text argues to be a better, official vernacular of French. The Limousin's speech announces— indeed, prefigures—the moment when Pantagruel encounters Panurge (ch. 9), in which the trickster's thirteen translations of the same introduction produce a verbal cartography reaching out to each of the four corners of Europe all the while, in doing so, they define a Parisian center. Where the first encounter with the Limousin ignoramus was a "failed" meeting, the second, with a polyglot rogue, comes as a "success" marking how a new conjugation of space and discourse can be attained. In both chapters of *Pantagruel* a standard language remains at the axis in order to note the verbal meridian of the book's *mappemonde*. In chapter 33 of *Gargantua* remembrance of the spatial measure of France, seen through the recurrence of *transfréter*, serves to control the outrageous ambition of Picrochole's men.

Soubdain works analogously but leads into different areas. The adverb jumps off the page when, all of sudden, it appears to spin off the counselors' mention of Jerusalem, the Great Sultan of Egypt, and the Holy Land. The advisors envisage the East under Picrochole's grasp: "Nous la tenons. Sainct Treignan, Dieu gard Hiérusalem, car le *Soubdan* n'est pas comparable à votre puissance!" (99), but when he wishes to erect Solomon's temple on those lands, they retort, "—Non (dirent-ilz) encores, attendez un peu. Ne soyez jamais tant *soubdain* à vos entreprinses . . ." (99). The similiarity of *Soubdan* to *soubdain* (both displaying mirrored letters in *b-d*) binds the movement of the discourse to a name marking a place. In the parabolic dimension of the chapter, it can be argued that the sin of covetousness is being parodied where we see mirages of things in words, but further, that the word traces the crossing of textual and spatial vectors in both the episode and the book as a whole.

Soubdain-Soubdan becomes, in the combination that typography elicits, the very *festina lente* that the three generals invoke erroneously to moderate the ambitions they are projecting onto Picrochole. The visibility of the two words in the greater context shows how the dialogue amounts to a logic resembling what Freud studies in the story of the negotiations between a vendor and a buyer arguing over a broken kettle. And elsewhere, *soubdain* generally marks a decisive shift in space, as in the beginning of the following chapter, where it spurs action: "En ceste mesme heure, Gargantua, qui estoyt yssu de Paris *soubdain* les lettres de son père leues . . ." (102), announces retaliation where it coordinates the movement from one point to the next. In chapter 33, *Soubdan* personifies the realm of the world beyond Christian—hence, for the ideology being advanced, rational—grounds of the world. Picrochole and his men always act *suddenly*, if not gratuitously, and always fail to heed the emblem of the *festina lente* that goes with the King (e.g., Francis's Royal Salamander that moves slowly but spits fire). Grandgousier wonders why Picrochole acts without temperance that comes from the conflation of the speed and deliberation: "Adoncques . . . fut conclud qu'on envoirroit quelque homme prudent devers Picrochole sçavoir pourquoy ainsi *soubdainement* estoit party de son repous et envahy les terres ès quelles n'avoit droict quicquonqes" (89). His action contrasts that of Frère Jean. After having appealed to the nincompoop monks in his midst, unable to negotiate action, the monk "*soubdain*. . . donnoit dronos" (86). The word sums up the gratuitous cause of the dispute over the *fouaces*, as in archaic scenes where different cultures encounter each other, the line between war and exchange is blurred with difficulty.[13]

Quite possibly, when it dilates space through typographical means, as it does with these and other vocables, the text shows how cartography is mobilized through print culture. Each toponym underscores the topos of details reflecting and reproducing the cosmos. Such *abymes* are well known and explained comically in *Pantagruel*. But they also indicate how mapmaking, in contrast to description, is limited by absence of verbs, discourse, or fabulation. Maps lack means to animate themselves, or to impugn or correctively distort their form. They display a paucity of iterative formulas. In other words, just as they cannot attain illusion of extensive depth or perspective in their representation of masses of land and water,[14] the text suggests that, unlike itself, maps are unable to make space move. They lack interlocutors who can mobilize them. To avoid becoming static accumulations of proper names, they require animation coming from without. By predicating spatial relations among its proper and common names, verbs, and adjectives, the design of this chapter of *Gargantua* appears thus to be showing how maps produce ideology by a propensity that strives to fix words or human subjects to places.[15] The work concomitantly unfixes the order that Picrochole's men would like to make of the world through their plans for conquest.

Up to this point we have seen that chapter 33 manifests what we have called "Gray's Law" of creation. Orthogonal representation of geography is not tranferred into discourse as one might read in an *itinerarium*. It is bent and twisted by means of varied degrees of inventive analogy. A verbal fabulation performs what cartographers seek to do with the transfer of curvilinear surfaces onto a flat plane, but contrary to their work, Rabelaisian cartography of *Pantagruel* and *Gargantua* yields effects that *increase* aberration of language and space. It can also be argued that the chapter obtains a spherical contour by other means. If, in 1535, the text was disseminating Evangelical materials[16] and allegorizing the wars of France and Spain, its display of new and extensive spaces can be linked with what Humanists were drawing from the Psalms to encourage readers to find the presence of God in and through the expanse of nature. In the program religious and cartographical missions combine. Because the chapter bends up and around the northern coast of Europe as it also moves down and around southern Europe and over Africa, it implies how much its discourse wills to reflect the curvature of the globe itself.

An especially significant sign is marked with reference to the island of Greenland. In most standard versions of Ptolemy, Greenland is not included along the western periphery. Hibernia, England, and Scandinavia are at the edge of the extreme longitude that runs north and south from the Canary

Islands. Why, if Ptolemy's conical projections seem to order the sequence of the counselors' units of speech, is an "absent" island included? Why do they advise Picrochole to lead his troops way off the mark, "sus Lubek, Norwerge, Swedenrich, Dace, Gotthie, Engroneland, les Estrelins, jusques à la mer Glaciale" (100), when they should merely skirt the Northern shores before descending the plains to the East of Germany? Is the text making an ostentatious enumeration telling us that it "knows" the names of the islands to the North and West? Is it insisting that students of nature must be versed in hydrography no less than cartography, as a 1513 hydrograph of Ptolemy indicates?

The text is quite possibly espousing not only Ptolemy but other projections, of more recent vintage and closer to home, associated with the Humanist cause of experimental cartography and typography. In the 1530s, one of the more decisively spherical and clearly organic projections of all available world-maps was recently drawn by Oronce Finé (Orontius Finaeus) and no doubt figures in a similar program that simultaneously represents and distorts the globe through language and perspective. In 1519 Finé, who would become the royal mathematician in the Collège de France, gave to Francis I a cordiform projection of the world (see Cimerlinus 1566 copy).[17] Later, in 1531, he executed a double cordiform map that soon led to Mercator's projection of 1538.[18] Finé draws the meridion along the edge of the Canary Islands, down to Antarctica, and up through Greenland to the North Pole. In the double projection Greenland radiates outward from the pole (whose meridian is now drawn from the Eastern extremity of Madagascar down to Antarctica and up through the *Sinus Persicus* and Caspian Sea).

In both maps the island is located well beyond the European peninsula and is not, as it was in Ptolemy's earlier hydrography, a Scandinavian peninsula, like modern Norway, extending from the upper reaches of the Asian continent. Its presence in the counselors' litany in *Gargantua* indicates that perhaps the Rabelaisian "vision" of the world moves with the innovations of Finé's stamp. Parallels can be established: Finé "signs" his work emblematically, with the escutcheon of dolphins adjacent to the fleur-de-lys, that mark his origin in *Dauphiné*, subtended by salamandar-like canines spitting fire. The signature *Orontius F. Delph.* in the cartouche of the 1531 projection sets the name on an axis, leading to his coat-of-arms, perpendicular to the meridian. Self and world are united and divided in a way that elicits analogy with "Rabelais" and his anagrams melding into the toponyms of the Touraine, in which the author happens to be in and of the world he maps. Orontius's cordiform projection retains a highly corporal, if not even evangelical, relation to what it represents. The map is the world and the heart, the center and totality, or the pulse of creation, of a great body that is sensed to be beyond the mannered border to the left and right. The northern extremity curves inward and outward at once, and appears virtually to generate the world's mass from its umbilicus. In terms that might be likened to botany, the North Pole is an "apical meristem," a point of embryonic growth that generates new surfaces but stands firm within its own point. Seen as a dynamic center, it works akin to the Rabelaisian letter that expands and extends in all cardinal directions all the while it is fixed in a grammatical montage.

The cartographic reading of chapter 33 reveals how new space is engendered through printed writing. Production figures, to be sure, in a program, aimed at a public of diverse degrees of literacy, that treats of the growing mass of a world in expansion. An allegory of contemporary politics is advanced, and so also is a lesson that teaches readers of the evangelical mission that uses geography to preach self-containment. In fact, the size of the early editions of *Gargantua*, at first in-8° and later in-16, display their cartography with words on a miniature page, in obvious contrast to the folio editions of Ptolemy or the greater size of Finé's cordiform map (211mm x 580mm). The textual map makes the infinitely small englobe the greater representations of the planet.

We can add that the overall plan of the thirty-third chapter of *Gargantua*, when seen beyond the points of view of the interlocutors, the narrative of the allegory, or in relation to literary and historical sources—but within the movement of style developing from montages of words and space—in fact generates a kind of "cordiform" text: whose at once mystical and rational orders extend and contain themselves; go beyond their means and yet hold to a bodily figure of mapping and writing; imply corporal orders within and without; sustain a graphic means of binding the world, typography, and the body. In respect to the last point, we must recall that Finé produced historiated letters that the Vascosan atelier often used, and that incorporate the configurations of the planets in the play of straight and curved lines.[19] These letters constitute miniature "worlds" of both personal and collective signature. Seen from that angle, comparison of the chapter, typographic letters, names, and the cordiform map shows how an aura of Humanism and Gallican Evangelism is conveyed; both move outward to new worlds and horizons, from Greenland to the New World and back; they also measure the globe in ways that disallow appropriation into centered units of "nation" or "self." Both are generative and, like the work of Floyd Gray, entirely *generous* creations that teach us, in their respective languages, how the work of creation will lead us to lose ourselves in the more dynamic play of language in the toss of space.

Notes

[1] *The Standard Edition of the Complete Psychological Works of Sigmund Freud*, ed. and trans. James Strachey (rpt. London: Hogarth Press, 1986) 23: 71.

[2] Rabelais, *Œuvres complètes*, ed. Jacques Boulenger (Paris: Gallimard-Pléiade, 1955) 97ff. All direct reference to *Gargantua* and *Pantagruel* will be made to this edition and cited in the text.

[3] Floyd Gray, *Rabelais et l'écriture* (Paris: Nizet, 1974) 99.The remark merits comparison with what, from a formal bias, Frank Lestringant studies in terms of spatial metonymy in "Rhétorique et dispositif d'autorité," *Littérature* No. 32 (Dec. 1978) 21ff. and "Rabelais et le récit toponymique," *Poétique* No. 50 (1982) 207-25.

[4] In Lucian, *Dialogues* 7, ed. and trans. M. R. Macleod, Loeb Classical Library (Cambridge: Harvard UP, 1961) 142-55. Rabelais may have found a French source of Lucian's dialogue in a printer's atelier. Geoffroy Tory published a French translation in *La Table de l'ancienne philosophe Cebes*, natif de *Thebes et Auditeur Daristote. En laquelle est descripte et paincte la voye de lhome humain tendant a vertus et parfaicte science. Avec Trente Dialogues moraulx de Lucien autheur iadis Grec. Le tout pieca translaté de Grec en langue latine par plusieurs sçavans & recommandes autheurs. Et nagueres translaté de Latin en vulgaire françois par maistre Geofroy Tory de Bourges* ... (Paris: Jehan Petit, 1529). Tory's introductory tale contains what might be the origin of the Limousin student episode. And Jehan Petit is also a printer who disseminated Oronce Finé's writing. Tory, also a publisher of itineraria, may indeed play an important cartographic role for Rabelais.

[5] M.A. Screech, *Rabelais* (Ithaca: Cornell UP, 1979) 165.

[6] Gray (92) notes that the enumeration serves as "negative aspect" of writing set in the text to contrast other modes of writing, such as the grandiloquent letter from *Gargantua* (202-06). In contrast, Lestringant shows that the serial effect pertains to contemporary itineraria, such as Bernhard von Breidenbach's *Voyage au Jérusalem* (11 editions and translations between 1486 and 1522), Jacques Signot's *Description* of alpine passages (1515) and, later, Charles Estienne's *La guide des chemins de France* (1552), noted in "Suivre la guide," in *Cartes et figures de la terre* (Paris: Centre Georges Pompidou, 1980) 424-35, a study informing his "Rabelais et le récit toponymique." The most accessible and handsome reprint of Breidenbach can be found in Kenneth Nebenzahl, *Maps of the Holy Land* (New York: Abbeville, 1986) 64-65. Mireille Pastoureau offers a quasi-complete bibliography in *Les Atlas français XVI-XVIIe siècles* (Paris: Bibliothèque Nationale, 1984).

[7] A. E. Nordenskiöld's *Facsimile-Atlas to the Early History of Cartography* (New York: Dover Reprint, 1973), includes a complete version of the 1490 Rome edition from which later copies were made (142 ff.).

[8] David Woodward shows that when they wanted to insert toponyms into map blocks, printers encountered difficulty in aligning spaces cut into the wood surface with the names printed on lead forms, as shown in "The Manuscript, Engraved, and Typographic Traditions of Map Lettering," in *Art and Cartography: Six Historical Essays*, ed. David Woodward (Chicago: U of Chicago P, 1987) 194-95. See also R. A. Skelton's discussion of type-set names in his introduction to Münster's edition of *Claudius Ptolemaeus Geographia* (Basle, 1540), Third Series 5 (Amsterdam: Theatrum Orbis Terrarum, 1966) xii-xiii.

[9] As Samuel Y. Edgerton, Jr. notes about the quincunx in designs of the body and the world, in "From Mental Matrix to Mappamundi to Christian Empire: The Heritage of Ptolemaic Cartography in the Renaissance," in *Art and Cartography* 12-13.

[10] On the equilibrating function of puns, see Guy Demerson, "Les Calembours de Rabelais," in *Cahiers de Varsovie* (1981) 73-95. I wish to thank Jan Miernowsi for obtaining a copy of this important article.

[11] See for example the Lubeck map reproduced in Tony Campbell, *The Earliest Printed Maps* (Berkeley: U of California P, 1987) 121.

[12] In *Le texte de la Renaissance* (Geneva: Droz, 1982), François Rigolot argues that a visual rhetoric informs *Pantagruel*. Following Charles Singleton's studies of center and circumference in Dante, Rigolot notes that a center is reserved for an enigma that generates textual production or an *événement poétique majeur* (145-46). The same holds here, except that now the identities at the periphery leave open an entirely mobile textual center that scatters everywhere through the toponyms. Hence the strange orthography of *cyre* for *sire* marks the moment where discourse anticipates its concurrently spatial and verbal movement. M. A. Screech notes rightly that the unusual spelling "increases the comedy, suggesting that Picrochole is a new Cyrus the Great, as well as indicating the current (false) etymology of *Sire* from *Kurios*, 'lord'" (*Rabelais* 166-67n31). He shows that Picrochole's last words in the chapter, "Qui s'aymera, si me suyvra," parody those of Cyrus. In doing so, the parting shot is placed in clear visual counterpoint to the beginning. In between these poles, the words vary on the incipit before returning to the five characters of the surname hidden in Picrochole's last remark.

[13] Lévi-Strauss reenacts it at the end of the famous chapter, "Leçon d'écriture," in *Tristes tropiques* (Paris: Plon, 1955), in which a successful meeting develops slowly, in such a way that in passage from night to day "conflict gives way to exchange."

[14] See Svetlana Alpers, "The Mapping Impulse in Dutch Art," in *Art and Cartography* 70-72.

[15] No doubt more extensive work remains to be done in the ideologies of cartography. Frank Lestringant shows how conquest and naming go hand in hand with the ruses of historians and travelers (hence confirming Gray's point about naming amounting to arrogating), in *Pratiques de la carte*, the conclusion to his "Fictions de l'espace brésilien à la Renaissance: l'exemple de Guanabara," in *Arts et légendes d'espace* (Paris: Presses de l'Ecole Normale Supérieure, 1981) 242-47. His work shares theoretical bases with Louis Marin's *Utopiques: jeux d'espace* (Paris: Minuit, 1973) and Michel de Certeau's remarks on cartography in *L'Ecriture de l'histoire* (Paris: Gallimard, 1975) and essays collected in *La Fable mystique* (Paris: Gallimard, 1982). An important point of departure in English is J. B. Harley's introduction to *From Sea Charts to Satellite Images*, ed. David Buisseret (Chicago: U of Chicago P, 1990) 3-15. The historical background in which human subjects are "fixed" in space is noted in François Rigolot, *Poétique et onomastique* (Geneva: Droz, 1977) 24 ff. In *Rabelais's Carnival* (Berkeley: U of California P, 1990), Samuel Kinser shows that the *Quart Livre* verbalizes scenes adorning Olaus Magnus's 1539 (Venice) *Carta marina* (64-66 and 99-103). His observations confirm that the writer uses maps to generate textual distortions of space and language. The relation of image and text also tells us why, despite the array of knowledge that Abel Lefranc offers in *Les Navigations de Pantagruel* (Paris: Henri Leclerc, 1905), the material cannot be used. He does not problematize the distortions engaged in mimetic transfer when materials of one medium are mapped onto others. For Lefranc *Gargantua* does not claim cartographic interest: "En résumé, il apparaît clairement que, dans ce premier livre, tous les éléments d'ordre géographique ou topographique sont *strictement empruntés à la réalité* et que l'imagination du conteur n'est intervenue en rien pour les transformer ou les combiner arbitrairement" (5-6, stress added).

[16] Skelton notes that Sebastien Münster used the Psalms (e.g., 104) that "praise God's work on the face of the earth to justify geography" (ix).

[17] Rodney Shirley underscores its historical importance by placing it in great evidence on the inner cover of his authoritative compendium, *The Mapping of the World* (Amsterdam, 1983). In his discussion of the map he calls special attention to the depiction of the North: "Four islands make up the north polar regions. The separate island of Greenland is named, and a large promontory marked *baccalar* (supposedly Labrador) extends from the North American land mass into the Atlantic" (75). The most complete overview of Finé's life and work is probably Richard Ross's

doctoral dissertation, "Studies of Oronce Finé" (Columbia, 1971). I am grateful to Robert Karrow, curator of maps at the Herman Dunlap Smith Center for the History of Cartography, Newberry Library of Chicago, for providing access to this and other materials relating to Finé and early mapping.

[18] It can be found in Simon Grynaeus, *Novuus Orbis Regionum ac Insularum veteribus incognitarum, unò cum tabula cosmographica . . .* (Paris: Jehan Petit, 1532), that relates accounts of travel up to Vespucci and Columbus. If a biographical approach were to be taken, the book could be said to figure in the world of Rabelais's knowledge.

[19] Finé develops the relation in his *Protomathesis* (Paris: Jehan Petit, 1532), a compendium of mathematics and cosmography that stood strong throughout the sixteenth and seventeenth centuries, that Finé both wrote and illustrated. It uses his own drawings, ornamental borders, historiated initials and allegorical frontispiece to allow the signature of the author to dissolve into the greater logic, mechanics and, too, image of the world. Later, in the *Lesphere du monde* (Paris: Vasconsan, 1551), Finé charts ptolemaic astronomy in the French vernacular that, like the discourse of Rabelais of the 1530s, promotes association of letters and pictures in and between the typography and illustrations.

Terence Cave

The Death of Guillaume Du Bellay: Rabelais's Biographical Representations

In a sonnet published posthumously, although probably written as early as April 1553,[1] Du Bellay records a troubled night spent at Saint-Symphorien. His long-dead uncle Guillaume Du Bellay, sieur de Langey, appears to him in a dream, "plus grand que de coustume"; waking in fright, he recalls that this was the very place where Langey had died in January 1543.

The reference emerges unexpectedly from what appears to be a case of amorous insomnia: Du Bellay is suffering from the "regret" of leaving both France and the "beaux yeux" of his mistress.[2] The structure of the sonnet might easily have led the reader to expect a dream image of the beloved; instead, it contrives a deviation into the political world of Du Bellay's family, the world of his more celebrated "regrets."

In the concluding lines, Du Bellay evokes Langey's role as a defender of the French monarchy against Charles V; the theme is developed at greater length in a companion sonnet:

> Langé vivant fut à ceux de sa part
> Fosse, tranchee, & muraille & rempart:
> Mais à la fin sa vertu fut contrainte
>
> De nous laisser pour aux astres courir:
> Et en mourant feit encores mourir
> L'espoir François & l'Espagnole crainte.[3]

A decade or more after it occurred, Langey's death is still seen as a critical disaster, a turning point in the fortunes of France.[4] The return of the great man's soul to its celestial home is mentioned at the end of both sonnets, yet the return of his dream image to the place where he died is marked by a sense of supernatural horror. Despite the consolations of immortality, a suffering mortal is left behind to face the endless political problems that Langey might perhaps have averted had he lived a few years longer.

A similar after image of Langey is conjured up in two extended and thematically rich episodes of Rabelais's later books: chapter 21 of the *Tiers*

Livre, in which Pantagruel proposes that Panurge should consult the dying poet Raminagrobis, and chapters 26 and 27 of the 1552 *Quart Livre*, which form part of the sequence on the isle of the Macraeons. One may assume that Du Bellay had read these chapters; the sonnets quoted above were probably written only a year or so after the publication of the expanded *Quart Livre*, and in the month following Rabelais's own death.[5]

It is not a question here of establishing literary influence. By the end of his life, Rabelais's position as a writer protected by the Du Bellay family was not so different from the one Du Bellay was to enjoy; despite the differences between them in age and in cultural formation, they clearly shared many perceptions of the way history was being made in their day, and in particular of the significance of Langey's premature death. The shock of that event must have continued to reverberate within the Du Bellays' milieu long afterwards; like a handful of well-preserved archaeological fragments, the sonnets of Du Bellay and—especially—the passages from Rabelais provide us with a representation of how it was felt, what its imaginative structure might have been.

The analyses of Krailsheimer and Screech go a long way towards clarifying the philosophical and Christian allusions of the two Rabelais passages.[6] They are indispensable to any historical reading of the texts, and I take them for granted as a point of departure. My own approach is, however, intended to be historical in a slightly different sense. It is based on the supposition that belief-systems such as Christian neoplatonism do not and cannot exhaustively define the mode of thought and perception of any individual; they should rather be conceived as enabling structures that provide a coherent frame for the shifting and often conflicting apprehensions of which subjective and even public experience is in *practice* made. I should like, then, to capture something of the elusive play of a sixteenth-century mind on a traumatic event, to follow the weaving of that event into patterns of reference and image which we would now call "literary" but which are, again, no less a historical phenomenon than is a certain kind of neoplatonism.

The reduplication of the reference in Rabelais is, to say the least, striking. If the episodes are considered separately, the evocation of Langey's death in each appears almost accidental; it plays an illustrative role which is clearly subordinate both to the narrative itself and to the themes raised by the narrative. Yet once the parallelism has been noticed, the perspective may well be reversed: it begins to look as if, in two successive books, Rabelais has developed a major episode out of the imaginative material provided by Langey's death. Raminagrobis on the one hand, the Macraeons and their dying

Heroes on the other, appear as fictional transpositions of the real but already near-legendary figure of Langey. All the more, indeed, because the episode to which the later passage belongs is much longer and composed of many more strands: in retrospect, the Raminagrobis episode has the air of a trial run. Or, to put it another way, the *Tiers Livre* raises a ghost that cannot be prevented from returning and having its full say.

In comparing the two references to Langey's death, one may first ask to what extent one is in fact a repetition or reduplication of the other. Most obviously, both are embedded in a sequence of *exempla*, classical topoi, adages and analogies. In the *Tiers Livre*, these illustrate the prophetic powers of those approaching death, whereas in the *Quart Livre* the predominant topic is the portents that accompany the death of "Heroes"; the connection between the two types of supernatural phenomenon is, however, extremely close and is reinforced by the neoplatonizing provenance of both themes and examples. In terms of *dispositio*, there is again a slight difference overridden by a much deeper similarity. The case of Langey is given a privileged status in the *Tiers Livre*: it is the final and decisive example in Pantagruel's preamble on the divinatory powers of the dying; it is long and detailed; and it emerges from a *praeteritio* which not only shows that Langey's death is wholly worthy to belong to the sequence of antique topoi but which also asserts its priority and self-sufficiency: "Je ne vous allegueray exemples antiques [eight examples are then listed] . . . seulement vous veulx ramentevoir . . . ."[7] In *Quart Livre* 26, a first brief evocation of Langey's death (cited by Epistemon)[8] follows an extended platonizing analogy and opens a sequence of examples of disturbances surrounding the death of great men; in chapter 27, Pantagruel develops the same theme through further analogies and examples and finally gives the cue for Epistemon to return to the death of Langey (ll. 49-67). This time the narration of the event is longer than in *Tiers Livre* 21 and no less detailed. It also closes the sequence of instances specifically concerning portents: the dialogue moves on to the question whether Heroes die, to the length of their lives, and eventually, in chapter 28, to the celebrated story of the death of Pan. Thus the death of Langey plays a key role in structuring the whole episode: the earlier brief reference may be read as the introduction of a theme which is central to the imagination of the characters, a *memory* to which they cannot help reverting.

The internal similarities between the two accounts of Langey's death are likewise striking. In *Tiers Livre* 21, he is referred to as "le docte et preux chevalier Guillaume du Bellay, seigneur jadis de Langey" (ll. 45-46), in *Quart Livre* 26 as "[le] preux et docte chevalier Guillaume du Bellay" (ll. 41-42), and in *Quart Livre* 27 as "[le] docte et preux chevalier de Langey" (ll. 50-51). This quasi-formulaic phrase recalls a long tradition of French epic narrative and thus endows Langey with an exemplary status which is significantly different from

that of the "exemples antiques"; it is one of the signs by means of which a shift
of temporal and cultural perspective is effected in these passages.

Another is the implied change in the function of first-person pronouns. In
introducing learned materials, Pantagruel characteristically uses first-person
formulas: "J'ay . . . souvent ouy dire," "Je ne vous allegueray exemples
antiques," "Je croy que toutes ames intellectives." He may also use a rhetorical
"nous" to suggest shared experience when adducing comparisons: "Car comme
nous, estans sur le moule . . . ."[9] By contrast, the first-person forms used within
the Langey passages denote the presence of the speaker as eyewitness at the
great man's death: "nous prædisant ce que depuis part avons veu . . . ," "Ce que
veismes plusieurs jours avant le departement de celle tant illustre, genereuse et
heroïque ame," "Il m'en souvient . . . et encores me frissonne et tremble le cœur
. . . quand je pense es prodiges . . . lesquelz veismes apertement. . . ."[10]

This use of deictic, eyewitness pronouns is closely linked to the shift from
present to past definite forms of the verb, informing the reader not only that the
events narrated are "historical," like the story of the death of Herod in *Quart
Livre* 26, but also that they derive from the living memory of the speaker. A
further distinctive feature is the recording of eyewitness *response* to indicate
the power and above all the authenticity of the experience narrated: "combien
que pour lors nous semblassent ces propheties aulcunement abhorrentes et
estranges" (*Tiers Livre* 21, ll. 52-54); "encores me frissonne et tremble le cœur
dedans sa capsule, quand je pense es prodiges tant divers et horrificques
lesquelz veismes apertement . . ." (*Quart Livre* 27, ll. 52-55). The sense of
strangeness, the physical manifestations of horror, are themselves the very
proof that these events occurred; this is the rhetoric of the "true story."

Even these features, however, are secondary to the central and most visible
mark of authenticity. In each case, Rabelais is scrupulously careful to provide
a quasi-legal documentation of the event. In the *Tiers Livre* version, he specifies
the place of death and then, with almost redundant precision, the date: "le 10
de Janvier l'an de son aage le climatere et de nostre supputation l'an 1543 en
compte Romanicque" (ll. 47-49). Langey may not have died on 10 January, and
he wasn't at a "climacteric" (he was 51, not 49 or 63). But accuracy is here much
less important than precision.[11] Rabelais is providing the reader simultaneously
with an indication of the symbolic importance of the event and with the proof
that it actually happened in recent recorded time. By contrast, even celebrated
figures like Isaac, Jacob, Hector, Achilles, Alexander the Great, cited in the
preceding *praeteritio*, seem to belong to a vague, distant, and barely even
chronological domain of the past. Even more dramatic is the listing, in *Quart
Livre* 27, of sixteen named eyewitnesses, signatories as it were to Epistemon's
affidavit; the naming of Rabelais himself among them is of course a special sign
for the reader, the ultimate indication that the text has momentarily moved out
of the fictional mode into a privileged realm of both private and public
experience.

It might be objected that Rabelais is a master of the comic and parodic list, that the use of his own name might be read as a sign of irony rather than authenticity. Rabelais's writing plays strange tricks, and these passages are certainly not immune to its habitual complexity; but the massing of effects, the recourse to pathos and a sense of supernatural terror, support the view that Rabelais cannot simply be "playing" here (whatever that might mean). Nor need the sense be inverted or even undermined by the more-than-legal redundancy. It is more plausible to say that Rabelais's proliferating and deviant language is exploited for a special moment of intensity in honor of Langey and the almost unspeakable charge of meaning carried by his death.

We may now move outwards again towards the integration of these passages into the wider context of the episodes to which they belong. The *Quart Livre* chapters will necessarily predominate here, simply because they supply so many more interconnections; but the complementary relation between the earlier and the later version of Langey's death will be presupposed throughout.

We have seen that the death is presented as both exemplary and actual, and the same double perspective governs Langey's participation in the natural and supernatural realms. In *Tiers Livre* 21, he is said to have reached a symbolic age, a turning point for the world at large as well as for himself; yet he certainly appears primarily as a dying mortal. He is not (as the footnote to the TLF edition has it) himself a Hero: Pantagruel's preceding exposition speaks of Heroes as belonging to the category of quasi-supernatural beings who welcome and console dying men, communicating to them the art of prophecy; Langey is a beneficiary of this gift. Even in the *Quart Livre*, Langey figures in a large and loose category of great men whose death is marked by portents or other perturbations. However, the whole discussion arises here from Macrobe's suggestion that the storm suffered by Pantagruel and his company was a portent associated with the death of a Hero. At the beginning of chapter 27, Pantagruel calls the souls of departed great men "Heroïques," and it is the same epithet that he subsequently applies to the soul of Langey. There is thus every reason to suppose that, by 1552, Rabelais had promoted Langey to the rank of Hero, which of course not only adds to his ex-patron's supernatural aura, but also, conversely, makes the category of "Hero" a more tangible, less theoretical one.

If Langey is both a man who died at a particular, recent moment and a member of the transtemporal class of Heroes, he is also by the same token drawn into the imaginative theme which founds the Macraeon episode as a whole: the theme of ageing which is also that of antiquity and of the loss of some former glory. The ancient ruins and inscriptions the companions find on the island, together with the fact that Macrobe communicates in "languaige Ionicque," bespeak a venerable origin (ch. 25, ll. 25-36, 46); yet the population of the island is very much reduced, and those who remain are all "charpentiers et . . . artizans" (ll. 19-24). Macrobe subsequently makes the decline explicit:

> Amys peregrins icy est une des isles Sporades . . . jadis riche, frequente, opulente, marchande, populeuse, et subjecte au dominateur de Bretaigne; maintenant, par laps de temps et sus la declination du monde, paouvre et deserte comme voyez. (ch. 26, ll. 1-8)

The temporal pathos of the isle is equally embodied in the Daemons and Heroes who inhabit the forest, "les quelz sont devenuz vieulx" (ll. 11-12). Their life guarantees the welfare and abundance of the island; when they die, afflictions come (16-22). Thus the history of the island and its civilization is recapitulated in the (admittedly distended) life span of each individual Hero.

Pantagruel and his company arrive on the island at a critical moment, a kind of climacteric portended by the storm they have just endured and embodied in the death of a Hero. As Pantagruel himself says, in reply to Macrobe's explanation of the portents, the passing of these "ames nobles et insignes" is marked not only by celestial perturbations but also by "lamentations des peuples, mutations des religions, transpors des Royaulmes, et eversions des Republiques" (ch. 26, ll. 31, 37-39). And it is at this point that Epistemon recalls the death of Langey:

> Nous . . . en avons naguieres veu l'experience on decés du preux et docte chevalier Guillaume du Bellay, lequel vivant, France estoit en telle felicité que tout le monde avoit sus elle envie, tout le monde se y rallioit, tout le monde la redoubtoit. Soubdain après son trespas, elle a esté en mespris de tout le monde bien longuement. (ll. 40-45)

The imaginative context in which this allusion occurs suggests that Rabelais is attempting to make sense of the critical historical moment in which he lived in terms of wider temporal structures. Whereas in the first two books, a burgeoning and enlightened present was compared with a benighted past, and Utopia (or utopian Thélème) seemed almost within reach, the vision is now reversed: the *translatio imperii et studii* ("transpors des Royaulmes") to France has come and gone, an unfavorable "mutation de religion" has supervened in so far as the cause of moderate gallican reform has failed.

Epistemon's later gloss—like Du Bellay's sonnets—represents the passing of Langey as both the cause and the embodiment of this turning point. Witnessing the portents that preceded his death, his friends and servants foresaw "que de brief seroit France privée d'un tant perfaict et necessaire chevallier à sa gloire et protection" (64-66). When one juxtaposes this passage with the earlier account, in *Tiers Livre* 21, of Langey's prophecies, a discrepancy appears. Pantagruel claims that Langey spent the last hours before his death nous prædisant ce que depuys part avons veu, part attendons advenir: combien que pour lors nous semblassent ces propheties aulcunement abhorrentes et estranges, par ne nous apparoistre cause ne signe aulcun præsent pronostic de ce qu'il prædisoit. (*Tiers Livre* 21, ll. 51-56)

Assuming that the "nous" of this passage is not distinct from the eyewitnesses listed in *Quart Livre* 27, one might think it odd that, after five or six days of portents, Rabelais's friends lacked any "signe present" to corroborate his prophecies. However, the difficulty is only superficial and is no doubt due to a difference of emphasis. In the earlier version, the theme of prophecy is uppermost; the significant point is that Langey's predictions seemed implausible at the time because nothing then indicated the traumatic changes which were about to take place. In the later passage, the discussion centers on the portents that made the death of Langey seem inevitable; his prophecies are not mentioned. The actual consequences of that calamitous event could only be observed in retrospect, as in the passage in *Quart Livre* 26.

What emerges overall from this configuration of texts is the sense of a very precise, personally experienced historical moment which is also a critical turning-point in the affairs of France; the cosmic perturbations that accompany it appear as a projection of the shock and dismay it caused as well as of its quasi-apocalyptic character. Past, present and future are gathered together at a single juncture: the prosperity of a past civilization, the living memory of a great man and his achievements, the present shock of his death, the prophecies that spell out a strange, abhorrent but all too certain future—all these are apprehended in retrospect as a nexus of historical meaning.

It goes (almost) without saying that a central preoccupation here is the correct reading of signs. These may be disconcerting, strange, or unnatural, as when Pantagruel refers to "prodiges, portentes, monstres, et aultres precedens signes formez contre tout ordre de nature" (*Quart Livre* 27, ll. 47-48). They reveal their dark or obscure side to those who witness them, but the signs at issue here are by definition carriers of the truth; they are a divine script. A great deal has been said about the question of signs in Rabelais, particularly in the third and fourth books,[12] and I only propose here to touch on one local aspect of the topic. Pantagruel's account of Langey's prophecies in *Tiers Livre* 21, quoted above, mentions the lack of any "cause ne signe . . . præsent pronostic de ce qu'il prædisoit." His general discourse on portents at the beginning of *Quart Livre* 27 reverts to the same phrasing, while giving the word "prognostic" a more specific connotation. He embarks on a lengthy simile to explain the function of the heavenly signs that accompany the death of a Hero: "Et, comme le prudent medicin, voyant par les signes prognostics son malade entrer en decours de mort . . ." (ll. 9-11); the comparison closes as follows: ". . . telz cometes et apparitions meteores, les quelles voulent les cieulx estre aux humains pour prognostic certain et veridicque prediction que, dedans peu de jours, telles venerables ames laisseront leurs corps et la terre" (ll. 22-26). The analogy, then, introduces the figure of a doctor who interprets natural bodily signs to make a prognosis.

The figure can hardly be a mere illustration in this context. The scene evoked in the simile, where the doctor is seen exhorting the family and friends of his patient to come to the deathbed and ensure that everything is left in order after his demise, is precisely relevant to the case in hand—more so, a modern reader might think, than a celestial firework display. Furthermore, the witnesses at Langey's deathbed include one "maistre Gabriel medicin de Savillan,"[13] and no sixteenth-century reader could have been unaware that Rabelais himself, whose name follows Gabriel's, was a doctor. In consequence, the practice of medicine becomes linked to the art of prognostication and vice versa. Langey's suffering body was studied with a doctor's eye for signs of dissolution; the heavens sent portents which all those present could interpret; and Langey himself uttered prophecies as if reading signs that other mortals could not see. The three levels seem to represent the transition from this world to the next, from natural or physical to supernatural or celestial. Otherworldly signs become more reassuringly tangible, physical signs point towards an event of historic and cosmic significance. And, in a position which is both central and marginal, as a character in a simile, a name in a list, or a displaced first-person pronoun, is represented the doctor whose testimony is here recorded in an act of both homage and interpretation.

Another striking, and crucial, example of a simile whose meaning reaches beyond its immediate context is the comparison in *Tiers Livre* 21 between those who, from the safety of shore, watch mariners out at sea and pray for their safe arrival in harbor, and supernatural beings (Angels, Heroes, good Daemons) who guide dying humans to their last rest. This simile is of course very close in its structure and purport to the "doctor" analogy of the *Quart Livre*. What it introduces, however, is not a glimpse at one or more removes of a real deathbed scene, but only, it would seem, a timeworn topos: life as a dangerous maritime excursion, death as a safe harbor. In the *Tiers Livre*, this is indeed all it is, apart from the platonizing references. But in retrospect it may well look like a trailer (or "signe pronostic"?) for the great storm scenario of the *Quart Livre*, to which the Macraeon episode is intimately linked: the storm is explained as one of the portents accompanying the death of a Hero, and Pantagruel's mouth in that episode is full of references to stormy weather.[14]

The cause of the storm which nearly shipwrecks Pantagruel's company is in fact not unequivocal. The explanation just referred to is given by Macrobe in chapter 26, in reply to Pantagruel's question (ch. 25) as to whether the seas adjacent to this island are particularly subject to tempests. The question might suggest that no other cause than a physical one had ever been implied. This is, however, not the case. At the height of the storm, Frere Jan says of Panurge: "Ce diable de fol marin est cause de la tempeste" (ch. 20, ll. 24-25). The remark is enigmatic: does it simply mean that he is the reason why they have embarked on the voyage (see Pantagruel's remarks, ch. 25, ll. 53-57)? That would be an odd reading of the phrase "est cause de la tempeste." The only other plausible reading is an allegorical one: the tempest is a manifestation of Panurge's "folly," his mental and moral confusion ("Ce diable de fol marin . . .").

A nonliteral reading becomes essential, in fact, from the very beginning of this episode, which is arguably the most patently allegorical sequence Rabelais ever wrote. It will be recalled that the company encounters several boatloads of monks and assorted ecclesiastics making their way to the "concile de Chesil," easily identifiable as the Council of Trent: "Les voyant, Panurge entra en excès de joye, comme asceuré d'avoir toute bonne fortune pour celluy jour et aultres subsequens en long ordre" (ch. 18, ll. 7-10). So Panurge makes a favorable prognostication from this sign, throwing in some material donations as an insurance policy. Pantagruel, by contrast, remains "tout pensif et melancholicque" (l. 17). Frere Jan asks him why, but there is no time for a reply: the wind rises, and the pilot, "prevoiant un tyrannique grain et fortunal nouveau" (21-22), puts both crew and passengers on the alert; then a storm of fearful proportions arises. It is quite clear that Pantagruel's prognostication is the opposite of Panurge's; even though it is the practical pilot (rather like the doctor) who foresees the storm itself, the connections soon become clear. The encounter with the clerics was a sign clear enough for Pantagruel at least to read.

In chapter 18, then, it appears that the monks going to their council are a presage and perhaps even a cause of the storm; in chapter 26, by contrast, Macrobe connects the storm with the death of a Hero. Portents are involved in both cases, but the relations are reversed: in chapter 18, a specific event presages the storm, in chapter 26, the storm portends a specific event (although it is of course also an *effect* of the event). Is this simply an involuntary discrepancy, to be ascribed to the interval between Rabelais's composition of the storm episode for the 1548 edition and his development of the Macraeon episode for the 1552 edition?

The alternative view is that the double explanation creates a relationship between the threatening prospect of Chesil-Trent and the death of a Hero potentially identifiable with Langey. The storm, whether portending or portended, then becomes the allegorical expression of the religious and political crisis of the 1540s, of that turning point in the affairs of France referred to in chapter 26 and of the dire events foretold by Langey on his deathbed. Langey's death was a catastrophe for Rabelais because it deprived France of a major statesman, a man who would not only have championed the French cause against Charles V (as Du Bellay suggests) but might also have given weight to the moderate faction at Trent and thus prevented a reassertion of "hardline" orthodoxy. The allegorical landscape allows the writer to understand and explore a series of events which, in their raw experiential form, are both traumatic and uncontrollable.

This last remark could be extended to the third and fourth books as a whole. In the first two books, problems are raised, the giants and their friends are threatened by hostile forces, but Gargantua and Pantagruel visibly dominate their world, dwarfing and defeating their opponents with gigantic ease. In the third and fourth books, problems become chronically difficult to resolve; the monsters and alien forces of the *Quart Livre* (not least the storm) present serious threats and may prove impossible to evacuate; the safest course, in more than one episode, is evasion. One indicator of this shift is the repeated advocacy, from early in the *Tiers Livre*, of a neostoic disaffection in the face of externals, a topos which may perhaps better be regarded as a symptom of disquiet than as a comprehensive philosophical solution. Another is the emergence of the themes of prophecy and portents, largely absent from the earlier books: when the present looks confused and murky, the desire for a knowledge of the future becomes critical. And yet another is the reversion to images of old age and decline, already present in the ageing anxious Panurge of the *Tiers Livre*.

Of course there are many other themes and emphases in Rabelais's later books; of course it is a critical commonplace that the tone of these books is more somber and the role of the giants more subdued, less exuberant. I would argue only for a reading that makes the shock of Langey's death and the quasi-supernatural aura of that "real" experience central to the renewal of Rabelais's imaginative powers in the last seven years of his life. It may well be, indeed, that it was not until after the events of the mid-1540s— France's reversals in the imperial wars, the affirmation of conservative orthodoxy at Trent—that the passing of his patron began to take on, for Rabelais, truly cataclysmic proportions; and to become, by the same token, the nucleus out of which whole segments of his later books grew.

Krailsheimer has pointed to the probability that, from the beginning of the *Tiers Livre,* Rabelais drew on his experience of Langey's government of Piedmont in constructing his fictional scenarios (229, 233, 243-44); he has even suggested that the accuracy of Langey's prophecies may be credited to the extremely efficient intelligence service of the Du Bellay family (130). We know, too, that many of the new episodes in the 1552 *Quart Livre* have to do with the Tridentine insistence on the observance of fasting, with the repressive and materialistic policies of the Papacy, with French gallican policy, and other related issues. These are the wider reverberations of the group of themes and episodes we have been considering. The object of evoking them here is not to suggest that the *Quart Livre* (let alone the two later books as a whole) is coherently structured as a kind of historical allegory, but that the imaginative energies released in the later part of Rabelais's career may often be traced back to the seismic upheaval of his patron's demise. A crack opens up, first—more simply—between the earlier and the later books, then at the very heart of the composition of the *Quart Livre*. The storm episode in its first version is the last complete episode in the 1548 *Quart Livre*, written not very long after the *Tiers Livre*; it conjures up a brief image of the prospects at Trent and raises a portentous wind. A sequel—the Isle des Macraeons—is begun but abandoned in mid-sentence after a few lines. Did Rabelais already know how he was going to complete it? Did he already have the reference to Langey in mind? Did he perhaps foresee the great complexity of the materials he had embarked on and not have the leisure until much later to work them out fully? This is idle speculation, of use only as a way of drawing attention to this most spectacular crack or fault line in the composition of the *Quart Livre*. Those two episodes are deeply related; yet they are also riven apart, like fragments of a disquieting experience that cannot easily be made coherent.

One last fragment needs to be recalled here. In the prologue to the *Tiers Livre*, Rabelais famously and enigmatically speaks of his book, his writing, as the only thing left to him after the "naufrage faict par le passé on far de Mal'encontre" (ll. 170-71). It is hard not to read this as a reference to some actual personal disaster. The allegory is banal, but it contains in miniature the very scene that will recur, first as an extended simile in *Tiers Livre* 21, then as a full-blown episode in the *Quart Livre*: the scene of the mariner adrift on a perilous sea. And in each case, the topos is associated with the death of Langey. The "naufrage" may not be directly identifiable with that event, but the juxtaposition and recurrence of these motifs can only be read as a textual representation of the shock and disorientation set in train by the loss of a revered patron.

The curious interplay in these two passages of *exempla* and analogies, allegories, philosophical and literary topoi, and subjectively perceived histori-cal occurrences, is not without parallels in Du Bellay's Roman poetry; the two Langey sonnets cited at the beginning of this paper belong to the same family. The amalgam is characteristic of the mid-sixteenth century, and it might be said also to anticipate Montaigne's (or, of course, d'Aubigné's) oscillation between literary and personal materials. The death of La Boétie and the accident recounted in "De l'exercitation" are represented in the same textual world as the quotations from Lucretius, Seneca and others in "Que philosopher, c'est apprendre à mourir": the difference between I, 20 and II, 6 is primarily one of emphasis, since "personal" and "non-personal" materials are to be found in both. What we have to ask here is not what *really* happened to the writer, or what his text *really* means, but how the process of representation works in early modern France. On the other hand, there is no reason to think that the process can only be traced if the text is sterilized and considered as a self-sufficient act of writing. On the contrary: we only read the text because it gives us a sense of life, of history, of something beyond itself. We read for the trace of unseen and often obscure happenings; we listen for the seismic tremor, the first faint sounds of rising wind; we remember an experience utterly foreign to us and feel—at however many removes—something of the numinous power of a long past event: "Il m'en souvient, et encores me frissonne et tremble le cœur dedans sa capsule. . . ."

NOTES

[1] This sonnet, entitled "D'un songe qu'il feit passant à S. Saphorin," is the fourth of the *Sonnets divers* in Joachim Du Bellay, *Œuvres poétiques*, vol. 2, *Recueils de sonnets*, ed. Henri Chamard, Société des Textes Français Modernes (Paris: Cornély, 1910) 257-58. Chamard plausibly conjectures that it refers to an overnight stop made during Du Bellay's journey to Italy in 1553 (see below, note 2), but one should bear in mind that this group of posthumous sonnets was brought together by Chamard from various sources; the sequence and dating cannot therefore be taken as certain.

[2] See sonnet III of the *Sonnets divers*, entitled "Du regret de l'autheur au partir de la France" (257), lines 3 and 6. It is again reasonable to assume, as does Chamard, that sonnets III and IV belong together because of their titles and internal references; they were printed thus, with the following six *Sonnets divers*, in the first sixteenth-century edition (1568).

[3] *Sonnets divers*, sonnet V, "Sur ce mesme propos," 258-59.

[4] Du Bellay's historical reflection is introduced in the quatrains by a reference to the Trojan War: Troy would have been swiftly defeated, and many years of destructive war avoided, had Agamemnon had ten Nestors; thus too the effects of Charles V's twelve-year campaign against France would have been nullified had Langey been accompanied by ten others like himself.

[5] For evidence that Rabelais died in early March 1553, see Jean Dupèbe, "La Date de la mort de Rabelais (suite)," *Etudes Rabelaisiennes* 18 (1985) 175-66.

[6] A.J. Krailsheimer, *Rabelais and the Franciscans* (Oxford: Clarendon Press, 1963) 118-23, 125-33, 229, 233-34, 243-44, 247, 314; M.A. Screech, *Rabelais* (London: Duckworth, 1979) 350-57, and notes to ch. 21 of the *Tiers Livre* in the Textes Littéraires Français edition.

[7] François Rabelais, *Le Tiers Livre*, ed. M.A. Screech, Textes Littéraires Français (Geneva: Droz and Paris: Minard, 1964) ch. 21, lines 39-45. All passages from this chapter will henceforth be quoted according to this edition and identified by line-numbers.

[8] François Rabelais, *Le Quart Livre*, ed. Robert Marichal, Textes Littéraires Français (Geneva: Droz, 1947) ch. 26, lines 40-45. All passages from this sequence of chapters will henceforth be quoted according to this edition and identified by line-numbers.

[9] *Tiers Livre* 21, lines 20, 39; *Quart Livre* 27, lines 99-100; *Tiers Livre* 21, line 25.

[10] *Tiers Livre* 21, lines 51-52; *Quart Livre* 27, lines 49- 50, 52-55.

[11] An entertaining medieval example of the use of a precise but apparently fictional formula to prove age is given by Keith Thomas in "History and Literature," The Ernest Hughes Memorial Lecture (University College, Swansea, 1988) 9-10.

[12] See in particular Screech, *Rabelais* 414 ff.

[13] On this figure, see Richard Cooper, "Maistre Gabriel medicin de Savillan," *Etudes Rabelaisiennes* 17 (1983) 115-18.

[14] Krailsheimer (128-29) claims that "there is no detail of the nautical simile in the *Tiers Livre* omitted from this description," namely, the description of the safe landing of Pantagruel and company in the port of the Isle des Macraeons.

Marcel Tetel

Le Physetère bicéphale[1]

Dans sa globalité le *Quart Livre* de Rabelais est encore à déchiffrer. Cette exigence s'explique du fait que ce livre est le plus allusif et enchevêtré de l'œuvre rabelaisienne, car le tissu textuel s'avère dense et emblématique. En outre, c'est un ouvrage des plus épisodiques, c'est-à-dire un texte se composant d'une succession de segments à l'allure disparate sauf qu'ils sont souvent reliés par une binarité antithétique. Récemment pour décrire cette structure on a trouvé l'heureuse formule de "l'insulaire" ou "la fiction en archipel."[2] En effet, il est une donnée que le *Quart Livre* figure une série d'escales et procède en grande partie au moyen d'une binarité antithétique, tels les Andouilles et Quaresmeprenant, Physis et Antiphysis, les Papimanes et les Papefigues… Or, la portée globale du *Quart Livre* ne peut s'articuler que par une analyse systématique des épisodes afin d'en relever sans doute une organicité structurale et sémantique, une marqueterie en fait bien jointe. De même, au cours de ce genre d'étude totalisante, il faut tenir compte de toutes les manifestations narratives ou textuelles: les édifices verbaux, les narrés, les dialogues, les intertextes… Il va sans dire que la démarche multivalente d'un texte de la Renaissance, en somme la démarche de l'esprit humaniste, exige et produit des significations sur plusieurs registres: religieux, philosophique, historique, autobiographique, inscriptions dans le passé et le présent, résultant en une métatextualité égocentrique, voire narcissique.

Pour illustrer ce défi que Rabelais lance au lecteur il suffit de se pencher sur l'épisode exemplaire et emblématique du physetère, épisode quelque peu négligé par la critique et à l'intérieur duquel on délaisse toute une masse textuelle lorsqu'on en fait l'analyse. Les deux chapitres consacrés à cet épisode figurent une division nette loin d'être fortuite. Le premier chapitre (33) représente les réactions des voyageurs (surtout celle de Panurge) devant l'apparition de ce monstre marin et s'inscrit essentiellement dans une représentation de la tradition, l'archéologie sémantique, à laquelle appartiennent les diverses significations de cette créature métaphorisée. Par contre, le chapitre suivant s'axe autour du nouveau, de l'exceptionnel, surtout par le biais des prouesses de Pantagruel triomphant du physetère, et de cette façon réécrit et met à jour le chapitre précédent et se pavane d'une narrativité métatextuelle.

La rencontre d'un monstre est un topos du même ordre que la tempête au cours d'un voyage. De prime abord, ils servent d'épreuves pour tester le for intérieur des voyageurs; ensuite c'est au lecteur de démêler les résonances particulières de cette confrontation. Or, Rabelais situe d'emblée cette scène sous le signe de l'Y pythagoricien, ce qui signifie qu'elle figure le carrefour herculéen, existentiel, devant lequel on doit choisir le vice ou la vertu, la folie ou la sagesse, la jeunesse ou la maturité:[3] "A cestuy son, toutes les naufz, guallions, ramberges, liburniques (scelon qu'estoit leur disciple navale) se mirent en ordre et figure telle qu'est le Y grégeois" (672).[4] Mais qui doit faire face à ce choix? Panurge? Pantagruel? le narrateur? La seule peur de Panurge ne le privilégie pas à être le seul à qui incombe le choix.

Pour Pantagruel en tant que capitaine de la flotille, de la quête, du voyage, ce sera, entre autres, l'épreuve de se soustraire à l'influence de son père Gargantua, c'est-à-dire du passé, ce qui représente le dilemme de l'humaniste qui ne veut pas rejeter la paternité de sa culture mais plutôt de l'incorporer dans un présent, dans une nouvelle culture qui se distingue en fait des précédentes (antiquité et moyen âge). Quant au narrateur, l'acte de l'écriture l'oblige sans cesse à faire face au choix de la logorrhée, du débordement verbal (ses pulsions naturelles) et par ailleurs à une contrainte d'expression afin de convaincre plus directement mais plus dangereusement; en somme, un choix entre déraison et raison scripturales. Par contre, c'est Panurge qui profère deux intertextes; il évoque d'abord le Léviathan et ensuite Andromède.

Or, pour le lecteur de la Renaissance ou pour celui de nos jours la présence de ces intertextes peut évoquer des significations supplémentaires qui font partie intégrante de la référence biblique ou du mythe et n'annulent pas nécessairement celles déjà citées ci-dessus. Dans le cas du Léviathan, si on ne choisit pas d'extrapoler simplement la référence à ce monstre, on remarque pour commencer que le livre de Job consacre soixante-huit vers à la description physique et allégorique de cette créature marine (40: 25-30, 41: 1-26), d'abord au moyen d'une *quaestio*, une série de questions dont la réponse sous-entendue est censée être négative et ensuite par une description anatomique (40: 21; 41: 4, 7). Compte tenu de la portée moralisatrice et de la condition humaine se soumettant à la volonté divine qui se dégagent de cet épisode biblique, il en émane également une narrativité, une volonté de narrer et de séduire au moyen d'une répétition formelle (les questions) et d'un écoulement de raconter et de décrire.[5] Ce genre de narré intertextuel préfigure d'ailleurs le chapitre suivant et représente de même dans une grande mesure l'écriture de Rabelais.

Si Panurge allègue "le noble prophète Moses en la vie du sainct homme Job" (673), il évoque ainsi la faiblesse de Job et explique de même sa propre peur et humilité devant le physetère, allégorie de Antiphysis (dans le chapitre précédent) et du mal. De même, Panurge allègue Andromède pour s'identifier à elle ("Je croy que c'est le propre monstre marin qui feut jadis destiné pour dévorer Andromède"), car elle représente dans la mythologie de la Renaissance les bons et les innocents que Dieu protège et empêche de périr, dans son cas à elle sauvée par Persée, et dans notre épisode ce sera Pantagruel/"Perseus" qui exercera cette fonction et dont la retorte sous forme de jeu de mots annonce le chapitre suivant: "Persé jus par moy sera . . . N'ayez paour." En effet, nous retrouverons le monstre tué et renversé par les flèches du géant. Par ailleurs, l'intertexte ovidien, allégué précisément par Panurge, relève littéralement d'un tout autre contexte, car Persée ne sauvera Andromède, ne combattera et ne tuera le monstre, que si ses parents lui donnent la main de leur fille: "'Ut mea sit seruata mea uirtute, paciscor.' / Accipiunt legem (quis enim dubitaret?) et orant / Promittuntque super regnum dotale parentes" (IV, 703-05).[6] La peur de Panurge devant ce monstre peut donc aussi signifier allégoriquement la réaction devant sa libido qui resurgit et dont il ne peut se défaire (un retour au *Tiers Livre*).[7] Il incombera à Pantagruel, à la raison et à l'ordre, de contrôler ce désir libidinal et cette pulsion incessante de la quête qui relie le *Tiers* au *Quart Livre*.

La peur multivalente qui domine ce premier chapitre de l'épisode se manifeste non seulement chez Panurge et indirectement chez Pantagruel mais fait percevoir également un Rabelais autobiographe. C'est l'intertexte du chariot de Phaéton, le seul évoqué par Pantagruel, qui sous-tend et contribue à cette multivalence de la peur. Effectivement, le géant en guise de réconfort à Panurge allègue les quatre chevaux de ce chariot: "vous doibvez paour avoir de Pyroeis, Heou, Aethon, Phlegon, célèbres chevaulx du Soleil flammivomes, qui rendent feu par les narines; des physetères ne doibvez paour avoir" (673). Ces quatre chevaux représentent dans la tradition patristique les quatre saisons, les quatre parties du jour et les quatre âges de l'homme, et dans ces contextes ils figurent l'ordre et la perfection. Et dans la tradition néoplatonicienne et chrétienne, l'ascension de ce chariot devient analogue à celle d'Elie et symbolise le baptême et la purgation de l'âme à travers le feu.[8] Or, ne faut-il pas également tenir compte d'une signification mythologique et plus littérale de cet intertexte ovidien, puisque entre autre, l'ordre de l'énumération des chevaux suit exactement celui qui se trouve dans les *Métamorphoses*: "Interea uolucres Pyrois et Eous et Aethon, / Solis equi, quartusque Phlegon hinnitibus auras / Flammiferis inplent pedibusque repagula pulsant" (II, 153-55),[9] tout en décrivant précisément la tentative de Phaéton, fils de Soleil/Apollon, dieu de la médecine et de la poésie, de voyager outre ses capacités. En effet, Phébus avait admonesté son fils de ce danger, et lorsque Phaéton réussit à convaincre son père, il se rend vite compte de sa condition, et une peur vertigineuse s'empare de lui:

Sed leue pondus erat nec quod cognoscere possent
Solis equi solitaque iugum grauitate carebat . . .
    Ut uero summo despexit ab aethere terras
Infelix Phaethon penitus penitusque patentis,
Palluit et subito genua intremuere timore
Suntque oculis tenebrae per tantum lumen abortae;
Et iam mallet equos numquam tetigisse paternos,
Iam cognosse genus piget et ualuisse rogando;
Iam Meropis dici cupiens ita fertur ut acta
Praecipiti pinus Borea, cui uicta remisit
Frena suus rector, quam dis uotisque reliquit.
Quid faciat? . . . (II, 161-62, 178-87)[10]

Or, en dialoguant avec Panurge, Pantagruel va lui indiquer qu'il n'a pas à craindre autant l'ambition et la gloire terrestre que son immortalité extra-terrestre. Rabelais lui-même se pose ainsi un dilemme fondamental humain: comment réconcilier la vanité d'ici-bas au salut de l'au-delà.

Par ailleurs, deux autres significations se dégagent de cette allégation mythologique dans le contexte apollonien. D'abord, selon le code médical. Rappelons l'appel du narrateur dans le prologue à propos de Rabelais: "Médicin, o guériz toy-mesme" (568). Evidemment un an avant sa mort Rabelais doit avoir des raisons de se soucier de sa santé physique et spirituelle. Ce qui explique aussi, dans une certaine mesure, la peur de Panurge face au Léviathan. De plus, le code apollonien se rapporte à l'inspiration créatrice, donc à l'écriture, et l'on sait que la problématique de l'écriture se pose certainement pour Rabelais par le biais du rapport entre la *rhetorica precisa* et la *rhetorica perpetua*, mesure et démesure verbale. Si la logorrhée et ici la peur de Panurge ne suffisent pas à convaincre le lecteur de cette dimension sémantique de cette peur, la narration débordante des prouesses de Pantagruel dans le chapitre suivant y parviendront.

Lorsque Panurge répond à l'intertexte multivoque allégué par Pantagruel, il ramène l'épreuve devant le danger non seulement au niveau théologique et hermétique, comme le fait le géant, mais aussi à l'échelle humaine, même à la littéralité ovidienne: "Vertus d'un petit poisson ne vous ay-je pas assez exposé la transmutation des élémens et le facile symbole qui est entre roust et bouilly, entre bouilly et rousti" (674). Théologiquement et hermétiquement, l'eau et le feu peuvent signifier soit un élément purificateur (notamment le baptême), soit un élément destructeur et de damnation. Or, Panurge réfute ici le dogme de la prédestination que Pantagruel avait proposé lorsqu'il déclara à Panurge que celui-ci n'avait rien à craindre de l'eau mais par contre tout à craindre du feu. D'ailleurs, la retorte finale de Panurge au cours de ce dialogue est des plus significatives, car elle s'appuie sur les principaux fondements de l'Humanisme. Panurge, lui, veut "mourir à son arbitraige" (674), veut choisir comment mourir, veut privilégier son libre arbitre. Et si le choix est vraiment possible, il

optera en outre d'être noyé dans un "tonneau de Malvesie" (674), car il
(Panurge/Rabelais) n'a aucune intention ici de délaisser la *rhetorica perpetua*.
Il serait peut-être légèrement outré de supposer que Panurge dans ces
circonstances ne figure que comme un simple repoussoir aux remarques de
Pantagruel. Au contraire, dans ce premier chapitre, le géant et son compagnon
dialoguent sur la condition humaine et sur le débat théologique qu'elle
engendre; à son tour, ce dialogue, y compris le narrateur au début du chapitre,
situe l'épisode dans une tradition littéraire et dans un code mythologique qui
en fait ressortir la portée existentielle et métatextuelle et se centre essentiellement
sur Panurge et ses réactions—un Panurge d'ailleurs incarnant les faiblesses et
les appréhensions de maints êtres humains aussi bien que celles de François
Rabelais lui-même et de sa persona créatrice.

Du domaine du dialogue, consacré à des propos idéologiques, on passe
ensuite dans le chapitre suivant au registre de la description, domaine du
narrateur qui focalise entièrement son attention sur le géant et ses prouesses; ici
le dialogue proprement dit cède à un dialogisme comparé entre les anciens et
les modernes. Une série d'exemples ou d'anecdotes d'archers habiles de
l'antiquité s'efface devant l'exemplarité et la précision des sagettes du géant.
Sur le plan le plus évident il est incontestable que la défaite du physetère par
Pantagruel annonce aussi le triomphe du pantagruélisme. Pour appuyer cette
certitude il suffit de retenir la façon dont il vainc le monstre. Les flèches qu'il
tire sur lui forment des groupes de trois ou quatre (pour dessiner un nouvel Y)
ainsi que deux rangées de cinquante. Or, puisque la tradition pythagoricienne
et chrétienne confère à ces chiffres une signification de perfection et d'intégralité
(voir Masters 149-51), Pantagruel et le pantagruélisme incorporent, certes, ces
mêmes qualités. Dans ce cadre, et dans ce chapitre, le géant conserverait ainsi
sa fonction plus ou moins allégorique et s'opposerait à la représentation plus
humaine de Panurge dans le chapitre précédent, dichotomie ou binarité polaire
qui s'accorde parfaitement avec une démarche structurale du *Quart Livre*.[11] Sur
un autre plan, le Chaos, le Mal représenté par le physetère, du premier chapitre
est opposé à la perfection, la vertu, du second, un topos de la Renaissance que
l'Arioste, par exemple, avait déjà exploité.[12] De plus, le décousu narratif
apparent dans l'Arioste ou dans Rabelais, autre Chaos, se propose comme
nouvel ordre. Or, la perfection pantagruéline dans le second chapitre va
surpasser celle des anciens, mais est-elle simplement supérieure au débit
dyonisiaque de Panurge ou est-elle censée coexister avec elle? Au niveau de
l'énoncé, cette lecture du deuxième chapitre est irréprochable, mais suffit-elle
sur le plan de l'énonciation?

Effectivement le gros de ce deuxième chapitre se compose de narrés. Ceux
se rapportant à l'exemplarité de l'antiquité débutent tous par une apostrophe à
un *Vous*: "Vous dictez, et est escript. . . . Vous nous racontez aussi. . . . Vous
nous dictez aussi merveilles.. . . . Vous faictez pareillement narré des Parthes

. . ." (674-75). Le destinataire ou narrataire est ici au moins double. D'une part, c'est peut-être le lecteur coopté par le narrateur. D'autre part, ce sont les auteurs des intertextes allégués (Arrien, Sabellicus, Hérodote) et toute une tradition littéraire qui sont interpelés et mis en question par le narrateur puisque Pantagruel va les surpasser. Les quatre exemples semblant louer les archers des temps passés s'allongent de plus en plus si bien que le dernier est même dramatisé, donc privilégié, au moyen d'un dialogue et oppose la dextérité des Parthes, qui tiraient par derrière, à celle des Scythes qui tiraient en avant. Et ce narré où "Aussi célébrez-vous les Scythes en ceste dextérité; de la part desquels jadis un ambassadeur envoyé à Darius, roy des Perses, luy offrit un oyseau, une grenouille, une souriz et cinq flèches, sans mot dire" (675) se transforme en des propos sur l'interprétation des signes et leur virtualité:

Par ces dons et offrandes vous disent tacitement les Scythes: Si les Perses comme oyseaulx ne volent au ciel, ou comme souriz ne se cachent vers le centre de la terre, ou ne se mussent on profond des estangs et paluz comme grenouilles, tous seront à perdition mis par la puissance et sagettes des Scythes. (675)

Sans la présence d'un autre mot, le texte passe à la description de la virtuosité de Pantagruel pour indiquer en fait comment on doit lire les prouesses du géant. Pour commencer, le nouveau est représenté comme tout puissant et peut paraître, tels les Scythes, sauvages, et barbares au lecteur insuffisant.

En outre, l'entrée en scène de Pantagruel nationalise le nouveau et écarte rhétoriquement le passé, car selon une formule narrative propre à la littérature populaire du gigantisme, la grandeur des flèches du géant est comparée à des particularités géographiques françaises: "(lesquels proprement ressembloient aux grosses poultres sus lesquelles sont les pons de Nantes, Saulmur, Bergerac et à Paris les pons au Change et aux Meusniers soustenuz, en longueur, grosseur, poisanteur et ferrure)" (675-76). Ensuite les virtuosités du géant glissent du registre de l'extraordinaire à un plan bien emblématique:

de mil pas loing il ouvroit les huytres en escalle sans toucher les bords; il esmouchoit une bougie sans l'extaindre; frappoit les pies par l'œil; dessemeloit les bottes sans les endommaiger; deffourroit les barbutes [cagoules] sans rien guaster; tournoit les feuilletz du bréviaire de Frère Jean, l'un après l'autre, sans rien dessirer. (676)

Effectivement les deux dernières merveilles peuvent s'inscrire dans le registre d'une certaine portée religieuse, notamment l'amélioration et l'épuration sans endommagement qu'apporte, par exemple, l'Evangélisme. D'ailleurs ce genre de glissement contextuel et sémiotique sans paraître perturber une écriture séquentielle se remarquait déjà dans la succession des prodiges des archers de l'antiquité. Aussi cette empreinte fréquente de l'écriture rabelaisienne pose-t-elle une question d'importance primordiale pour la critique rabelaisienne, notamment quel est le rapport entre le signifié explicité, d'une part, et d'autre part, l'excrescence verbale ou narrative du signifiant. Question qui se pose justement dans ce chapitre-ci et que nous abordons obliquement.

En fin de compte, les prouesses de Pantagruel aboutissent à une articulation de son pouvoir de transfigurer un objet en un autre. Le physetère, une fois anéanti et paré de flèches, devient un navire, et les flèches sont elles-mêmes francisées ou rabelaisées puisque la métamorphose, suggérée par une première analogie géographique, est désormais complétée: "De manière que le corps du physetère sembloit à la quille d'un guallion à troys gabies, emmortaisée par une compétente dimension de ses poultres" (676). En effet les flèches ont disparu et sont remplacées par les poutres, signes du nouveau, que le lecteur dorénavant reconnaîtra.

L'épisode du physetère s'articule donc essentiellement en deux moments. Dans le premier, le chapitre 33, on se trouve dans un domaine surtout existentiel: devant le choix de subir ou agir contre son destin—la mort, et ce choix est accompagné d'une peur inhérente également générée par le souvenir de Phaéton. Ici Pantagruel ne contrecarre pas Panurge; au contraire, ses actions dans le chapitre suivant lui confèrent une personnification du bien et du nouveau triomphant du mal. Lecture des plus évidentes. C'est alors que s'impose la lecture métatextuelle, car ce chapitre (34) s'avère comme une succession de narrés soulignant l'insolite, le prodigieux, et la dextérité. Aussi Pantagruel représente-t-il le livre même qui incorpore ces qualités au moyen desquelles le narrateur transfigure, réécrit le passé et s'inscrit lui-même auprès de la postérité grâce à sa virtuosité narratrice. L'épisode du physetère figure par conséquent, entre autre, un art poétique de Rabelais: forger de nouvelles voies dans le brouillis de l'existence (religion, vieillesse, écriture).[13] Face à cet "Y gregeois," les solutions résistent; elles ne sont pas toujours recherchées, d'ailleurs. Ici Rabelais se contente de coopter et de tenir en éveil le lecteur en lui conseillant d'apprendre à lire la fécondité des signes.

Notes

[1] Le mot "physetère" est un néologisme tiré de *L'Histoire naturelle* de Pline: "Maximum animal in Indico mari pristis et ballaena est, in Gallico oceano physeter, ingentis columnae modo se attollens altiorque navium velis diluviem quandam eructans." Ed. et trad. E. de Saint-Denis (Paris: Société d'Edition "Les Belles Lettres," 1955) IX, iv, 8, p. 40. Bien que Rabelais au début du chapitre 33 traduit par moments Pline, il amplifie également pour souligner le visuel et le sonore (souffleur) d'où provient l'étymologie grecque.

[2] Voir la très fine étude de Frank Lestringant, "L'Insulaire de Rabelais ou la fiction en archipel (pour une lecture topographique du *Quart Livre*)," *Rabelais en son demi-millénaire*, eds. Jean Céard et Jean-Claude Margolin (Genève: Droz, 1988) 249-74. En ce qui concerne l'épisode du physetère, l'auteur se limite à démontrer très justement que Rabelais s'était inspiré, outre d'André

Thevet, également du cartographe suédois Olaus Magnus et a bien connu sa *Carta Marina* (262, 264).

[3] Pour la tradition et la signification de ce mythe dans un contexte global de la Renaissance, voir Ervin Panofsky, *Hercules am Scheidewege und andere antike Bildstoffe in der neueren Kunst* (Leipzig et Berlin, 1930); une étude plus italianisante se trouve dans Ronald G. Witt, *Hercules at the Crossroads: The Life, Works and Thoughts of Coluccio Salutati* (Durham, NC: Duke UP, 1983); et pour Rabelais voir G. Mallary Masters, "Panurge at the Crossroads: A Mythopoetic Study of the Pythagorean Y in Rabelais's Satirical Romance (*QL*/33-34)," *Romance Notes* 15 (1973) 134-54; et Paul J. Smith, *Voyage et écriture: étude sur le* Quart Livre *de Rabelais* (Genève: Droz, 1987) 110.

[4] Les citations du *Quart Livre* sont tirées de l'édition établie par Guy Demerson dans la Collection "l'Intégrale" (Paris: Seuil, 1973).

[5] "Et Léviathan, le pêches-tu à l'hameçon, / avec une corde comprimes-tu sa langue? / Fais-tu passer un jonc dans ses naseaux, / avec un croc perces-tu sa mâchoire? / Est-ce lui qui te suppliera longuement, / te parlera d'un ton timide?… / Je parlerai aussi de ses membres, / je dirai sa force incomparable. / Qui a découvert par devant sa tunique, / pénétré dans sa double cuirasse? / Qui a ouvert les battants de sa gueule? / La terreur règne autour de ses dents! / Son dos, ce sont des rangées de boucliers, / qui ferment un sceau de pierre." *La Bible de Jérusalem* (Paris: Desclée de Brouwer, 1975), *Job* 40: 25-26, 41: 4-7).

[6] "'Qu'elle soit à moi et je m'engage à la sauver par ma valeur.' Acceptant cette condition (qui aurait pu hésiter?), les parents pressent le héros et lui promettent, outre leur fille, un royaume pour dot." Ovide, *Les Métamorphoses*, éd. et trad. Georges Lafaye (Paris: Société d'Edition "Les Belles Lettres," 1928) 119.

[7] Il n'est pas inconséquent de rappeler, ici, qu'Andromède est punie à cause de la vanité, la philautie, de sa mère, Cassiope, qui s'était vantée d'être plus belle que les Néréides. Or, l'apparition du physetère pourrait bien représenter pour Panurge cette hantise libidinale et généalogique du livre précédent.

[8] Voir Masters 144-45; Smith 110-11.

[9] "Cependant les rapides coursiers du Soleil, Pyrois, Eolis, Ethon et Phlégon, le quatrième, remplissent les airs de leurs hennissements et de leur souffle enflammé et ils frappent de leurs pieds les barrières."

[10] "Le char était léger; les chevaux du Soleil ne pouvaient le reconnaître; le joug n'avait plus son poids ordinaire. … Quand le malheureux Phaéton, du haut de l'éther, jeta ses regards sur la terre qui s'étendait si bas, si bas au-dessous de lui, il pâlit; une terreur subite fit trembler ses genoux et les ténèbres, au milieu d'une si grande lumière, couvrirent ses yeux; maintenant il aimerait mieux n'avoir jamais touché aux chevaux de son père; maintenant il regrette de connaître son origine et d'avoir vaincu par ses prières; maintenant il voudrait bien être appelé le fils de Mérops; il est emporté comme un vaisseau poussé par le souffle impétueux de Borée, à qui son pilote a lâché la bride impuissante, l'abandonnant aux dieux et aux prières. Que pourrait-il faire? …"

[11] V.-L. Saulnier a déjà bien précisé ce sens: "Rien ne sert de tirer au hasard. Ne gaspillez pas vos forces. Contre l'ennemi, sur le chemin du vrai, ce n'est pas le poids de l'artillerie qui compte, mais la précision d'un tir juste. Finesse fait plus que violence." *Rabelais dans son enquête* (Paris: SEDES, 1982) 92.

[12] Voir Smith 116 et Elizabeth A. Chesney, *The Countervoyage of Rabelais and Ariosto* (Durham, NC: Duke UP, 1982) 29.

[13] On a remarqué tout dernièrement que l'épisode du physetère est un interlude entre les épisodes de Quaresmeprenant et les Andouilles et lié par conséquent au conflit traditionnel carnavalesque (corps/esprit, viande/poisson) ainsi qu'à la fable Physis/Antiphysie. Voir tout dernièrement et globalement, par exemple, Samuel Kinser, *Rabelais's Carnival: Text, Context, Metatext* (Berkeley: U of California P, 1990, surtout p. 66, mais Kinser touche à peine à l'épisode du physetère. Or, c'est précisément ce statut d'interlude qui fait ressortir le caractère métatextuel sur lequel se déploie cet épisode et sur lequel en fait il finit par se replier.

Michel Jeanneret

Rabelais, les monstres et l'interprétation des signes (*Quart Livre* 18-42)

Le traitement de la littérature comme objet d'enseignement et de recherche a des conséquences que nous ne mesurons pas assez. Celle-ci par exemple: nous appartenons à une confrérie qui justifie son existence par l'explication des textes. Professionnellement, nous élucidons les zones obscures et découvrons des cohérences cachées. Nous devons être aussi malins que les auteurs, plus clairs que les œuvres et, bien sûr, paraître plus savants ou plus intelligents que nos collègues.

Il faut comprendre, ordonner, rationaliser. Que la critique porte sur un objet réputé complexe afin de le ramener à un principe simple, qu'elle dépasse au contraire la trompeuse simplicité de l'œuvre pour en déployer la complexité cachée, elle doit sa respectabilité à une opération de maîtrise. Si la littérature, engagée dans une lutte indécise avec des forces qui la dépassent, occupe un espace instable, à la limite du dicible et de l'indicible, le métadiscours interprétatif adopte, par vocation, le parti de la logique et de la clarté. Il objective—et désamorce—les difficultés, il travaille à dissiper la part de l'indéterminé.

Il y a là un risque de réduction auquel la critique rabelaisienne est particulièrement exposée. Parce qu'elle est nécessaire, l'explication érudite se croit également suffisante. Elle déchiffre des allusions, repère des intentions et, faute de reconnaître que son commentaire demeure partiel et univoque, tend à imposer son propre discours comme la vérité de l'œuvre. Le danger est de sacrifier la part du jeu, de censurer les ambiguïtés et de faire apparaître comme un système cohérent une vision du monde instable ou hétérogène. L'assurance de la critique positive exerce sur le texte littéraire une violence qui dénature son objet.

Le débat, à propos de Rabelais, n'est pas neuf. Je voudrais montrer une fois de plus, mais sur un objet nouveau, que le récit rabelaisien plaide lui-même, en la thématisant, pour une méthode interprétative multiple, expérimentale, qui respecte le mystère et fasse la part de l'obscur, de l'étrange. Je souhaiterais rappeler en même temps que cette approche relève, autant qu'une autre, de la recherche historique, tant il est vrai que l'histoire ne répertorie pas seulement des événements ou des idées définitivement acquises, mais rend compte aussi des tâtonnements, des incertitudes et des crises d'une époque.

On n'a pas remarqué jusqu'ici, à ma connaissance, qu'un thème et un problème continus occupent le milieu du *Quart Livre*. De l'île de Thohu Bohu (17)[1] à celle de Ruach (43-44) s'étend ce que j'appellerais une *séquence des monstres*.[2] Les deux épisodes qui encadrent la série, d'ailleurs reliés entre eux par une intrigue commune et par leur onomastique hébraïque, ne comportent pas spécifiquement le terme de *monstre*. Il reste, entre ces deux pôles, un ensemble solidement agencé, ne serait-ce que par la récurrence du même mot-thème:

18-28: la tempête, interprétée ensuite chez les Macraeons comme un des "prodiges . . . , *monstres* et . . . signes forméz contre tout ordre de nature" (27);

29-32: Quaresmeprenant, associé aux "*monstres* difformes et contrefaicts en despit de Nature" (32);

33-34: le physétère, "*monstre* marin" (33);

35-42: les Andouilles, dont le chef, Mardigras, est un "*monstre*" (41 et 42).

La diversité des phénomènes ainsi rapprochés s'explique par l'acception du terme dans la langue du XVIe siècle: est *monstre* toute manifestation insolite, un être ou un événement qui sort de l'ordinaire. L'étymologie latine habite encore le mot et lui confère une valeur supplémentaire: "Les *monstra*," dit St. Augustin, "tirent leur nom de *monstrare*, en ce qu'ils montrent quelque chose en le signifiant" (*De Civitate Dei* 21, 8). S'ils troublent l'ordre naturel, c'est pour être perçus comme signes divinatoires. Figure difforme, phénomène atmosphérique ou épidémie, le monstre est un accident chargé de sens, un message chiffré qui demande à être interprété.

Le concept implique donc la question fondamentale des signes et recoupe des problèmes majeurs de l'herméneutique antique et médiévale.[3] Tous les faits insolites ont-ils valeur symbolique, ou seulement certains? Dans cette dernière hypothèse, comment distinguer les choses qui ne signifient rien d'autre qu'elles-mêmes et les choses qui sont aussi des signes? Où passe la frontière entre les événements fortuits, dépourvus d'intentionnalité et ceux où il faut reconnaître une intervention surnaturelle? Sur cette première difficulté s'en greffe une autre: à supposer qu'on ait pu identifier tel signe, comment l'interpréter? Selon quelle méthode déchiffrer le sens caché? Le phénomène extraordinaire peut-il être entièrement expliqué, l'hésitation et l'inquiétude, surmontées?

A travers la séquence des monstres se déploie donc la question de l'interprétation et celle-ci peut être appréhendée à deux niveaux. La première dimension, patente et transitive, touche à la lecture du monde: les êtres et les choses inhabituels recèlent-ils un sens second, et pénétrable? A un second degré, latent et réflexif, la recherche se déplace vers le livre porteur: comment faire face aux singularités du texte? La fiction et ses signes fonctionnent-ils comme une allégorie? J'ai montré ailleurs qu'une autre série de chapitres, dans le *Quart Livre* (48-65), proposait une réflexion sur la figure et sur les niveaux de sens.[4] Avec une persistance qui ressort de mieux en mieux, Rabelais s'interroge sur l'interprétation des phénomènes et, du même coup, esquisse des modèles herméneutiques applicables à l'analyse des énoncés ainsi qu'au déchiffrement des récits.

La tempête (18-24) trouble l'ordre des choses et, par là, revendique en puissance la qualité de signe. Interpellés, les navigateurs adoptent successivement deux attitudes. A l'exception de Panurge que paralyse la peur, ils commencent par implorer l'aide de Dieu et luttent contre le fléau. Ils perçoivent d'abord l'événement au premier degré, comme une menace très réelle et très directe. La *praxis* précède le *logos*, l'exigence éthique renvoie à plus tard la question herméneutique.

L'étape chez les Macraeons (25-28) va fournir, dans un second temps, le calme et le recul qui favorisent l'interprétation. L'identification d'une cause permet d'assigner au cataclysme une signification cachée: un Démon vient de mourir, explique Macrobe, et l'événement a été précédé de deux phénomènes cosmiques à valeur prémonitoire—l'apparition d'une comète et, précisément, le déclenchement de la tempête. Ce qui tout à l'heure ressemblait à une simple contingence naturelle acquiert maintenant la profondeur du signe.

Le désordre apparent est ainsi récupéré dans un ordre supérieur. La tempête était l'un de ces "prodiges, portentes, monstres et autres précédens signes forméz contre tout ordre de nature" (27) que Dieu envoie aux hommes comme autant de messages codés, et finalement déchiffrables. Les interprètes détiennent un savoir surnaturel qui résout la difficulté: c'est un "prognostic certain et véridicque prédiction" (27) qui peut être traduit en termes clairs. Le "monstre", dès lors, ne fait plus peur: il répond à une nécessité logique et témoigne que les cieux sont "bénévoles" (27). A la tourmente répond ainsi le triomphe de l'esprit et de la méthode. Une herméneutique sûre d'elle-même a permis de transférer la donnée brute dans la catégorie des signes; elle désamorce la menace et rend à l'univers son harmonie.

Il est vrai que les Macraeons, entourés de forêts, de monuments symboliques et d'inscriptions cryptiques (25), ressemblent à des sages antiques et paraissent initiés à des mystères dont seuls ils détiennent la clé. Ce sont aussi des vieillards, comme figés dans un décor archaïque, dans un temps régressif; leurs temples sont ruinés et leur terre, dévastée. Est-ce à dire qu'ils incarnent un passé perdu et que la juste lecture des signes relève d'un savoir désormais oublié? Le récit de la mort du seigneur de Langey (27) dément cette hypothèse, puisque ici et maintenant, sous les yeux de Rabelais lui-même, des présages ont annoncé l'événement et ont été correctement interprétés. Aujourd'hui encore, la nature se donne à lire comme un livre où Dieu inscrit ses intentions. Dans sa réflexion sur les signes, l'épisode des Macraeons est donc foncièrement optimiste; de la transcendance à l'immanence, de l'idée cachée à sa manifestation visible, un système de correspondances garantit l'intelligibilité des phénomènes. Dans le monde et dans le livre, des figures nous interpellent, et nous sommes capables de les comprendre.

Le physétère, une énorme baleine qui menace la flotte, est lui aussi, en puissance, un monstre[5] et soulève à son tour la question du signe (33-34). La problématique est constante, mais la réponse, on va le voir, varie du tout au tout.

Le scénario ressemble à celui de la tempête: Pantagruel affronte le danger et, à force d'habileté, finit par le surmonter. La différence est qu'il n'y aura pas ici de regard rétrospectif ni de retour interprétatif. En dépit de son apparence prodigieuse, le physétère n'est qu'un vulgaire animal: il "se renversa . . . comme font tous poissons mors" (34) et, une fois liquidé, ne retient pas davantage l'attention, car Pantagruel en a déjà vu d'"aultres assez pareilz, voyre encores plus énormes" (35). La nature, ici, ne signifie rien d'autre qu'elle-même. Ce qui aurait pu être un monstre ne montre rien; il n'est qu'un objet insignifiant et passif, non montrant mais montré, pris en charge par un héros qui seul détient le pouvoir de désigner et signifier: "Pantagruel le *monstra* au pilot" (33); "Pantagruel . . . *monstre* ce qu'il sçavoit faire" (34).

Contrairement à tout à l'heure, la dimension transcendante et, avec elle, l'authentification surnaturelle du signe font complètement défaut. Pour sa défense, Pantagruel adopte une stratégie spécifiquement humaine: il compte sur sa force, son adresse et la précision géométrique de ses manœuvres; son combat se présente comme la victoire emblématique du calcul et de la raison sur la menace de l'irrationnel. L'événement est contingent, immanent et la méthode, résolument profane.

Il n'est peut-être pas indifférent que cette démonstration de maîtrise se situe exactement au centre du *Quart Livre* (33 chapitres de part et d'autre). Au cœur du récit, Rabelais inscrit la démystification du monstre. Là où la superstition, illustrée par Panurge, pensait voir un signe surnaturel et un présage funeste, il n'y a qu'un incident fortuit, banal, que la compétence technique de l'archer suffit à neutraliser. Il règne dans cet épisode comme un écho de Lucrèce et de sa croisade contre les impostures: l'hypothèse d'un sens caché s'effondre et il apparaît finalement que le monstre n'existait que dans l'imagination des esprits crédules.[6]

S'opposent ainsi, dans la question du signe, deux solutions extrêmes: tel objet ne représente que soi, tel autre est porteur d'un sens second. Mais ces deux positions ne sont pas incompatibles; elles attestent la coexistence, largement reconnue par l'exégèse traditionnelle, de choses qui ne sont que choses et de choses qui sont aussi des signes (voir n. 3) Les deux démonstrations, dans leur simplicité, partagent en outre un optimisme commun: elles expliquent pleinement le phénomène interrogé, elles vident le mystère et désamorcent la peur. Qu'il fonctionne ou non comme signe, le "monstre" est élucidé et son étrangeté, résorbée. Chacun à sa manière, l'épisode de la tempête et celui de la baleine résolvent, sans reste ni ambiguïté, le problème du sens. La raison est satisfaite.

Mais Rabelais n'a pas dit son dernier mot. Les deux autres épisodes de la séquence des monstres, Quaresmeprenant et les Andouilles, relèvent de la même problématique et pourtant, ils brouillent les pistes, ils disqualifient les solutions simples. Ces êtres étranges ont-ils statut de signe? D'où parlent-ils? Et de quoi? La confiance herméneutique affichée jusqu'ici se heurte à de fortes résistances et la question de l'interprétation, du coup, se complique singulièrement.

Au lecteur qui cherche à construire une explication, les deux histoires fournissent, il est vrai, quelques indices familiers et rassurants. Des paradigmes du discours moral, des stéréotypes de la satire émergent, qui semblent inviter à reconnaître, dans les figures et les conduites bizarres des monstres, des aberrations identifiables. Avides de certitudes faciles, la plupart des commentateurs isolent ces données, les traitent comme des indices aisément décodables et réduisent ainsi le récit à l'économie d'une fable.[7]

Le texte lui-même marque la voie: le couple antagoniste Quaresmeprenant/ Andouilles est visiblement construit sur le modèle de l'opposition traditionnelle Carême/Carnaval, qui à son tour emblématise la dissension catholiques/ protestants. Le régime maigre de Quaresmeprenant, sa carcasse décharnée figurent à l'évidence les mortifications, la rigueur des jeûnes et, par delà, désignent indirectement la bigoterie de l'Eglise romaine, le respect littéral d'une loi sectaire et pharisienne. Grasses et dissolues, les Andouilles incarnent logiquement la Réforme et son rejet des observances; elles aussi, d'ailleurs, succombent à l'excès: leur refus de la règle est une autre manifestation de fanatisme, leur libertinage, un dogmatisme inversé. Il n'en faut pas plus pour rassurer le lecteur: un lieu commun du folklore qui allégorise un débat d'époque, un principe de la pensée évangélique hostile à toutes les formes d'intolérance et de violence institutionnelle, il a reconnu tout cela; dans le labyrinthe, il a trouvé le fil rouge.

La méthode paraît d'autant plus légitime que l'épisode de Quaresmeprenant s'achève précisément sur une moralisation de ce type. L'apologue de Physis et Antiphysie propose une traduction en règle: la hideuse anatomie du monstre représente les forces du mal qui dénaturent l'ordre du monde et pervertissent les proportions harmonieuses de l'homme et de l'univers. A peine plus loin, une explication complémentaire resserre encore la perspective: les "monstres difformes et contrefaicts en despit de Nature" (32) sont à comprendre comme allégories des calomniateurs, censeurs et autres fanatiques qui, de part et d'autre de la barrière confessionnelle, répandent la terreur. Les véritables ennemis sont les adversaires du plaisir et du rire, les diffamateurs qui, souillant ce qu'ils touchent, taxent d'hérésie et envoient aux tribunaux des livres joyeux et innocents.[8] La laideur physique est donc l'image de la noirceur de l'âme. La vraie monstruosité réside dans la haine et l'intolérance, dans la perversité d'une loi aveugle qui paralyse la liberté de l'esprit.

Ces rationalisations sont commodes; elles déplacent l'inconnu sur le terrain du connu et, de la sorte, évacuent la surprise, balaient le trouble de la première lecture. Il a suffi de quelques opérations bien rodées pour exorciser l'inquiétante étrangeté de Quaresmeprenant et neutraliser la loufoquerie des Andouilles. La nébuleuse opaque a acquis la transparence du signe institué.

Cette méthode, on vient de le dire, trouve dans le texte des amorces; elle est également illustrée par Pantagruel qui, comme témoin et commentateur des événements, s'emploie à élucider et domestiquer la bizarrerie ambiante. C'est lui qui, troublé par le portrait saugrenu de Quaresmeprenant, invoque à la fin de l'épisode la fable d'Antiphysie, de manière à conclure sur une morale qui, stabilisant un sens diffus, résorbe les difficultés. C'est lui aussi qui, dialoguant avec Epistémon et Macrobe, explique le prodige de la tempête et, de l'arbitraire apparent, dégage la logique d'une symbolique providentielle.

Sa technique revient à aligner l'insolite sur le familier. A force d'expérience et d'érudition, il établit des parallèles, il cite des précédents et des exemples, de façon que le phénomène nouveau n'apparaisse que comme la répétition de l'ancien. En bon humaniste, il considère qu'une référence savante tient lieu d'explication; la mémoire encyclopédique et la médiation des livres lui fournissent des modèles et lui permettent de classer l'inconnu dans des systèmes sémantiques ou idéologiques déjà constitués. Connaître, pour Pantagruel, c'est donc reconnaître; c'est ranger la donnée brute dans la grille immuable des connaissances acquises et, du même coup, lui conférer le statut de signe.

Ce réflexe de récupération fonctionne d'autant mieux que le défi intellectuel est plus fort. Pour parer à l'extrême bizarrerie des Andouilles, qui semblent bousculer toutes les catégories reçues, Pantagruel se lance par exemple dans un "notable discours sus les noms propres" (37); il cite Platon, invoque Pythagore, et parvient ainsi à plaquer un système de signes déjà éprouvé—la valeur prémonitoire des noms—sur un phénomène sauvage et, comme tel, inexplicable. La manœuvre de diversion et le mécanisme de défense sont patents. Qu'il tue le monstre ou qu'il le rationalise, Pantagruel s'arrange pour détourner la provocation. Dans un récit qui reflète en abyme les problèmes de la lecture et de l'interprétation, il incarne le parti des idées claires et des significations logiques—principe qui commande, aujourd'hui encore, les travaux de la critique positive.

L'inadéquation de la méthode saute pourtant aux yeux. L'intérêt d'épisodes comme ceux de Quaresmeprenant et des Andouilles est de montrer combien est partiale et appauvrissante l'explication de type allégorique. Elle tire un seul des fils de l'écheveau, elle prélève quelques éléments reconnaissables, censure le reste, et tente de faire passer son coup de force pour une solution globale. Or il y a des pages entières, des masses de détails qu'elle occulte—l'interminable anatomie de Quaresmeprenant, la complexion des Andouilles, leurs sombres manœuvres, leur burlesque bataille contre les maîtres queux… Ces curiosités foisonnent, elles interpellent constamment le lecteur, sans pourtant se laisser forcer dans le réseau des signes traduisibles. Est-ce suffisant pour leur dénier tout impact? pour n'y voir que jeux gratuits, produits sans conséquence d'un esprit ou d'une plume fantasques? Invoquera-t-on, une fois de plus, l'argument débile du sucre qui fait avaler la potion?

Non, car ces restes ne sont ni subordonnés ni innocents. S'ils gênent, c'est qu'ils ouvrent la zone trouble du non-sens ou découvrent plutôt un autre système de sens—le territoire inquiétant de l'étrange et de l'irrationnel. Ce que la critique positive ne veut pas voir, c'est la part de l'ombre, les créatures délirantes de l'imagination, tout ce non-dit du discours raisonnable qui frappe les affects et réveille les fantasmes refoulés. Si la Tempête et le Physétère réussissaient à détourner la menace du monstre, les deux autres épisodes lui font face, sans la sauvegarde d'une herméneutique rassurante. Le vase de Pandore est ouvert. Osons regarder ce qui s'y cache.

Quaresmeprenant et les Andouilles exhibent d'abord leur laideur, leur difformité. Corps hybrides, organismes composites, ils brouillent la distribution ordinaire des espèces, ils dépouillent chaque classe de ses qualités spécifiques. Un premier coup est porté à la dignité de l'homme: sa différence s'estompe, la suprématie de l'esprit chancelle.

Débité en longues listes d'organes ou de fonctions discontinus, le corps de Quaresmeprenant, désarticulé, apparaît d'abord comme la juxtaposition de morceaux hétéroclites. L'unité de la personne se désagrège en une poussière de parties disjointes. Mais l'effet de déshumanisation, dans le portrait du monstre, tient encore à une autre aberration. Chacun des membres de l'anatomie est comparé à un objet—un ustensile, un appareil. Le mariage troublant de l'animé et de l'inerte, l'invasion saugrenue du règne des choses vivantes par des matières dures et hostiles, tout cela évoque le spectre de la machine qui prend le contrôle de l'homme. Comme les visages réifiés d'Arcimboldo, le corps de Quaresmeprenant est un montage d'instruments, une mécanique aveugle, une carcasse désertée par l'esprit. Reste le cauchemar de l'automate.

Etrangement métissées, les Andouilles occupent elles aussi, dans l'échelle des êtres, un espace mixte et indéterminé. La barrière des sexes vacille: ce sont des femmes, mais elles font la guerre et arborent la forme du membre viril.[9] Sont-elles hermaphrodites? incarnent-elles la figure de la mère phallique?[10] Une chose est sûre: une image de rêve s'affiche agressivement, un tabou sexuel défie le silence. Mais la contamination des classes ne s'arrête pas là. Les Andouilles participent de trois règnes: par leur comportement, leur discours, elles relèvent de l'humain. Dans leur corps, en revanche, se croisent des traces de femme, des marques animales—elles ressemblent à des "escurieux, belettes, martres ou hermines" (35) et surtout à des serpents—et les propriétés de l'objet—ce sont des saucisses. Des fantasmes d'alliances contre-nature, d'accouplements interdits produisent une figure polymorphe et monstrueuse. On dirait une effigie onirique qui se forme, se déforme, se transforme, une ébauche en gestation, dont les contours ne seraient pas encore arrêtés. A travers les corps ambigus de Quaresmeprenant et des Andouilles se profile l'image d'un monde primitif, un chaos dont les êtres, transitoires, chercheraient leur moule définitif. Tout se passe comme si la création poursuivait son cours, en quête d'un équilibre encore à conquérir: *natura naturans*, foyer d'énergies au travail, brassage de matières malléables, à l'opposé des configurations stables de l'idéal classique—*natura naturata*.

Morphologies archaïques et corps en mutation, mariage de l'homme et de la chose, brouillage des sexes, ces différentes représentations ébranlent chez le lecteur des affects qui, pour être d'ordinaire réprimés, n'en sont que plus puissants. L'image surdéterminée des Andouilles, plus qu'aucune autre, met à jour des fantasmes d'angoisse ou de plaisir, qui submergent toute tentative d'explication rationnelle; elle nous bombarde de suggestions symboliques qui défient la totalisation. Si ces dames ont une allure de pénis, elles ressemblent aussi à des étrons animés: "en Andouilles plustoust l'on trouvoit merde que fiel" (42). Phalliques et fécales, elles n'en demeurent pas moins des saucisses, conjuguant ainsi les jouissances de la bouche, celles du sexe et celles de l'excrétion. En elles se cristallisent deux solidarités d'ordinaire inavouées: l'affinité du plaisir alimentaire et du plaisir érotique, la parenté secrète des activités orales et anales.

Le mitraillage d'images choquantes ne s'arrête pas là. La figure du dieu porcin, le cochon ailé Mardigras, emblématise la relation troublante du sacré et de l'animal, de l'esprit et de la tripe. Le chapitre 38 surtout associe les Andouilles à une galerie d'effigies monstrueuses—archétypes des forces obscures du mal. Les géants du mythe grec, surgis des profondeurs de la terre pour détrôner les dieux de l'Olympe; le sinistre serpent de la Genèse; Priape, le satyre au sexe érigé; Mélusine, la femme reptile… , ces différentes figures évoquent à leur tour un monde primitif, dominé par l'instinct, livré à des puissances animales et traversé par la peur. Chacun de ces symboles résonne de vibrations affectives très fortes et devrait être interrogé de près. Il aura suffi de suggérer que Rabelais propose des représentations extrêmement troublantes, qui ouvrent une brèche dans les contenus obscurs de l'inconscient. On n'a pas quitté la problématique du signe, mais, de l'idéal de transparence posé tout à l'heure à l'exploration des profondeurs menée ici, quel chemin parcouru!

L'inquiétante étrangeté qui sature ces pages n'est pas seulement une affaire de vision. Si elle tient à des effets de signifiés, elle se joue aussi au niveau des signifiants. Il arrive que le travail sur la matière verbale récuse l'antériorité de l'idée et, à force de bricoler du sens à partir des sons, subvertisse la logique du discours. Les mots, comme affranchis des contraintes habituelles de la signification, prennent alors l'initiative du récit. La bizarrerie s'en trouve redoublée.

Quaresmeprenant "travailloit rien ne faisant, rien ne faisoit travaillant . . . Se baignoit dessus les haulz clochers, se sechoit dedans les estangs . . ." (32). Comme à travers les listes qui composent l'essentiel du portrait, le texte se fige dans l'application machinale de procédés formels—la comparaison, le chiasme, le paradoxe… De même que le monstre est un corps sans âme, un homme envahi par l'instrument, de même l'histoire semble livrée à la mécanique des mots et des stéréotypes. La langue en liberté fabrique des représentations, mais celles-ci échappent à la sanction du vraisemblable, elles inversent le rapport de la forme et du fond. Autant que le contenu des images, les moyens de le produire engendrent le malaise.

A la figure extravagante des Andouilles se superpose, également, une bonne dose de loufoquerie verbale. Les noms des guerriers, le détail de l'action militaire sont déterminés par une série de jeux de mots; ici encore, l'atelier des signifiants—appel des homonymes et des paronymes, création cocasse d'une onomastique culinaire—détermine le sens. Pantagruel en tire argument pour prouver la théorie de Cratyle; on a le droit d'y voir plutôt l'exploration farcesque des ressources et des ridicules du calembour.

La pratique insistante de la parodie—échos burlesques de la geste héroïque, imitations facétieuses du discours savant, réécriture bouffonne du mythe et de la légende—contribue à la même impression. Tout se passe comme si l'intrigue, au lieu d'obéir à une logique de l'action qui en garantirait la vraisemblance, n'était que le produit artificiel d'un collage intertextuel. De même qu'elle paraissait tout à l'heure conduite par l'impulsion des mots, l'histoire semble ici dépendre d'opérations strictement littéraires. Les événements, les personnages, l'intention présumée du récit ne seraient que des effets de répétition, le simple résultat d'une manipulation de formes et d'idées déjà constituées.

Le phénomène est à double tranchant et son évaluation, douteuse. Reconnaître que les monstres ne sont que de purs effets d'écriture, c'est les démystifier; l'exhibition des trucs du métier lève la crédulité et la peur; l'illusion référentielle s'abolit dans la conscience du jeu. Mais il n'est pas sûr que les fantaisies de la lettre soient aussi inoffensives que cela. Les mots et les formes en liberté engendrent des visions saugrenues qu'il n'est pas facile de disqualifier. Surtout, on comprend mal que des techniques apparemment gratuites puissent susciter des représentations aussi troublantes. Ce sont des artifices, et pourtant ils prennent corps et hantent l'imagination. Faut-il rire d'un bricolage sans conséquence? S'abandonner à la trouble fascination de scènes saturées d'affects? Jeu ou enjeu? Le malaise est d'autant plus grand que la question est indécidable.

Pareille ambivalence s'étend à l'ensemble des deux épisodes et contribue à l'hésitation du lecteur. Le cocasse et le sinistre se superposent; des images surgissent qui, à la fois factices et contraignantes, défient la logique du tiers exclu. Les occasions de rire abondent: complicité avec un écrivain qui s'amuse, profusion joyeuse de mets et de mots, déploiement euphorique d'une inventivité sans borne... Et pourtant, on frise la répulsion: hideur d'une carcasse déshumanisée, duplicité de figures traîtresses et insaisissables, afflux de fantasmes inavouables... Quaresmeprenant et les Andouilles sont *drôles* dans les deux acceptions du terme: comiques et inquiétants, plaisants et déplaisants, ni vraiment ceci, ni tout à fait cela. Toute position unilatérale demande à être inversée; le sens bascule, il vacille dans un tourniquet de contradictions.

Si Pantagruel et, comme lui, le lecteur précautionneux se protègent à force de coupures, de rationalisations et d'interprétations édifiantes, il y a une autre manière de lire, plus aventureuse, qui s'expose au questionnement de l'étrange. L'auteur donne l'exemple. Parti avec ses personnages à la découverte d'un autre monde, il accepte, sans chercher à l'expliquer ni le maîtriser, le surgissement de phénomènes extraordinaires. Le voyage, pour ces témoins-là, ne consiste pas à expliquer le nouveau par l'ancien, mais à pousser jusqu'au bout la surprise et le dépaysement. Disponibles, fondamentalement curieux, ils recueillent des singularités qui ébranlent l'édifice de la sagesse et du savoir reçus: hantises réprimées et scories de l'imagination, monde sans foi ni loi, soumis à des forces sauvages et à d'obscurs accouplements.

S'ouvre ainsi dans le texte, avec des pages comme celles-là, un espace où le sens s'élargit, se complique et se brouille. Les certitudes paraissent alors trop simples, la volonté de comprendre se heurte à la résistance d'une masse diffuse de signes opaques. A la façon des corps hybrides des monstres qui appartiennent à plusieurs espèces et ne se laissent épingler nulle part, le texte embrasse des matériaux si hétérogènes, et à ce point irréductibles, qu'il en devient insaisissable. Ce qu'il raconte n'est sans doute pas vrai, mais pas faux non plus; ça n'est ni sérieux ni futile; c'est irréel et pourtant incontournable; il y a du sens, mais ce sens défie l'analyse et la somme. Ce que Rabelais explore ici, c'est un chaos primitif d'intuitions à demi différenciées, c'est le foyer, opaque et fécond, des idées indéterminées.

La séquence des monstres, dans le *Quart Livre*, déploie la question du signe sous plusieurs faces, et sans concession aux solutions simples. Trois situations ont été distinguées, qui imposent chacune une méthode différente. Aux yeux des sages qui connaissent les affinités secrètes de la nature et de la surnature, la tempête apparaît comme la face visible d'un événement caché. Le monde est perçu ici comme un système symbolique cohérent et, pour qui connaît le réseau des correspondances, entièrement lisible. Les choses sont des signes dont la vérité peut être percée: la méthode allégorique s'impose, et elle fonctionne. A l'inverse, le Physétère ne montre rien que soi; ce qui aurait pu être un signe n'est qu'un animal banal, dépourvu de mystère; l'approche pertinente est ici la lecture littérale. Se complètent de la sorte deux solutions propices à la connaissance: l'extension du signe et, le cas échéant, sa signification peuvent être déterminées.

Dans les épisodes de Quaresmeprenant et des Andouilles pullulent des images qui sollicitent l'interprétation. Mais sont-elles des signes? Elles ne relèvent ni de la nature ni de la surnature; elles cachent sans doute plus qu'il ne paraît, mais le déchiffrement allégorique n'a pas prise sur elles. Quelque chose se donne à connaître, qui échappe cependant au crible des méthodes reçues. Parmi les objets qui s'offrent à l'investigation, il semble qu'il n'y ait plus seulement des messages transcendants et des phénomènes immanents, mais toute une zone mal définie—les chimères de l'imagination, les produits de l'art, les inventions de la langue—dont le statut et la portée sont incertains. Des sources mystérieuses émettent des signaux qui interpellent l'homme, dérangent sa quiétude et postulent une herméneutique différente.

Entre les trois modèles ainsi posés, rien n'indique qu'il faille choisir ni attribuer à Rabelais une préférence. Plusieurs modes de lecture sont possibles, qui varient en fonction des objets et des interprètes. Fidèle à sa vocation polyphonique, le texte rabelaisien ne cherche pas à imposer une vérité. Il répercute un débat d'époque, il présente les problèmes et les éventuelles solutions. D'un côté, il enregistre les données acquises, de l'autre, il découvre les points de résistance—et livre tout cela à la sagacité du lecteur.

Si la question déployée ici revient avec insistance dans les prologues, dans le *Tiers Livre* et partout, dans les récits, où il s'agit de regarder et d'écouter, de lire et de comprendre, c'est qu'elle recoupe un problème essentiel de la pensée humaniste. Le Moyen Age a élaboré une théorie générale du symbole qui, applicable à la lecture du monde comme témoin du Créateur, à l'exégèse de la Bible et, par extension, à l'interprétation des œuvres païennes, prétend fonctionner comme une grille universelle et infaillible. Quels que soient les moyens de la démonstration, la fin revient toujours à retrouver, sous l'apparence, la vérité unique de la Révélation. Parce qu'ils n'adhèrent plus à une conception monolithique de la vérité, les humanistes vont s'appliquer à assouplir ce système. S'ils travaillent, par la philologie, à établir la dignité du sens littéral et de la spécificité historique, ils ne contestent pas la présence, sous les choses et sous les mots, de valeurs latentes, qui entraînent la nécessité d'une interprétation "à plus haut sens." L'esprit anime la matière, des connaissances cachées gisent dans les textes sacrés et antiques, si bien que la recherche des significations secondes demeure essentielle. Mais cette opération, pour les hommes du XVIe siècle, ne saurait être formalisée; l'excès de méthode inhibe la vigilance du lecteur. La poursuite authentique du sens est une activité spirituelle, un don de l'inspiration ou, à tout le moins, une conquête de l'intuition, un effort de l'intelligence. La lecture avait pu prétendre autrefois épuiser la question du sens. Elle est conçue maintenant comme un exercice d'adaptation et d'écoute, une quête problématique, qui postule un engagement personnel. Elle reconnaît que la vérité ne se révèle que par détours et par bribes. Cette crise dans le système des signes anime en profondeur le texte de Rabelais. Si le débat sur l'interprétation des récits ne cesse de rebondir, c'est qu'il est constitutif de l'œuvre elle-même.

Notes

[1] Les chiffres désignent les numéros de chapitre. J'utilise l'édition de la Pléiade.

[2] Cela n'exclut pas que d'autres épisodes, dispersés, touchent de près ou de loin à la même problématique (e.g. Medamothi, Ennasin, Gaster).

[3] Outre l'ouvrage essentiel de Jean Céard sur les monstres, *La Nature et les prodiges. L'insolite au XVIe siècle en France* (Genève: Droz, 1977), voir, sur la question générale du signe, Henri de Lubac, *Exégèse médiévale: les quatre sens de l'Ecriture*, 3 vols. (Paris: Aubier, 1959-64) ainsi que les articles de Johan Chydenius, "La Théorie du symbolisme médiéval" et Armand Strubel, "*Allegoria in factis* et *Allegoria in verbis*," l'un et l'autre dans *Poétique* 23 (1975) 322-41 et 342-57.

[4] Voir "Les Paroles dégelées: Rabelais, *Quart Livre* 48-65," dans *Littérature* 17 (1975) 14-30 et "Polyphonie de Rabelais: ambivalence, antithèse et ambiguïté," dans *Littérature* 55 (1984) 98-111. Voir aussi Gérard Defaux, *Marot, Rabelais, Montaigne: l'écriture comme présence* (Paris et Genève: Champion-Slatkine, 1987) chap. 2.

[5] Il est désigné dans les deux titres de chapitre comme "monstrueux physétère" et, par Panurge, comme "monstre marin" (33).

[6] Sur la démystification du monstre, dans cet épisode, voir Paul J. Smith, *Voyage et écriture. Etude sur le "Quart Livre" de Rabelais* (Genève: Droz, 1987).

[7] Voir par exemple Verdun-L. Saulnier, *Rabelais*, vol. 2 (Paris: SEDES, 1982) chap. 13 et 15 et Michael A. Screech, *Rabelais* (Londres: Duckworth, 1979) 367-71.

[8] En écho à la fin du chap. 32, l'épître dédicatoire du *Quart Livre* à Odet de Châtillon ainsi que le Prologue de 1548 traitent de monstres et cannibales les calomniateurs responsables de la condamnation du *Tiers Livre*.

[9] La *Briefve Déclaration* traduit le nom de la reine des Andouilles, Niphleseth: "membre viril. Héb."

[10] Voir Françoise Charpentier, "La Guerre des Andouilles. *Pantagruel* IV, 35-42," dans *Etudes seiziémistes offertes à V.-L. Saulnier* (Genève: Droz, 1980) 119-35 et Gisèle Mathieu-Castellani, "Bisexualité et animalité fabuleuse," dans *Corps Ecrit* 6 (1983) 159-69.

Part II

Marot, Pernette du Guillet, Du Bellay, Ronsard

Gérard Defaux

Clément Marot:
poésie, autobiographie et roman

> CLOV. —Oh, à propos, ton histoire?
> HAMM. (*très surpris*) —Quelle histoire?
> CLOV. —Celle que tu nous racontes depuis toujours.
> HAMM. —Ah, tu veux dire mon roman?
> CLOV. —Voilà.
>
> Beckett, *Fin de partie*

Comme ce dialogue emprunté à *Fin de partie* l'aura peut-être déjà fait comprendre, mon propos est ici de montrer que si, à la Renaissance, le roman n'est pas véritablement un genre littéraire, que s'il est vraiment difficile, à quelques exceptions près, que nous connaissons tous, de parler du "roman" du XVIe siècle comme on parle du roman du XIXe ou du XXe siècle, il existe en revanche, à l'époque d'Erasme, de Rabelais, de Budé et de Marot, comme à celle de Montaigne et d'Agrippa d'Aubigné, ce qu'on pourrait appeler une irrépressible *pulsion autobiographique*, un désir essentiel de se dire, de se loger dans l'écriture. Il est ensuite de montrer que ce désir, ou plutôt les apories dans lesquelles il conduit l'écrivain qui en est possédé, favorise dans une large mesure l'épanouissement de la fiction, engendre une écriture spécifiquement *romanesque*, une écriture grâce à laquelle, au XVIe siècle, le roman, sans être véritablement nulle part, sans avoir son espace et son lieu, est positivement partout: présent, non seulement dans l'épopée burlesque de *Pantagruel* et dans les romans de chevalerie qu'elle parodie et dont souvent elle s'inspire, dans les nouvelles, les contes, les histoires sentimentales, pastorales ou tragiques, voire dans le récit de voyage, la chronique historiographique ou le discours humaniste, chez Rabelais, Marguerite, Helisenne, ou Bonaventure des Périers, Aneau, Belleforest ou Boaistuau, Erasme, Montaigne ou Budé, mais aussi bien dans la poésie de Clément Marot.

Pour essayer de montrer pourquoi et comment, à propos de l'œuvre de Marot, la poésie tend à générer une écriture proprement *romanesque*, à préparer les triomphes et l'hégémonie future du roman—c'est-à-dire pour montrer pourquoi et comment, au fond, cette œuvre, en dépit des apparences, en dépit aussi de la situation historique qui est la sienne, est étrangement et résolument *moderne*—, la meilleure stratégie est encore celle qui consiste, modestement, et dans un esprit très pratique, à s'interroger sur les éditions qui, parues du vivant de notre poète, s'échelonnent des *Opuscules et petitz traictez* de 1530-31 aux *Œuvres* publiées en 1544 à Lyon par Constantin, en passant naturellement par *l'Adolescence clementine* de 1532, *La Suite* de 1533-34, la traduction du *Premier livre de la Metamorphose d'Ovide* de 1534, le *Recueil* préparé en mars 1538 pour le connétable de Montmorency, et les éditions Dolet de 1538, 1542 et 1543;[1] à examiner la forme qui est la leur, l'économie qui les caractérise et les principes, les intentions et les motifs qui, consciemment ou non, ont dicté au poète l'ordre qu'il a choisi de leur donner.

On s'aperçoit alors très vite, en effet, parallèlement à un souci très humaniste et très apparent de tenir compte des genres, de l'existence de ce que je viens juste d'appeler une pulsion autobiographique. Si Marot tient de toute évidence à offrir à ses "tres chers freres" et autres "Enfans d'Apollo" un véritable "jardin poétique" à la française, bien peigné et bien entretenu, avec son imposant massif de traductions virgiliennes et dévotes, son majestueux "Temple de Cupido," ses allées d'Epîtres, de Complaintes et d'Epitaphes, ses alignements traditionnels de Ballades et de Rondeaux, son parterre coloré et fleuri de Chansons, le lecteur s'aperçoit vite, malgré tout, de la fragilité de cette architecture florale et de la présence en elle d'un mouvement impossible à maîtriser, d'un mouvement qui déplace continuellement les lignes, et qui bouscule l'ordre établi. Marot d'ailleurs ne s'en cache pas, qui affirme, dans son Epître liminaire de *L'Adolescence*, la volonté qui est la sienne de procéder en quelque sorte chronologiquement, en commençant par présenter ses "Œuvres de jeunesse," les "coups d'essay" de son "printemps," puis en ajoutant à ce bouquet un peu pâle et à bien des égards imparfait, "Ouvrages de meilleure trempe, et de plus polie estoffe."[2] Tellement soucieux de représenter ses progrès, son cheminement créateur et poétique, c'est-à-dire d'enraciner la poésie dans le moi, de la rattacher aux événements personnels qui lui ont donné naissance, que non seulement il offre d'abord au lecteur sa traduction de la première Eglogue de Virgile, travail si peu satisfaisant au plan du métier poétique que Jean Lemaire de Belges le "reprit" en y introduisant les "couppes feminines," mais que, pour l'essentiel, comme on s'en aperçoit sans peine à examiner ses Opuscules, ses Ballades ou ses Epîtres, il semble, dans sa présentation, avoir été surtout guidé par des considérations de chronologie, par un souci très évident de *représentation* des événements majeurs de son existence jusqu'à la fin de l'année 1526. A un tel point que l'édition *princeps* de son *Adolescence* s'ajoute déjà, de la façon la plus inattendue qui soit, un bourgeonnement quelque peu sauvage, les "Autres Œuvres de Clement Marot, Valet de chambre du Roy, faictes depuis l'aage de son Adolescence,"[3] amalgame informe et désordonné où, plutôt que de s'intégrer au corpus déjà existant, Ballades, Epîtres et Chants royaux, Huitains et Dizains se mêlent à l'"Eglogue sur le trespas de Loyse de Savoye" et à la fameuse "Deploration de Florimond Robertet." Et que quelques mois plus tard une nouvelle édition—la seconde—ajoute encore à ce désordre naissant un bouquet bigarré d'"Autres Œuvres faictes en sadicte maladie."[4]

On pourrait certes, face à ces "dangereux suppléments," à ce principe de désordre qui vient continuellement bouleverser l'ordre du classement par genres, invoquer l'intervention des imprimeurs, toujours soucieux, comme Marot lui-même d'ailleurs le reconnaît dans son épître à Etienne Dolet de juillet 1538,[5] d'ajouter aux éditions déjà existantes, en les "recueillant çà et là," toutes les "pieces" qui leur tombent entre les mains—"et par telles additions," commente Marot, "se rompt tout l'ordre de mes livres, qui m'a tant cousté à dresser." Mais, dans ce domaine, et en dépit même des déclarations que je viens de rappeler, l'intervention des imprimeurs, ce que le poète appelle leur "avare convoitise," n'explique pas tout. Marot est clairement, sinon le seul, du moins le premier responsable. La preuve en est qu'en 1534, ou à la fin de 1533, *L'Adolescence clementine* qui, de bourgeonnement en bourgeonnement, tient à ne pas grossir, à conserver son identité—voire son authenticité—se donne éloquemment une *SVITE* d'"Elegies," d'"Epistres differentes," de "Chants divers," de "Cimetiere" et de "Menu." Et que la traduction du *Premier Livre de la Metamorphose d'Ovide* s'ajoute un *item* autobiographique au titre des plus révélateur, le poète profitant d'une conjoncture politique et religieuse encourageante pour publier enfin "Certaines Œuvres qu'il feit en prison non encore imprimeez."[6] La preuve en est que le *Recueil* présenté en mars 1538 à Anne de Montmorency, *Recueil* qui est le produit de la seule volonté de Marot et qui exclut, par sa nature, toute intervention étrangère, obéit à des impératifs du même ordre et que, comme son titre nous l'indique—*Recueil des dernieres Œuvres de Clement marot, non imprimées / Et premierement / Celles qu'il fit durant son exil, Et depuis son retour / 1537 / En mars*—,[7] Marot s'y propose avant tout de présenter au nouveau Connétable, de l'aveu même de Claude Mayer, pourtant partisan déclaré d'une économie à caractère exclusivement générique, "une espèce de compte rendu de ses faits et gestes depuis sa fuite en 1534."[8]

On voit sans peine à quelles conclusions des observations de cette nature permettent d'aboutir. Comme je l'ai déjà fait remarquer, Clément Marot n'est pas pour rien l'exact contemporain d'Erasme. Pour lui aussi, comme plus tard pour Montaigne, l'œuvre est témoignage et miroir, voix et présence de l'ouvrier, représentation d'une subjectivité, inscription de cette subjectivité dans l'histoire et dans le temps. Elle devient de plus en plus, une fois passé le cap des "coups d'essay" de l'adolescence, la dépositaire de ses convictions et de son existence, elle semble avoir de plus en plus tendance, au fur et à mesure que les épreuves s'accumulent, à prendre une dimension personnelle et autobiographique, à se vouloir jaillissement irrépressible et spontané du moi. Là où le poète, dans un geste novateur qui doit sans doute beaucoup à l'exemple des *Opere toscane* de Luigi Alamani, trahit un souci bien compréhensible de distinction et de définition des genres, s'efforce tant bien que mal de maîtriser sa production, de la couler dans des moules tout faits, voire, quand le besoin s'en fait sentir, d'en créér de nouveaux, cherche à imposer *de l'extérieur* à son œuvre la forme et l'ordre qui, étant donnée sa nature, naturellement lui manquent, l'homme continue de se laisser conduire par des considérations de chronologie, à attacher plus d'importance, au fond, à sa vie qu'à son rôle, à son être qu'à sa *persona*. Un peu déjà à la façon dont Montaigne bâtira sa vie au troisième livre des *Essais*, le sujet Marot, le Moi Marot, d'édition en édition, construit sous nos yeux sa propre histoire, avec tout ce que celle-ci a d'imprévisible, de provisoire et d'inachevé, prenant sans doute lui aussi conscience, puisque sa poésie s'affirme de plus en plus clairement *speculum animi*, miroir de son âme, qu'il pourra continuer d'écrire ainsi "tant qu'il y aura de l'encre et du papier au monde." C'est pourquoi, le poète en Marot ne parlant pas assez fort pour réduire l'homme au silence, il faudra symboliquement attendre la mort de ce dernier pour voir enfin, en 1544, sur l'initiative de Guillaume Roville, l'œuvre elle-même se plier finalement aux exigences du classement par genres.[9]

Du vivant de Marot, celle-ci demeure au contraire, d'une façon très révélatrice, soumise à la pression des circonstances et des événements. Elle prend naissance dans l'histoire, l'histoire du siècle comme l'histoire du Moi, et c'est cette histoire même qu'elle se propose de traduire, d'exprimer et de représenter. Comme celle d'une Chronique, d'un *Registre* ou encore, disons-le, d'un *Journal*, sa réalité et sa vérité sont toutes temporelles. L'homme, l'homme vivant, se sert du poète pour raconter sa vie, rapporter ce qui s'y passe, s'expliquer, se défendre et se justifier. Le lecteur apprend ainsi que Marot ne parvient pas à se faire payer, qu'une femme inconstante l'a trahi, qu'il est en prison, qu'il est malade, que son valet lui a volé son cheval, ses vêtements et son argent, que les théologiens de la Sorbonne et les officiers de justice le persécutent, qu'il a dû s'enfuir à Ferrare puis à Venise, qu'il rentre en France en passant par Lyon, que le roi lui a fait cadeau d'une maison. Et chaque épisode majeur qui lui est ainsi rapporté s'inscrit pour ainsi dire tel quel dans le tissu de l'œuvre, dans une sorte de jaillissement immédiat, insouciant et direct. Somme toute, par le biais de ce désir de représentation, de ce vouloir-dire autobiographique, Marot remet en place, dans sa poésie, les structures narra-tives que son classement par genres risquait de lui faire perdre. Il renoue avec une tradition alors extrêmement vivante, et qui peut s'observer dans des sommes poétiques comme *Le Sejour* ou *Le Vergier d'Honneur*, *Le Jardin de plaisance et fleur de Rethoricque*. Dans la poésie, il réintroduit l'histoire, il réintroduit, plus exactement, une histoire qui est à la fois celle du Prince et de son royaume, et celle du poète. Son histoire à lui.

Cette présence du sujet dans son discours poétique est si réelle et si pesante qu'elle finit d'ailleurs par ébranler sérieusement la notion même de genre qui, dans l'économie de l'œuvre, lui servait de contrepoids. Paradoxalement, les expériences et les réflexions théoriques de plus en plus poussées auxquelles il se livre, poussé par ses lectures des grands modèles latins, Virgile, Horace, Catulle, Ovide, par ses fréquentations—Macrin, Bérault, Tory, Macault, Bourbon, Brisset, Mellin de Saint-Gelais, Dolet, etc.—et par les ferments de renouvellement qu'il respire tous les jours, dans sa résidence parisienne ou à la Cour, aboutissent chez lui à une sorte d'appauvrissement, voire à une déconstruction, à une remise en question extrêmement lucide de tous les critères formels sur lesquels les poéticiens s'appuient. C'est ainsi que le poète qui cultive l'élégie, l'épigramme, le cantique et l'épithalame, est aussi celui qui révèle cruellement les insuffisances des genres qu'il cultive et qu'il introduit dans notre poésie, celui qui continuellement regimbe, refuse de se laisser enfermer, recherche la liberté dans les nuances que lui suggère autant son désir d'authenticité que l'acuité de son sens critique, ne parvenant plus finalement, au fur et à mesure que sa pratique s'affine, à distinguer nettement la "complainte" de l'"elégie," et cette dernière de l'"epistre," considérant le "coq-à-l'âne" comme une épître ordinaire, composant des élégies "en forme d'epistre," de "cantique" ou de "ballade," coulant même certaines de ses épîtres dans le moule de strophes lyriques ou leur donnant déjà, par leur densité et leur "pointe finale," quelque chose du piquant heureux de l'épigramme, trahissant au fond, dans ces hésitations apparentes, et dans ces "confusions" qui n'en sont pas, une subjectivité de poète à la recherche de la note juste, une subjectivité soucieuse de s'inscrire tout entière dans son écriture et qui, pour y parvenir, dispose avec élégance de toutes les conventions, de toutes les contraintes formelles susceptibles de constituer un obstacle à son expression. Semblable en cela au romancier, Marot est à la fois celui qui cultive tous les genres, et qui, en même temps, les liquide.

On pourrait, sans le moins du monde forcer les choses, presque dire qu'il en va chez Marot de la poésie comme il en va de la religion. De la même façon qu'il semble avec saint Paul accorder dans le domaine de la religion plus d'importance à la Foi qu'aux Œuvres, il s'attache davantage, dans le domaine de la poésie, à l'authenticité du sentiment, à la justesse et à la force de l'idée, à la précision nerveuse du trait d'esprit, qu'aux formes mêmes dans lesquelles ces sentiments et ces idées trouvent finalement leur corps, leur inscription matérielle et sensible. Toujours embarrassé, en vérité, par ces formes venues d'ailleurs que de lui, et toujours désireux de les abolir, pour mieux affirmer sa maîtrise, pour maintenir malgré tout, en dépit de tous les obstacles que la tradition poétique et le langage lui opposent, ce que Marc Fumaroli a justement appelé le primat sénéquien et augustinien de l'intériorité.[10]

C'est pourquoi ses *genres* de prédilection—mais sans doute conviendrait-il, à ce stade, de mettre le terme *genres* entre guillemets—ceux qui ont été pour lui l'occasion des plus grandes réussites et qu'il a sollicités le plus volontiers, sont indiscutablement la "chanson" et ses variantes, l'"hymne" ou le "cantique," parce que le poète y est le maître souverain de ses mètres et de ses strophes, l'"épigramme," qui offre, sur des genres comme le rondeau ou le sonnet, l'avantage de la variété, de la disponibilité et de la souplesse,[11] et l'"épître," celui de tous les genres alors à sa disposition qui autorise le plus de liberté. Ce qui nous mène à conclure que l'unité poétique de base qui s'accorde le mieux avec le génie de Marot, et avec son projet poétique, est le couplet de décasyllabes à rimes plates. Ou encore—ce qui revient au même—que ce n'est jamais, chez lui, la forme qui s'impose au poète mais, bien au contraire le poète qui, constamment, invente ou choisit les formes dans lesquelles il va s'exprimer. Formes qui toutes tendent au non-être, à la négation d'elles-mêmes, à ce qu'on pourrait appeler, après Robert Griffin, l'absolue *formlessness*.[12]

S'il fallait véritablement reconnaître à Marot, au moment où il fait son apparition sur notre scène poétique, une quelconque originalité, c'est très certainement là qu'il faudrait la situer, dans ce souci de présence et d'expression de son Moi. Avec le temps, Marot devient de plus en plus un poète qui se prend lui-même pour sujet de sa poésie, qui fait d'elle le lieu privilégié—le lieu unique—de l'extériorisation et de l'inscription de sa subjectivité, un moyen de *représentation*. Car l'intériorité, ce qu'il appelle volontiers "le cœur," la "vraye intention," le "vouloir," est bien pour lui, comme pour Rabelais, ce qui compte avant tout. Foyer, origine, source et principe de tout le reste. Et s'il lui arrive malgré tout de céder l'initiative aux mots, de lâcher joyeusement la bride au signifiant, de s'en griser au point de s'abandonner à sa magie, ces moments d'abandon s'accompagnent toujours chez lui d'une telle maîtrise qu'on s'aperçoit bien vite que l'abandon n'était que feint, et que Marot ne cultive ces moments que pour mieux affirmer sa présence.

Naturellement, une constatation de cet ordre ne peut que déboucher sur des questions de rhétorique et de poétique, plus précisément encore sur des questions de style. Questions qui elles-mêmes renvoient à une onto-théologie, à tout un système métaphysique sur lequel elles se greffent et sans lequel elles ne sauraient exister. J'ai tenté ailleurs[13] de décrire ce système et de traiter ces questions, en montrant comment, à partir de cette croyance logocentrique—certains diraient de cette illusion—, de cette attitude et de ce rapport nouveaux du sujet face au langage, tout, en définitive, dans la littérature de l'époque, s'enchaîne, se détermine, se structure et s'explique. Faute d'espace et de temps, je ne reprendrai pas ici ces développements, rappelant simplement cette évidence, que si le langage est présence, s'il est vérité, cette présence et cette vérité même acquièrent du même coup une importance considérable, deviennent ni plus ni moins les points de focalisation, les enjeux majeurs du discours humaniste, dans sa dimension écrite aussi bien que dans sa dimension parlée. Par quoi se pose, avec une acuité et une urgence exemplaires, un vieux problème, celui qui, si nous en croyons Jacques Derrida,[14] vouait déjà à l'impuissance l'auteur du *Phèdre*, incapable de réellement distinguer, quoi qu'il ait pu dire, entre le discours de la vérité et celui du mensonge.

Il est clair en effet, à partir du moment où l'on croit que la vocation du langage est d'être le miroir de l'âme, que sa seule raison d'être consiste à accueillir et à loger l'intériorité, que ce problème devient incontournable, et d'autant plus incontournable qu'il paraît pratiquement insoluble. Le cas Marot est à cet égard aussi éloquent qu'instructif, au double plan de l'œuvre et de la réception qui, depuis du Bellay, lui a été réservée. Quand la "transparence," l'"élégance" et la "simplicité" du style marotique n'ont pas suscité le mépris ou le doute, elles ont donné naissance à de véritables romans d'imagination. Et le premier paradoxe auquel se trouve encore aujourd'hui confronté l'apprenti qui, comme moi, se voit condamné par les contraintes du genre de l'édition critique à écrire une "biographie" de Marot, est celui de l'impossibilité dans laquelle il se trouve de pouvoir dire si ce qu'il écrit est vrai ou faux, si la "vie" qu'il est en train de reconstruire a la moindre valeur scientifique et n'est pas, à tout prendre, un roman—un roman peut-être un peu moins naïf que celui de Lenglet-Dufresnoy,[15] mais un roman quand même. Non seulement parce que, à quelques rares exceptions, les seuls "documents" que nous possédions sont les poèmes de Marot lui-même, et que nous ne savons jamais que croire et que ne pas croire de ce qu'il a bien voulu nous dire, mais aussi, et surtout, parce que "la commune maniere de parler" que l'auteur de la *Deffence et illustration* reproche à son aîné n'a, quand on la sonde, absolument rien de "commun," et encore moins de "simple" ou de "transparent." Si elle est en quoi que ce soit *miroir*, ce miroir dissimule l'auteur qui le tient, et il ne reflète en fin de compte que le lecteur qui essaye en vain de le traverser.

Il reste malgré tout possible, à certains moments précis, de surprendre le poète en flagrant délit sinon de mensonge, du moins de fiction, et de comprendre du même coup pourquoi une œuvre apparemment si "naturelle" et si "simple" a pu générer tant de lectures proprement romanesques. Lui aussi désireux de mettre son cœur à nu, mais en même temps contraint à la prudence et au calcul par la censure de la Sorbonne et les foudres du Parlement, et de surcroît voué à toutes les manipulations rhétoriques par ses fonctions de poète à gages et de valet de chambre, Marot a vite compris que la vérité, si impérieuse soit-elle, ne saurait se passer du secours de la fiction. Et il a construit lui-même sa vie pour nous, à la façon dont un romancier peut construire un roman. L'examen des éditions publiées de son vivant—et de son aveu—révèle qu'en lui le militant de la Foi et de la Vérité se double d'un stratège habile, d'un maître tacticien soucieux de créer de lui une certaine image et de l'imposer à ses lecteurs, et extrêmement conscient de ce qu'il peut et ne peut pas se permettre: désireux, par exemple, de faire croire, et Sebillet l'a cru, et Villey, et bien d'autres après Villey, que tous ses rondeaux, ses ballades et ses chants royaux sont "œuvres de jeunesse"; n'hésitant pas, quand le besoin s'en fait sentir, à adresser à "ma Dame la duchesse d'Alençon" une ballade initialement écrite au comte d'Etampes,[16] alors Prévôt de Paris; imaginant, pour expliquer son départ de Ferrare, une sombre et incroyable histoire d'agression contre sa personne, d'"oultraige / Que Ferraroys mal nobles de couraige" lui auraient "fait de nuyct, armez couardement"—alors qu'en réalité, des documents cette fois nous le disent, il n'a quitté Renée de France que parce que l'inquisition du lieu commençait à voir en lui un hérétique dangereux, un luthérien notoire; tellement convaincu que la vérité n'est pas toujours bonne à dire, et que tout, en elle, y dépend de celui à qui l'on s'adresse, que le *Recueil* manuscrit qu'il offre en 1538 au Connétable de Montmorency filtre soigneusement toutes les pièces compromettantes et sentant, même de loin, le fagot. Si bien que lorsque, à notre tour, nous nous mettons à écrire la vie de Marot, nous ne pouvons généralement que mimer, que répéter, la fiction ainsi soigneusement mise en place.

A ces flagrants délits, qui ne peuvent que légitimement faire naître le doute—la critique se souvenant alors soudainement que les poètes ont toujours eu la réputation d'être de grands menteurs—viennent s'ajouter d'autres constatations encore plus troublantes, je veux dire celles que ne peut pas manquer de faire tout lecteur tant soit peu averti face à l'impeccable enchaînement des causes et des conséquences, à la parfaite séquence narrative que Marot lui propose, récit où ce qui est dit a très évidemment moins pour fonction d'informer que de désarmer d'avance la curiosité en faisant oublier tout ce qui ne l'a pas été. La stratégie est patente dans l'affaire de la "rescousse"—nous ne saurons sans doute jamais *pourquoi*, pour quelle raison précise Marot "recourut ung certain Prisonnier" entre les mains du guet, ni *qui* était ce personnage auquel il prêta secours—, et tellement efficace que la lettre d'élargissement signée par le roi le 1er novembre 1527 reprend les termes mêmes de l'épître de Marot.[17] Elle est peut-être encore plus apparente dans l'affaire de l'emprisonnement du printemps 1526, puisque Dolet, quand en 1542 il publie *L'Enfer*, ajoute à cet *opus magnum* "aulcunes Ballades, Epistres & Rondeaux appartenant à l'argument,"[18] reconstituant ainsi l'histoire de "la Prinse de Marot" dans la version même que ce dernier en avait proposée. Quoi de plus satisfaisant pour l'esprit que d'apprendre 1) que Marot avait une maîtresse nommée Isabeau; 2) qu'abandonné par celle-ci, il avait écrit un rondeau dans lequel il dénonçait son inconstance; 3) que la dite dame, "de cueur faulse & lasche," avait décidé de se venger en l'accusant auprès de "je ne sçay quel papelard" d'avoir rompu le jeûne ordonné par l'Eglise; 4) qu'à la suite de cette dénonciation ("Prenez le, il a mangé le Lard!"), Marot aurait été emprisonné au Châtelet et interrogé par le lieutenant criminel Gilles Maillard; 5) qu'il aurait, de sa prison, appelé à l'aide successivement le docteur en théologie responsable de son emprisonnement, à savoir Nicolas Bouchart, et son ami Lyon Jamet; 6) que grâce, sans doute, à l'intervention de ce dernier, et à la complicité de Louis Guillard, évêque de Chartres, il put enfin sortir de son "enfer" et être transféré "en la prison claire et nette de Chartres"; 7) qu'il fut finalement délivré "le premier jour de la verte sepmaine" de l'an de grâce 1526. A découvrir ainsi cette histoire, le lecteur reste somme toute sur une impression identique à celle que lui laisse le style "naturel" de Marot: convaincu et charmé, mais réduit au silence, n'ayant plus rien à dire et plus rien à demander, puisque, apparemment, toutes les réponses et tous les faits lui ont déjà été fournis. Si bien qu'une accusation de Luthéranisme se voit, par l'habileté de Marot, ramenée à l'insignifiance amusée d'une vengeance de femme, en quelque sorte banalisée, et transformée en littérature, par un poète qui a compris que le jeu, l'humour et l'esprit, et cette façon qu'il a de maîtriser les mots, constituent encore pour lui la meilleure des défenses, le plus sûr des plaidoyers.

Car, nous le savons tous, c'est bien de littérature qu'il s'agit, d'*imitatio* plus que de *mimesis*.[19] Littéralement, Marot nourrit son récit de tous les prestiges de la fable. Non seulement parce qu'il sollicite Esope, qu'il donne à ses poèmes une dimension réflexive et allégorique, mais aussi parce qu'il nous refait le coup de François Villon et qu'il utilise les recettes les plus éprouvées de la tradition courtoise, allant même jusqu'à dater sa mise en liberté du premier jour du mois de mai, et à inscrire dans le tissu de son rondeau "parfaict" le refrain d'une ballade de Charles d'Orléans. Et ce qu'il fait en cette occurrence précise se répète en vérité partout. Des voix se sont récemment fait entendre pour suggérer, par exemple, que lorsque Marot se plaint de ses malheurs—il est malade, et son valet s'est enfui avec son argent, ses habits et son cheval—il utilise toute une série de topoi éprouvés, ceux de la "rhetoric of misfortune," topoi mis depuis longtemps en place par Deschamps, Taillevent, Molinet—et naturellement ce mauvais garçon de Villon. Et que ce n'est pas parce qu'il nous le dit que nous devrions croire qu'il ait réellement eu un "valet de Gascogne," puisque ce valet est avant tout "a literary stereotype."[20] Marot a certes été jeté en prison, il a sans doute été malade et volé, mais tout le reste est littérature.

La littérature est pour Marot tellement vitale qu'à chaque fois qu'il s'efforce de l'abandonner, de se dire dans son secours, il se trouve soudain démuni et gauche, confronté à tous les obstacles insurmontables que suppose sa rhétorique de l'intériorité. Je pense ici particulièrement à cette épître qu'en novembre 1535 il fait parvenir "Au Roy nouvellement sorti de maladie." Etrange et fascinante épître, qui nous met en présence de deux discours brutalement juxtaposés. L'un que nous connaissons bien, puisqu'il est par exemple celui des épîtres qu'en 1527-28 il adresse au roi et à d'autres grands

personnages de la Cour pour se faire payer ses gages et être "bien couché";
l'autre, que nous sommes surpris de découvrir en tel voisinage, puisqu'il est
celui du prédicateur évangélique et du martyr de la foi. D'abord comme il se
doit tout entière occupée par l'expression d'une "lyesse" convenable en
pareille circonstance, l'épître tourne ensuite assez vite à la requête intéressée
et à l'offre de service. Marot tâte le terrain, il voudrait bien faire mentir ses
ennemis, recevoir ses gages, savoir que le roi ne l'a pas réellement abandonné.
Il lui fait part de ses progrès en italien et en latin, des cours qu'il suit à
l'académie de Ferrare. Mais soudain, sans la moindre transition, et comme si
ce langage—ce badinage, on pourrait dire non ce mari-, mais ce *marovaudage*—
ne le satisfaisait plus, ne l'exprimait plus, le ton change et devient plus pressant,
le lecteur est confronté à un autre registre, un registre où le désir de convaincre
se substitue à celui de séduire, et où la passion remplace l'esprit:

> O Sire, donq renverse leurs langaiges;
> Vueilles permettre (en despit d'eulx) mes gaiges
> Passer les montz et jusque icy venir,
> Pour à l'estude ung temps m'entretenir
> Soubz Celius, de qui tant on aprent,
> Et si desir apres cela te prent
> De m'appeler sur la terre gallique,
> Tu trouveras ceste langue italique
> Passablement dessus la mienne entée,
> Et la latine en moy plus augmentée,
> Si que l'exil, qu'ilz pensent si nuysant,
> M'aura rendu plus apte et plus duysant
> A te servir myeulx à ta fantaisie,
> Non seullement en l'art de poesie,
> Ains en affaire, en temps de paix ou guerre,
> Soit pres de toy, soit en estrange terre.
>   Je ne suis pas si laid comme ilz me font;
> Myré me suis au cler ruysseau profond
> De verité, et à ce qu'il me semble.
> A Turc ne Juif en rien je ne ressemble.
> Je suis Chrestien, pour tel me veulx offrir,
> Voire plus prest à peine & mort souffrir
> Pour mon vray Dieu et pour mon Roy, j'en jure,
> Qu'eulx une simple et bien petite injure;
> Ce que croiras, Sire, je t'en supplye . . .[21]

Marot dépasse ici son rôle de poète courtisan. Il s'agit pour lui de proclamer son innocence, de faire partager à son maître les certitudes qui sont en lui. Et, comme il en a lui-même conscience, tout, dans ce domaine, est affaire de croyance. De croyance et de persuasion.

Ce qui naturellement revient à dire que le problème essentiel qui, en cette conjoncture, se pose à Marot est un problème de rhétorique. Puisqu'il lui faut avant tout convaincre, et persuader, le poète se trouve réduit à la nécessité de mobiliser toutes les ressources du langage, toutes ces "fleurs" et ces "couleurs," ces artifices et ces fards, ce souci tout extérieur et tout sophistique des formes que son projet de représentation justement exclut. Car, comme le mensonge, la vérité, non pas la vérité qui est, mais celle qu'il s'agit de faire partager, de communiquer, se fabrique. Elle est elle aussi le fruit d'une technique.

Or si l'œuvre de Marot, et son style, nous enseignent quelque chose, c'est bien que le poète s'est toujours ingénié à fuir cette technique, à refuser de l'utiliser. Marot est ce poète qui constamment "rime en prose," qui n'éprouve que réticence et qu'ironie envers tout ce qui est "hault style," "parolle fardée" ou "grande levée / de Rethorique." L'équation, pour lui, va de soi. La hauteur est toujours nécessairement pour lui "enflure" et artifice, la "rime" antithèse obligée du "Cueur" et de la "Raison." Vérité et rhétorique sont chez lui ce qu'elles sont chez Lefèvre d'Etaples ou Marguerite de Navarre: des termes qui s'excluent. Celle-ci n'est décidément rien d'autre que l'outil de Rhadamante et de "Folle Amour," "Diable cornu en forme d'un bel Ange," "faincte doulceur," source de mensonge, d'erreur et d'illusion.[22] Obstacle fatal à la communication, à la parfaite communion qu'il rêve d'établir entre son lecteur et lui.

Ainsi pris entre la nécessité de convaincre et la méfiance qu'il a toujours manifestée envers la rhétorique et ses artifices, Marot commet maladresse sur maladresse. Fidèle à ses partis pris, à son style et à sa propre rhétorique, celle du cœur, du *pectus* et de l'*ingenium*, il s'embarrasse dans des déclarations et des justifications pathétiques et d'autant plus insuffisantes qu'il sait, au moment même où il les énonce, qu'elles ne convaincront personne: car rien, absolument rien, ne permet de distinguer le langage de la vérité de celui du mensonge. Il essaye donc de s'en sortir en accusant les autres, les juges, la Sorbonne, le Parlement. Il va même, nous l'avons vu, sous le manteau respectable qu'il s'est confectionné et qu'il endosse parfaitement, ce style si "naturel" et si "transparent," jusqu'à mentir, poussant même la plaisanterie jusqu'à dire que c'est le Ciel, "l'esprit de Dieu," son "courroux" tout "paternel," qui l'ont finalement chassé de Ferrare. Suffisamment honnête cependant, et conscient du jeu qu'il se voit contraint de jouer—il n'est pas Tartuffe, ni Dom Juan—, pour avouer au Dauphin François que sa fréquentation des Lombards lui a enseigné la circonspection, lui a appris à "parler froid," à répondre seulement "de la teste," voire à "poltroniser."[23] Ce qu'il veut par dessus tout, c'est rentrer en France et tous les moyens, ou presque, lui semblent bons.

Le malaise qui est alors le sien, la gêne qu'il éprouve à se trouver pris au piège d'une situation pour laquelle il ne se sent pas fait, devant laquelle il se sait vulnérable et désarmé, se découvrent peut-être le mieux dans le fait que, pour la première fois de sa carrière d'épistolier, il se met à parler un langage qui n'est pas le sien. Les deux épîtres qu'il envoie de Venise à François Ier et à sa sœur la Reine de Navarre sont toutes deux nourries des plaintes d'Ovide.[24] Pour demander la permission de rentrer en France, Marot ne trouve rien de mieux que de piller les *Tristes* et les *Pontiques*. Comme si, finalement, il baissait les bras, ne trouvait plus en lui-même, en cet esprit qui l'avait pourtant si bien et si longtemps servi, les ressources nécessaires pour se faire accorder le laissez-passer dont il a besoin. Comme si, finalement, il confiait au langage d'un autre, ou à l'autre tout court, la responsablité de satisfaire à son désir. L'aveu d'impuissance, ici, est patent. Marot non seulement se prend plus que jamais au piège de la rhétorique, mais il ne fait même plus confiance à son propre discours pour exprimer ses angoisses et ses doutes, ses craintes et son espoir. L'expression du moi intime est ouvertement devenue littérature, et l'écriture du moi plus que jamais écriture romanesque.

Notes

[1] Voir à ce sujet l'ouvrage de C.A. Mayer, *La Bibliographie des Œuvres de Clément Marot. Tome I: Manuscrits; Tome II: Editions* (Genève: Droz, 1954), ainsi que sa réimpression du Tome II, *Bibliographie des Editions de C.M. publiées au XVIe siècle* (Paris: Nizet, 1975).

[2] Texte de cette importante épître dans le Tome I de mon édition des *Œuvres poétiques de C.M.*, Classiques Garnier (Paris: Bordas, 1990) 17-18.

[3] *LADOLESCENCE CLEMENTINE. Autrement, Les Œuvres de Clement Marot de Cahors en Quercy, Valet de Chambre du Roy, composees en leage de son Adolescence. Avec la Complainte sur le Trespas de feu Messire Florimond Robertet. Et plusieurs autres Œuvres faictes par ledict Marot depuis leage de sa dicte Adolescence. Le tout reveu / corrige / & mis en bon ordre. . . .* On les vend à Paris, devant Lesglise Saincte Genevieve des Ardens, Rue Neufve Nostre Dame. A Lenseigne du Faulcheur. (Achevé d'imprimé du "Lundy .xii. jour Daoust. Lan. M.D. XXXII. pour Pierre Roffet, dict le Faulcheur. Par Maistre Geofroy Tory, Imprimeur du Roy.") B.N., Rés. Ye 1532, Mayer, no. 9.

[4] Il s'agit de l'édition du 13 Novembre 1532 (Paris: Geofroy Tory, pour Pierre Roffet) B.N. Rés. Ye 1533, Mayer no. 11. Voir l'admirable travail de Pierre Villey, "Tableau chronologique des publications de Marot," *Revue du Seizième Siècle* (1920) 74-75.

[5] Texte de cette épître dans l'édition citée *supra* 5-7.

[6] *Le Premier Livre de la Metamorphose D'Ovide, translaté de Latin en François par Clement Marot de Cahors en Quercy, Valet de Chambre du Roy. Item certaines œuvres qu'il feit en prison, non encore imprimeez* (Paris: Estienne Roffet, 1534) B.N. Rés. Ye 1563, Mayer no. 21.

[7] *Recueil* conservé au Musée Condé, Chantilly, sous la cote ms. 524/748, XIX-B 28.

[8] C.A. Mayer, "Les Œuvres de C.M.: l'économie de l'édition critique," *Bibliothèque d'Humanisme et Renaissance* 29 (1967) 364.

[9] *Les œuvres de clement marot de cahors, vallet de chambre du roy. Plus amples, & en meilleur ordre que paravant* (A Lyon: à l'enseigne du Rocher, 1544) B.N. Rés. Ye 1484-1485, Mayer no. 129. Sur le rôle joué par Roville dans l'édition dite "Constantin," voir mon Introduction au tome II des *Œuvres poétiques complètes de C.M.*, Classiques Garnier (Paris: Bordas, 1992).

[10] Voir, de Marc Fumaroli, "Genèse de l'épistolographie classique: rhétorique humaniste de la lettre, de Pétrarque à Juste Lipse," *Revue d'Histoire Littéraire de la France* 78 (1978) 886-905; "Michel de Montaigne, ou l'éloquence du for intérieur," in *Les Formes brèves de la prose et le discours discontinu (XVIe-XVIIe siècles)*, Etudes réunies et présentées par Jean Lafond (Paris: Vrin, 1984); et surtout *L'Age de l'éloquence. Rhétorique et "res literaria" de la Renaissance au seuil de l'époque classique* (Genève: Droz, 1980).

[11] Tous les théoriciens de l'épigramme insistent au XVIe siècle sur la plasticité du genre. Voyez notamment Jules César Scaliger, *Poetices libri septem*. Voir aussi Pierre Laurens, *L'Abeille dans l'ambre: célébration de l'épigramme* (Paris: Belles Lettres, 1989), notamment les "Prolégomènes," 7-30. L'épigramme est, pour Marot, symbole de liberté poétique.

[12] L'expression est de Robert Griffin, *Clément Marot and the Inflections of Poetic Voice* (Berkeley: U of California P, 1974) 191.

[13] Cf. mon *Marot, Rabelais, Montaigne: l'écriture comme présence* (Paris et Genève: Champion/Slatkine, 1987).

[14] Voir sa "Pharmacie de Platon," in *La Dissémination* (Paris: Seuil, 1972).

[15] Allusion à la "Préface historique" (sic) placée par Lenglet-Dufresnoy en tête de son édition des *Œuvres de Clément Marot* (La Haye: chez P. Gosse & J. Neaulme, 1731).

[16] Texte de cette Ballade (Ballade V de *L'Adolescence*), édition citée 114-15; variantes et commentaire 503-06.

[17] *Œuvres poétiques*, édition citée 716.

[18] *L'Enfer de Clement Marot de Cahors en Quercy, Valet de chambre du Roy. Item aulcunes Ballades, & Rondeaulx appartenans à largument. Et en oultre plusieurs aultres compositions dudict Marot, par cy devant non imprimees* (A Lyon: Chés Etienne Dolet, 1542) B.N. Rotschild no. 618, Mayer no. 102.

[19] Allusion à l'admirable *finale* du livre de Michel Jeanneret, *Des mets et des mots* (Paris: Corti, 1987).

[20] Voir l'étude de Christine Scollen-Jimack, "Marot and Deschamps: The Rhetoric of Misfortune," *French Studies* (1988) 21-32; et le livre d'Annwyl Williams, *Clément Marot: Figure, Text and Intertext* (Lewiston: Edwin Mellen Press, 1990).

[21] *Œuvres poétiques complètes*, tome II, Ep. VIII. Dans l'édition C.A. Mayer des *Epîtres* (Londres: Athlone Press, 1958) Ep. XXXVII, 208-10.

[22] Voyez sur ce point l'évidence textuelle accumulée dans mon *Marot, Rabelais, Montaigne* 77-83.

[23] Texte de cette épître "Au tresvertueux prince, Françoys, Daulphin de France," dans l'édition C.A. Mayer des *Epîtres*, Epître XLV, 240-43.

[24] Edition Mayer, Epîtres XLIV, 232-39, et XLVI, 243-51.

Robert D. Cottrell

Pernette du Guillet
and the Logic of Aggressivity

The Old Scar

In the poem that opens Pernette du Guillet's *Rymes* (1545), the speaking
subject "recalls" the moment of its coming-into-consciousness:

> Le hault pouvoir des Astres a permis
> (Quand je nasquis) d'estre heureuse et servie:
> Dont, congnoissant celuy qui m'est promis,
> 4   Restée suis sans sentyment de vie,
> Fors le sentir du mal, qui me convie
> A regraver ma dure impression
> D'amour cruelle, et doulce passion,
> 8   Où s'apparut celle divinité,
> Qui me cause l'imagination
> A contempler si haulte qualité. (Epigram 1)[1]

A divinity appeared, the text says, and, drawing the subject irresistibly away
from what it had been, propelled it towards what it was to be. The text, then,
figures coming-into-consciousness as the transcendence of one order—which,
retrospectively and diacritically, is marked by passivity, pain, and lack—and
entry into another order.

The second poem retraces the trajectory laid out in the first poem.
Originally situated in the order of darkness, muteness, confusion and
disempowerment, the subject, obeying the imperatives of the mysterious force
that shaped its destiny, transcended the order of somnolence and passivity and,
with a gesture of triumph, acceded to the order of jubilation, of day, of light, of
voice and language (". . . commençay louer à voix haultaine," Epig. 2, line 9),
in short, the order of the Symbolic:

> La nuict estoit pour moi si tresobscure
> Que Terre, et Ciel elle m'obscurissoit,
> Tant qu'à Midy de discerner figure
> 4   N'avois pouvoir, qui fort me marrissoit:

> Mais quand je vis que l'aulbe apparoissoit
> En couleurs mille et diverse, et seraine,
> Je me trouvay de liesse si pleine
> 8   (Voyant desjà la clarté à la ronde)
> Que commençay louer à voix haultaine
> Celuy qui feit pour moi ce Jour au Monde. (Epig. 2)

The speaking subject, situated now in the Symbolic, acknowledges that its being is marked by the scar of an old rift or split. However, it does not fix its gaze on the past. In the poems that follow these two introductory poems, it celebrates the present, identified as the locus of consciousness and selfhood, the site of privileged knowledge and of power.

The Return of the Repressed

The first two poems in the *Rymes* recount the splitting of the subject in such a way that it can be read as a rearticulation of the neoplatonic problematic. The passage from darkness to light, from a lower to a higher order, from ignorance to knowledge coincides with the movement from matter to form that is the central feature of neoplatonism. At the same time, the text's account of the origin of subjectivity, that is to say, the splitting away of the subject from what it was initially and its subsequent accession to consciousness and joy, has faint but distinctly audible biblical echoes, for the drama of subjectivity is staged in the text as a resurrection not unlike that recorded in the Book of Revelation. In du Guillet's text, as in the Book of Revelation, the essential trope is a definitive turning away from darkness, from "le sentir du mal" (Epig. 1, line 5), and the emergence into light.

Recalling its accession to consciousness and voice, the speaking subject positions itself firmly within tradition, figured first by neoplatonism and the Bible and then, in subsequent poems, by classical authors (especially Ovid), by Petrarch and numerous petrarchist poets (both Italian and French), by the doctrine of *fin' amors*, and by contemporary French poets. But even as the speaking subject fixes its selfhood within the parameters of tradition, the text formulates, almost indistinctly at first, another discourse that little by little subverts the speaking subject's implied claim that its self is inscribed unproblematically in the dominant discourse of tradition. The first poem tells us, for example, that the subject is female. However, we do not learn this information (at least, not with any degree of certainty) by listening to the speaking voice, for, at the acoustic level, the signs of gender are inconclusive; phonically, "heureuse et servie" is scarcely distinguishable (if distinguishable at all) from "heureux et servi," and of course the "e" at the end of "restée" is not sounded. The subject's gender is disclosed, therefore, not by the system of meaning generated within the second order, the system of meaning controlled by voice, by *phonè*, which, following Lacan, we can call conscious discourse, but by the more archaic system of meaning generated within the first order, a system of meaning governed by the non-being of voice, by the seen instead of the heard, by matter, by the body of the text, by (in Pauline terms) the "letter" rather than the "spirit" (II. Cor. 3.6), by writing, by *graphie*, by unconscious discourse.[2]

Encoding gender in its script but not in its phonics, the first poem posits *graphie* (the world of matter, of the body) as original presence, as the primal order of subjectivity. This corporeal order is marked by "le sentir du mal." Accession to the second order does not mean elimination of the first order. On the contrary, the subject, having acceded to voice, says that it is the supposedly transcended "sentir du mal" that compels her to write, that drives her to "regraver [sa] dure impression," to reinscribe on the body of the text the malaise, "le mal," that was already inscribed on the (female) subject's body. Initially the text defines the female as an object ("sans sentiment de vie") that is looked at by a subject who possesses the gaze. Being an object that is *seen*, she is associated with inertness, with graphicity, with a pictorial language, a writing in images that makes of her a hieroglyph, an iconic sign. The subject who "looks" is necessarily positioned at some distance from the object, for sight requires distance. At the end of the first poem, the Guilletian *je*, guided by "celle divinité" who possesses the gaze, begins to "contemplate," to *see*. She establishes a distance between the object she was (and in one sense always will be, for the *je* inscribed in a text is alway the object of a representing, of what the Germans call a "setting-before," a *Vor-stellen*) and the subject she would become. Affirmation of distance between the object seen and the subject who sees is, in the economy of the text, preparatory to a shift away from the iconic sign towards the phonetic sign as the privileged system of representation, for what distinguishes the iconic sign is the absence of distance between signifier and signified whereas it is precisely distance between signifier and signified that marks the phonetic sign and thus defines language "proper."

Beginning with the second poem, the subject, having assumed language, represses both "le sentir du mal" and the body, that is to say, the text on which "le sentir du mal" had already been imprinted. Nearly all commentators on du Guillet have remarked that hers is a poetry of contentment; indeed "contentement" is a word the speaking subject reiterates with such insistence one might legitimately argue that it is overdetermined. If the speaking subject manages so quickly to repress "le sentir du mal" and the passion of the body, it is because, as the first line of the first poem makes clear ("Le hault pouvoir des Astres a permis"), it follows a path laid out for it by sovereign others who possess and wield power. At the most obvious level, this verse alludes to the widespread sixteenth-century interest in astrology.[3] But behind this manifest content, the line contains, I suggest, a latent content. From the outset, the text establishes an economy of power. If we read the text narratively as the story of its own writing, then the "Astres" represent the *auctores* whose canonical texts make up tradition. The nearest of these stellar divinities (or, in Bloomian terms, "strong" authors) is Scève, whose name is inscribed anagrammatically in the fifth epigram. Du Guillet's first poem, which functions as a kind of pre-text in the *Rymes* for it establishes the base over which the speaking voice will introduce its distinctive melody in the second poem, can be read as a re-writing of the prefatory poem of the *Délie*, the words "dure impression" in the sixth line of du Guillet's poem repeating the words "durs Epygrammes" in the sixth line of Scève's poem.

But the power that establishes its presence and its efficacy in the first line of du Guillet's text is not only linguistic power, i.e., the power of literary convention. It is also sexual power. The "stars" that wield power are male, first of all, by virtue of the masculine gender of the word "astre," and then, to the extext that they represent literary tradition, by virtue of the fact that that tradition is indisputably patriarchal. More cunningly, the text engenders sexual difference diacritically; that is to say, it sets up a clear difference between the passive, virtually lifeless *je*, who dares not speak her gender, and the powerful Others who police the space within which the subject seeks to fashion her self through voice. By inscribing her gender silently in the text, the female subject, diacritically, consigns the Others—those from whom she differs, those who, unlike her, possess power—to the male sex. Emerging into light, the subject begins to praise the "esprit celeste" (Epig. 4) through whose agency she was allowed access to the Symbolic. He is "la source, et l'onde" of all "vertu" (Epig. 4). In him she discerns a beauty and a grace ascribable only to Apollo. In the economy of the text, the image of Apollo dissolves quickly into that of Scève, the Scève who is the author of the *Délie*, of course, but more importantly the Scève who metaphorically figures literary tradition and male power, the Scève in whom inheres the apollonian virtues—"eloquence," "haut sçavoir," and "faconde" (Epig. 4), the latter term rendered by Cotgrave as "graceful speaking, sweet deliverie"—that the text's conscious discourse seeks to appropriate.

Located securely in traditional literary space, the speaking subject, in poem after poem, manipulates the conventions handed down to her. However, these conventions, dependent as they are on a male speaking subject and a female object, become problematic when the speaking subject is female. This problematization produces what Ann Rosalind Jones calls "contradictions" in the Guilletian text,[4] "contradictions" that in turn produce a tension, or an anxiety, that does not find expression openly in the text's manifest content. As the text unfolds, however, this latent content makes itself heard in a discourse that rises up and speaks through the gaps and breaks that increasingly disrupt the sovereign, imperturbable flow of patriarchal discourse. This disruptive discourse signals the return of what was written into the first poem but repressed by the speaking subject who sought to fix her self within the grid of patriarchal discourse: namely, material that relates to the libidinal economy of the female body and to an economy of power that can grant and withhold access to textual production.

Epigrams two through eight in the *Rymes* establish a semantic field shaped by the words "esprit" and "louer." Despite the serene abstraction that gives a surface calm to much of du Guillet's poetry, the demands of the desiring body make themselves heard with increasing urgency, stridency even, as the text unfolds, accounting for "[le] ton d'une sensualité ardente" that, in Françoise Charpentier's words, "parcourt souterrainement ce texte."[5] The ninth epigram, for example, which begins with the words "Plus je desire," suggests that desire may cloud the subject's vision and prevent her from seeing "him," i.e., the Good, making it impossible for her to realize the neoplatonic project that the text had seemed to posit as its goal. The eleventh epigram ("Comme le corps ne permect point de veoir / A son esprit, ny sçavoir sa puissance") states in even bolder terms that the body opposes and thwarts the spirit, for the spirit, unlike the body, seeks only to gaze humbly and adoringly on "celuy là," a pronoun that alway has multiple referents in du Guillet's poetry, for it signifies simultaneously Scève, the neoplatonic Good, and the space of literary tradition.

Subsequent poems are marked by an ever more powerful rhetoric of violence, which, I would argue, must not be neutralized and read out of the text by appealing to petrarchist and neoplatonic topoi. With a persistence that is obsessional, the text evokes fleeting images of nudity, of female rage so intense it becomes a wish to strangle the Other, of a female body being violated by a powerful Other, usually called "celuy là." In the following quatrain, which is a complete poem, the female subject finds "contentement," which Cotgrave translates as "full pleasure," in the spectacle of *his* pleasure when he torments her:

> Pour contenter celuy qui me tourmente,
> Chercher ne veulx remede à mon tourment:
> Car, en mon mal voyant qu'il se contente,
> Contente suis de son contentement. (Epig. 15)

Saulnier reads this and similar poems as an expression of woman's "tendre humilité"[6] and finds it touching. Situated in the context of du Guillet's poetic project, this poem and others like it disclose, however, a different meaning. How, we might ask, is a woman to read such a poem, indeed, petrarchist poetry in general? How can she read her self into a literary tradition that defines the male as the agent of the gaze, the emblem of subjectivity, and the female as the fetishized object that is caught in the gaze of the powerful male viewer? In

Epigram 15 and in similar poems, the female subject "reads" her self into the petrarchist grid by a narcissistic, even masochistic, identification with the fetishized female figure. One might argue, borrowing from Mary Ann Doane, who theorizes female spectatorship in the context of cinema,[7] that the female speaker in Epigram 15 identifies so blatantly and aggressively with the fetishized female figure and underlines so heavily the usually latent masochistic impulse that inheres in this identification that her identificatory gesture, excessive and overdetermined, represents not a passive and humble acceptance of the role patriarchal discourse demands of her, but, rather, in its flaunting of "femininity," of "tendre humilité," an ironic comment on the function of the female figure in patriarchal discourse.

Because she is female, then, the Guilletian subject identifies narcissistically and masochistically with the reified woman that petrarchist and neoplatonic discourse figures as an object of desire. But since in this discourse, invocative power and scopic power are invested in the male, sole possessor of the voice and the gaze, the Guilletian subject, appropriating voice, appropriates also the gaze (". . . voyant qu'il se contente," Epig. 15). Indeed, in several poems she puts herself in the position of the male spectator. She "masculinizes" herself and "looks at" the female figure from the "male" perspective. Thus, in Epître 1, which is a *coq-à-l' âne,* a genre associated closely with Marot and therefore with a male speaker, the Guilletian subject claims that "she"—disguised as a "he" by a kind of transvestism—would be dishonored if "he" did not seize the opportunity to rape a virgin. "Seroit ce pas grand deshonneur / De la laisser ainsi pucelle?" (93) "he" asks rhetorically. In the rest of the poem the subject, in male garb and speaking from the site of masculine subjectivity, focuses on the troubling and exciting nudity of female bodies. Claiming that "l'eau de Saone / Faict le beau tainct aux Damoiselles," the subject fixes "his" gaze on "leur blanche et delicate peau" (94). In "his" fantasy, the desirable woman is, significantly, a stranger, a foreign woman whose nakedness harbors mystery and the promise of unknown pleasure: "une estrangere / Sera tousjours la mieulx venue, / Pour autant que, quand elle est nue, / Elle change d'accoustrement" (93-94). Articulating "his" pleasure in the lexicon of commerce ("Nul n'est tenu de rendre compte / (Apres la paye) du receu" (94), the speaking subject identifies the desired female as a harlot. In the next two lines of the poem, however, the subject drops momentarily her male disguise and, speaking now from the site of female subjectivity, claims triumphantly that the male visitor to a brothel, even though he may think that by putting down his money he retains the position of power, has in fact been duped, lured into a trap set by females: "O qu'il est bien pris, et deceu / Le doux Pigeon aux Tourterelles!" The fact that the *coq-à-l' âne* is a satirical genre underscores the mockery of the female subject, whose male posturing throughout the poem is marked so outrageously by signs of exaggerated masculinity that—like her identification with the violated female figure—it becomes a dismissive gesture that disrupts patriarchal discourse.

The problematic of the Guilletian text—a problematic shaped by repressed material relating to the libidinal economy of the female body and an economy of power—comes sharply into focus in the relatively long and remarkably rich poems situated precisely in the center of the text: Chanson 6, Epigram 34 (the only short poem in this group), Chanson 7, Elégie 2. I turn to these poems now.

Chanson 6: Apollo's Archers

Chanson 6 is haunted by an earlier scene, that of the text's own beginning, for, driven by a compulsion to repeat, the speaking female subject narrates once again what she had recounted in the first poem: her coming-into-consciousness. Whereas the first poem had located the beginning in Scève, the later expanded version situates origin in an earlier canonical source, in Petrarch himself; indeed, Chanson 6 *recollects* the famous twenty-third poem of Petrarch's *Rime sparse*, the text in which the Petrarchan subject relates how Love aroused him from non-being and enflamed him with a desire not for Laura herself (she has no corporeal reality in the *Rime sparse*), but rather for "a green laurel" ("un lauro verde"), emblem of linguistic production and everlasting literary fame.[8]

The Guilletian subject, yielding at first to the pressure of the Petrarchan text, tells how she, too, was aroused from non-being by the appearance of an irresistibly attractive and powerful Other. In Petrarch's text, this Other is, at the narrative level, "Amor," whose figure dissolves later in the poem into that of "a powerful Lady" ("una possente Donna"). The Guilletian subject claims that even though she was attacked repeatedly by "Amour," i.e., Eros, she successfully resisted him. Soon, however, a more powerful opponent appeared, for she was besieged by the forces of the "Archiers de Vertu" (53, line 19). In the shifting imagery of the text, the figure of Cupid with his ineffectual arrows dissolves into that of the far more potent and effective "Archiers de Vertu." Behind these "Archiers" stands the figure of their god, Apollo, for Apollo is the god of archery. In Chanson 6, Apollo is perceptible only through the effects produced by the archers he commands. Throughout the Guilletian *œuvre,* however, Apollo is more than the god of archery, this being one of his secondary functions. He is above all the god of "Vertu," the divinity who, in the first poem of the text, appeared to the subject and, illuminating her consciousness, made it possible for her to "contempler si haulte qualité," to accede to the *haulte Vertu* of which he is the emblem. Unable to resist the "Archiers de Vertu," the subject, whose "cueur forcé fut soubdain abattu," surrendered to her conqueror, to the Apollonian force figured by the "Archiers de Vertu," a surrendering that, she says, "m'a hors de moy ravie" (line 25). Split off from what she was, the

Guilletian subject, tracing the trajectory laid out by the Petrarchan text, was thrust into an order of being marked by desire.

Through displacement, the Guilletian text shifts the agency of desire from Amour, or Eros, where it was first situated, to the "Archiers de Vertu" and then finally to the embodiment of Vertu, i.e., the Apollonian Scève (this by means of the Latinized form of Scève's name, *saevus*, which means "sévève"). Having identified Scève as the agent of desire, the text focuses on the arousal of the female who is subjected to the pressure of the Scevian gaze. Fleetingly, images of nakedness, violation, blindness, even bondage surface in the text. Through them desire speaks. She who had been the object of the Scevian look exults in the pleasure she experienced when she was delivered, blindfolded, into the hands ("es mains") of him who knew how to arouse her passion so that she could "gouster [le] bien" that, she says, "j'ayme, Dieu sçait combien" (line 30). The Guilletian text, unlike the Petrarchan text, defines the aim of desire as the conjunction of two bodies.

Having articulated desire in terms of carnal pleasure, the text, with a gesture that is repeated in poem after poem, retreats in its conclusion from its bold exposure of the body as the site of pleasure.[9] In the Guilletian text, poetic closure has the function of lowering a veil over what has just been disclosed, of neutralizing the transgression. In the verses that are located in the middle of Chanson 6, the subject, by speaking of the effects desire traced on her body and by identifying Scève's hand as the agent of her pleasure, created a context in which Scève's hand can—indeed, must—be read literally, that is to say, as a hand that moved amorously across her body, on which it inscribed pleasure. However, through metonymic slippage, which occurs constantly in Guilletian discourse, producing (to borrow once again from the vocabulary of cinema) one dissolve after the other, Scève's hand moves now not across her body but across a page on which it inscribes "ses escripts divins." Scève, deified and rendered "chaste" (line 35), an adjective that appears in the conclusion of a significant number of du Guillet's poems, has been metamorphosed into the principle of creative energy, into the god of archers, into Apollo. Narrative ceases, verbs in the past tense disappear, and the subject, speaking in a serene voice located in the present, *remembers* Scève only as the god who engendered in her, immaculately she would now have it, the power of speech, which she now exercises through a voice that, however, is pitched in a key decidedly different from his.

Epigram 34: Golden Words

Epigram 34 separates Chanson 6 from Chanson 7. Like so many of du Guillet's texts, it is a ten-line poem that displays the formal features of the

Scevian dizain. Epigram 34 picks up certain motifs enunciated in Chanson 6 and modulates them in such a way that they lead into Chanson 7. The speaking subject uses once again the strategy she had used in Chanson 6 to identify the "You" that is inscribed in the text; he is, she says, "de nom . . . severe" (55, line 1). In the verses located at the center of the epigram, the subject declares that since she is now busily engaged in producing texts she understands why he might choose to direct his "look" elsewhere. Implicit in this statement is the hint that she, no longer willing to be the object that is "looked at," has begun, though quietly and unobtrusively, to extricate herself from the grid within which the reified object is confined. Deploying the strategy observed in Chanson 6, the epigram's closing lines, however, obscure this transgressive gesture, which is "contained" (I use the word in its full force) in the center of the text. In its conclusion, the text withdraws the image of the female producer of texts. It superimposes on the effaced (though only partially so) image of the female writer that of the male writer, of Scève, whose exemplary texts, called "escripts divins" in Chanson 6, are now called "motz dorez" (line 10).

Chanson 7: Pursuing the Female

As if to suggest the pervasive, perhaps subliminal, power of "gold," the text retains the thematics of gold and extends it over to the next poem, Chanson 7, which opens by recalling Danaë's fate. Locked up in a tower by her father, who had been forewarned that his daughter would bear a son who would kill him, Danaë was visited in her prison by Zeus, who, in order to possess her, assumed the form of a golden rain that ran over the girl's body, impregnating her with a son who would be named Perseus. Of this myth, du Guillet retained only the scene of Zeus violating Danaë:

> Qui dira ma robe fourrée
> De la belle pluye dorée
> Qui Daphnes [sic] enclose esbranla:
> 4   Je ne sçay rien moins, que cela.

No allusion to Danaë appears in the rest of the poem. Nevertheless, each of the next three stanzas is a variation on the Danaë theme, for each depicts a situation in which libido breaks through—or is in danger of breaking through—the constraints placed upon it:

> Qui dira qu'à plusieurs je tens
> Pour en avoir mon passetemps,
> Prenant mon plaisir çà, et là:
> 8   Je ne sçay rien moins, que cela.

> Qui dira que t'ay revelé
> Le feu long temps en moy celé
> Pour en toy veoir si force il a:
> 12   Je ne sçay rien moins, que cela.
>   Qui dira que, d'ardeur commune
> Qui les Jeunes gentz importune,
> De toy je veulx, et puis holà:
> 16   Je ne sçay rien moins, que cela. (56)

The concluding line of each stanza is identical: "Je ne sçay rien moins, que cela." This verse constitutes a refrain by means of which the speaking subject disassociates herself from the violence she has just described, a violence that, at least in stanzas two, three, and four, she evokes with more than a hint of self-indulgence and vicarious pleasure. The negation reiterated in the refrain is not, of course, a denial of libidinal desire and the violence that the text associates with it. On the contrary, negation (*Verneinung*) is, as Freud points out, "a way of taking cognizance of what is repressed; indeed it is already a lifting of the repression, though not, of course, an acceptance of what is repressed."[10] Negation, therefore, affirms. It is always an admission.

Saulnier sees in the first stanza of Chanson 7 "une interprétation plaisante" (49) of the Danaë myth. According to him, du Guillet is here imitating the reworkings of the myth that had appeared in the *Greek Anthology*. In those reworkings, the "golden rain," Saulnier says, signifies money and therefore, although he does not put it this way, the interconnectedness of filthy lucre and libidinal drive. By denying any interest in, or knowledge of, the link between love and money, the subject, at least if we read the text through the Freudian grid, admits (unwittingly, of course) that the retailing of love, which was practiced not only by common prostitutes but also by the distinguished courtesans of du Guillet's day, some of whom were remarkable writers, has in fact a powerful, even dangerous, fascination.

Surely the most striking feature of the first stanza of Chanson 7 is the substitution of Daphne for Danaë. Critics have almost universally interpreted this as a mistake, observing that du Guillet, or perhaps an editor or a printer, confused either the two myths or simply the two names. Be that as it may, the text says "Daphne" not "Danaë," and we ought not, I believe, eliminate this "confusion" from the text by calling it an "error." Though from one perspective the substitution of "Daphne" for "Danaë" is clearly a slip or a "misnaming," such slips and "misnamings" draw, as we know, unexpected material into the text, potentially enlarging and enriching its semantic field.

In discussing Chanson 6, I suggested that the opening verses of that poem constitute on both the lexical and semantic levels a rewriting of the beginning of Petrarch's twenty-third *canzone,* which is itself a rewriting of an earlier text. Indeed, in his twenty-third *canzone* Petrarch restages the Ovidian myths of metamorphosis. The Petrarchan narrator, to express the sorrow he has experienced, casts himself successively in the roles of various Ovidian characters who suffered pain and frustration: he was Daphne (a laurel), Cygnus (a swan), Battus (a stone), Byblis (a fountain), Echo (a voice), Actaeon (a stag). Never, he says, was he transformed into a golden raincloud so that he, like Zeus, could partially quench his passion by inseminating the object of his desire. When we realize that the central scene in Elégie 2, the poem that follows Chanson 7, is a rewriting of the Actaeon-Diana myth, we begin to see that the four poems that occupy the center of the *Rymes* all reenact scenes that are narratively linked in Petrarch's twenty-third *canzone*. Petrarch called his rhymes *sparse*, that is, "scattered." Du Guillet performs the gesture that Petrarch's title seems to call for; she dismembers the Petrarchan text and "scatters" the fragments across a new textual space where each one generates its own distinct poem.[11]

Daphne figures much more prominently in the *Rime sparse* than does Danaë.[12] Indeed, Robert Durling has observed that "the first and basic metamorphosis in the *Rime sparse* reenacts the myth of Apollo and Daphne" (27). Scève's *Délie* also restages the Apollo-Daphne myth, although the *Délie*, like du Guillet's *Rymes*, dismembers the narrative and reconstitutes it in three discrete poems that are widely separated from each other in the Scevian text.[13] The *Délie* makes no mention at all of Danaë.

In the *Rime sparse*, transformation of the beloved into a laurel is effected easily, at least on the orthographic level: *Laura* become *lauro*. Because the apostrophe was not part of Petrarch's punctuation, *Laura* was orthographically and phonetically identical with *l'aura* (breeze), and *lauro* with *l'auro* (gold). The constant slippage from one term to another results in a superimposition of signifieds, creating within the Petrarchan text a remarkably rich semantic texture. In the Guilletian text, too, slippage occurs often, sometimes through orthographic or phonetic particularities but usually through semantic association. A series of terms and images issues associatively from the term "Apollo," the *deus absconditus* of Chanson 6. This associative chain leads from "Apollo" to "gold" (Apollo was of course the sun god), then, in Chanson 7, to "Danaë," inextricably linked to gold. Chanson 7, however, superimposes the image of Daphne on that of Danaë. The two names are, of course, linked alliteratively. More importantly, however, the two women are linked by virtue of the fact that both were objects of divine, male desire. That Daphne was pursued by Apollo prolongs the Apollonian character of the associative chain that began in Chanson 6 (actually in the first poem of the *Rymes*, but I am here considering these four poems as a discrete sequence) and plays itself out in Elégie 2, where the central passage is du Guillet's rewriting of the Actaeon-Diana myth.

Instead of reading the term "Daphne" in the first stanza of Chanson 7 as an "error" and thereby reading it out of the text, we can read it as a superimposition that produces a slippage from simple referential meaning to semiotic (contextual) significance. Because of this superimposition, the terms "Daphne" and "Danaë" (the latter term is never actually said by the text) lose to some degree the semantic characteristics they have outside the Guilletian text and acquire instead a semiotic function within the system of signs of this particular poem, this particular group of poems, this particular text.[14] Linked ambivalently, "Daphne" and "Danaë" together shape the significance that unfolds in Chanson 7. In stanzas two through four, the text actualizes what we might call the basic Danaë semes: rape, gold, *jouissance*. Part of the semiotic significance of these semes is determined, however, by the fact that they are played off against the Daphne semes—chastity, purity, female independence—which in the first four stanzas serve mainly as shadows that give relief and volume to the Danaë semes, which are foregrounded.

With the gesture characteristic of Guilletian closure, the text in its last two stanzas lowers a veil over the image of female desire and sexual fulfillment:

> Mais qui dira, que la Vertu,
> Dont tu es richement vestu,
> En ton amour m'estincella:
> 20   Je ne sçay rien mieulx, que cela.
>   Mais qui dira que d'amour saincte
> Chastement au cueur suis attaincte,
> Qui mon honneur onc ne foula:
> 24   Je ne sçay rien mieulx, que cela. (56-57)

The basic Danaë semes are repressed, and secondary semes, those that assimilate Danaë to Daphne, are now activated, generating a conclusion that stresses chastity, honor, and a love ("amour saincte") that conforms to the demands of male sovereignty.

Elégie 2: Appropriating the Phallus

The material that was repressed in Chanson 7 (and the same material is repressed time and again in du Guillet's poems) returns, predictably, in the next poem, Elégie 2. Elégie 2 enacts a desire; it frames a wish:

> Combien de fois ay-je en moy souhaicté
> Me rencontrer sur la chaleur d'esté
> Tout au plus pres de la clere fontaine,
> 4   Où mon desir avec cil se pourmaine
>   . . . .

Like so many of du Guillet's poems, Elégie 2 begins by situating itself in literary tradition, specifically in the tradition of the courtly lyric, represented here by one of its most characteristic images: *la dame au bord de la claire fontaine*. However, in the framed, carefully circumscribed space of its middle stanzas (lines 13-36), the text reveals that it is less a rewriting of the courtly lyric than a rewriting, albeit a deviant and transgressive one, of the Actaeon-Diana myth, which was codified in two canonical texts: Ovid's *Metamorphoses* and Petrarch's twenty-third *canzone* (not to mention Scève's *Délie*). Elégie 2, then, like other poems by du Guillet, at first foregrounds its status as the site of *reproduction* and only later discloses its status as the site of *production*.

In the economy of the Guilletian text, Elégie 2, coming after Chanson 6, Epigram 34, and Chanson 7, unfolds along lines determined in part by its textual past, dominated by the figures of Apollo, Danaë, and Daphne. The Actaeon-Diana myth, which is reinscribed in Elégie 2, might seem at first glance to have little to do with Apollo, Danaë, or Daphne; indeed, neither Ovid, Petrarch, or Scève linked them together. Du Guillet, however, situates the story of Actaeon and Diana in a semantic complex that was fashioned by Apollo, Danaë, and Daphne, who, though they do not appear explicitly in Elégie 2, remain in the text as memory traces, as the ghostly figures who fix the textual parameters within which the Actaeon-Diana myth acquires a distinctly Guilletian resonance.

On the most obvious level, the "D" at the beginning of Diana's name links her with Danaë and Daphne (with Délie, too, one might add). Reading the Guilletian text "retroactively" (Riffaterre: "A poem is read poetically backwards," 19), we can say that Diana was already present in Chanson 6, for if Apollo was the god of the "Archiers de Vertu," Diana, Apollo's sister, was figured from classical times on as the goddess of virtue, the emblem of chastity and female independence, precisely the features of the Actaeon-Diana myth that du Guillet will foreground in her rewriting of the story in Elégie 2. Furthermore, although no classical source associated Daphne and Diana, medieval exegetes, in an attempt to interpret Ovid from a Christian point of view, saw in both Daphne, who resisted Apollo's advances, and Diana, the virgin goddess, paradigms of chastity. The late Middle Ages saw in Danaë, too, an exemplar of chastity, indeed, a prefiguration of the Virgin Mary, for she, like Mary, conceived without sin and by divine intervention.[15]

Being the expression of a wish ("Combien de fois ay-je en moy souhaicté"), Elégie 2 has the structure of a fantasy (the hallucinatory reproduction of the Actaeon-Diana myth), the aim of which is to procure for the "dreaming" subject the satisfaction towards which the wish tends. In both Ovid's and Petrarch's versions of the myth, Actaeon, having spent the morning hunting, comes upon Diana at midday while she is bathing in a forest pool. Delighted by this lovely sight, he gazes at the naked goddess, seeing what no mortal man should see. Diana, ashamed and angry, splashes water in the transgressor's face, and he, the victim of divine vengeance, is transformed into a stag. Retaining the consciousness of the mortal man he once was (and in a sense still is, at least to the extent that consciousness defines the human), he tries to command his hounds, who,"keen with the lust of blood,"[16] now turn on him. To his horror, he discovers that in losing the appearance of a man he also lost the voice of a man. He tries to flee from the pact of enraged dogs, but they catch up with him and tear him to pieces.

Nancy J. Vickers ("Diana Described") points out the numerous and subtle ways in which Petrarch modified the Ovidian version of the myth. By shifting stress and accent, Petrarch produced a text whose resonance is distinctly different from that of the parent text. Du Guillet's recasting of the myth is more radical still. Eliminating the hunting motif, du Guillet pitches the myth in a courtly register and infuses it with a "badinage élégant" characteristic of Marot's poetry. More importantly, she plays with the gender relationships established in the older texts.

In the Ovidian and Petrarchan versions, Actaeon penetrates a hidden, secret space (Ovid calls it a "secret nook" ["antrum"], "a well-shaded grotto" ["recessus"] 134, line 157), which, because it belongs to Diana and her nymphs, is defined as female. That there is a sexual investment in this "cavern" with its pool of water is obvious. Indeed, there is a sexual investment in the Actaeon-Diana myth from the moment the story opens. Nicolas Perella has pointed out that, in the lyric tradition running from Ovid to Petrarch and beyond, "noon," figured as the hottest time of the day, often served to denote sexual excitement.[17] Ovid stresses the time of day when Actaeon saw Diana. He says that "midday had shortened every object's shade, and the sun was at equal distance from either goal" when Actaeon, finding himself "on a mountain stained with the blood of many slaughtered beasts" and himself, like his comrades, "dripping with [their] quarry's blood," decided to enter the inviting—and fateful—grotto to rest. He underscores the oppressive heat by observing ominously that "now Phoebus is midway in his course and cleaves the very fields with his burning rays" (135).

Petrarch, too, though less expansively (and less bloodily), emphasizes the heat of midday. (Since the Ovidian text subtends Petrarch's, Petrarch need not "repeat" Ovid, only "recall" him.) The Petrarchan Actaeon is still a hunter, although there is some ambiguity about the object of his hunt. The text makes no mention of his having slaughtered beasts during the morning chase. In fact, in Petrarch's version, which is cast as a first-person narrative, Actaeon remarks that he was pursuing not a beast but his *desire* ("I' segui' tanto avanti il mio desire," line 147). He points out that the sun was burning fiercely when he came upon Diana bathing. He was transfixed by what he saw. As Gisèle Mathieu-Castellani observes, the reader cannot be certain whether Actaeon's "crime" was an act of "impudence ou imprudence."[18]

In du Guillet's version of the myth, the female subject fantasizes that she was out walking with a man who remained indifferent to her. Actually, she doesn't say that *she* was walking with him but that her *desire* was walking with him ("mon desir avec [lui] se pourmaine"): a case of metonymic displacement, but also a case of making use of the ambiguity inherent in the Petrarchan text. The male, seemingly unaware of female desire, "exercite en *sa* philosophie / *Son* gent esprit" (lines 5-6, my emphasis). The word "gent," which by the sixteenth century had acquired an archaic flavor, helps to secure the medieval courtly framework within which the Guilletian narrative moves. Equally significant is the repetition of the possessive adjective ("sa," "son"). In the economy of the text's opening scene, female desire seeks an external object whereas male desire remains attached self-reflexively to the ego. As depicted at the beginning of Elégie 2, the Guilletian male is in fact another Narcissus and the Guilletian female, at least for the duration of the first stanza, another Echo.[19] Indeed, the story of Narcissus, who loved only himself, and of the unhappy Echo, who loved Narcissus but was scorned by him, has often been linked to the story of Actaeon and Diana, one myth being viewed as the reverse image of the other.

Beginning with the second stanza, the Guilletian subject abandons the role of Echo and assumes the role of Diana. Fantasizing, she tells how she would slowly move away from the beloved, not to leave him but rather to attack him from a more advantageous position. She would throw herself naked into a nearby pool of water. She imagines that she would have with her "son petit Luth," well tuned ("accordé au debvoir"). Accompanying herself on the lute, she would sing a siren song designed to envelop and entrap the unsuspecting male. Her lute and her song are instruments of aggression. They are her bow and her arrow.

The Guilletian subject says that the purpose of her song would be to see "quelz gestes il tiendroit." If he, she remarks, were to acknowledge her presence and move towards her, she would allow him to advance. However, if he wished to touch her, she would throw water in his eyes, hoping to transform him not into a stag, a "cerf," who would be torn apart by his own dogs but rather into a "serf," who, in accordance with the laws that governed the courtly lyric, would become her "serviteur."[20]

Her wish, grounded as wishes always are, in the regressive order of the Imaginary, culminates in an astonishing fantasy. It is not so much that she wants him to *be* her "serviteur." That would be little more than a reenactment of a scenario played out innumerable times in the courtly lyric. Rather, she wants him to *feel* that he is in her power. She wants him to be conscious of his transformation. He, like Actaeon, must fully remember what he once was and no longer is. Not content with stripping him of his power she demands that he acknowledge his deprivation:

32   Mais que de moy *se sensist* estre serf,
        Et serviteur transformé tellement
        Qu'ainsi *cuydast en son entendement*,
        Tant que Dyane en eust sur moy envie,
36   De luy avoir sa puissance ravie. (my emphasis)

The antecedent of the indirect object pronoun "luy" may be either the male beloved or the female goddess Diana, and the text surely invites both readings. If we read "luy" as referring to the humbled male, then we will hear in the female subject's discourse a desire to emasculate the captured male, to "lui ravir sa puissance," to appropriate male power. If we read "luy" as referring to Diana, then we will hear in the subject's speech a desire to appropriate the omnipotence and lethal power of the divine Diana, who, by exercising *her* power, deprived the male of his. Both readings end up stressing the loss of male power, and indeed the poem continues with a description of the mute, emasculated male poet who is no longer able to write. Immediately following the imaginary appropriation that is represented in the text, the jubilant female subject, invested with the power that was formerly "his" but that, having become hers, empowers her with the authority and potency of Diana, enjoys in fantasy a moment of triumph and joy: "Combien heureuse, et grande me dirois!" (line 37).

In the fantasmatic wish recorded in Elégie 2, the female's violation of the male and her claim to "puissance" (a word that links power, broadly understood, with sexual potency) is registered as an appropriation of the gaze and the voice. Whereas Diana punished Actaeon for seeing her naked, the female in Elégie 2 seeks to attract the male gaze by exposing and flaunting her naked body. The difference between the two women is that Diana was secure in her own subjectivity whereas the Guilletian female, at least throughout the first part of the poem, was not. The speaker in Elégie 2, before taking off her clothes and engaging in what Ann Rosalind Jones calls "erotic aquatics" ("Surprising Fame," 83), was denied "being" by virtue of the fact that the male Other refused to acknowledge her presence, refused to "see" her. We *are*, Lacan observed, because we are looked at. Unseen, we cannot acquire a "self."

Once the Guilletian female has induced the male to look at her, she appropriates the gaze and *looks back at him*. The woman who had been the Object that was looked at assumes mastery of the gaze and directs it towards him who had previously been the viewer. She becomes the Subject, possessor of the gaze, he the Object that is seen. Metaphorically, the water she throws in his eyes ("droict aux yeulx") is the gaze. Beneath the objectifying gaze of the female viewer, the male becomes an object robbed of identity and "puissance."

Freud maintained that the sight of the naked female body provokes anxiety in the male, for the female body, lacking the phallus, i.e., that by means of which the male identifies his being, represents for him the threat of castration. Indeed, several critics have observed that Actaeon's dismemberment can be read as an acting out of the fear of castration that is induced in the male when he sees the naked female body. Freud argued further ("Medusa's Head," *SE* 18: 273, and "The Uncanny," *SE* 17: 237) that male anxiety is heightened when the "castrated" and castrating woman (often figured in literature as the woman with the "evil eye") returns the gaze, an act the male perceives as a threat of emasculation. The fact that the Guilletian subject throws the water in the male's *eyes* brings to mind Freud's observation that castration anxiety is most commonly registered as a fear of blindness.

The text says that the Guilletian female scooped up water *with her hand*. This hand, however, does more than scoop up water. It also holds a pen. The jet of water that pierces the male's eyes is, I would argue, a metaphorical representation of the text the female hand has produced, of the textual body she is exposing to him and would have him "see," the text whose "being," whose "subjectivity," depends on being "looked at." The Guilletian female does not exhibit her nakedness in order to reveal her difference, her alterity. She does not take off her clothes to expose a lack. On the contrary, she displays her body to show the male that she has precisely what he has, that is to say, a lute, signifier of song, voice, presence, of textual performance, of phallic exuberance and of power.

As Elégie 2 moves towards closure, the Guilletian subject represses her fantasmatic wish. She puts her clothes back on, as it were, and assumes once more the role that tradition had assigned to women. "Ostez, ostez, mes souhaitz" (line 45), she says, observing that Apollo, representing now both literary tradition and societal forces, would ". . . contre moy susciter tout le Monde" if she failed to conceal her wish to appropriate male power.

Seeking to situate herself once again within the confines of a femininity endorsed by neoplatonism and, indeed, by society, she confirms her status as a being marked by lack, a being, therefore, that requires a "master" who will supply what she does not have. Because she is "sans grace, et sans merite" (line 49), she must derive her being, she says, from "celuy là" who, as she will say in Epigram 48, "est né pour estre sur moy maistre" (p. 77). Her "being" will be modeled on that of the master, on that of the "maître," or, as Lacan writes, the "m'être," a phonetic sign that fuses *master* and *being*.[21]

Desire, however, cannot be stilled. It circulates throughout the remaining *Rymes*, interrupting and contradicting the female's overdetermined expressions of socially endorsed modesty, self-sacrifice, and effacement. Time and time again it speaks through the interstices of a discourse that seeks to contain it. In Elégie 3, entitled "La Nuict," it assumes the shape of beasts ("bestes terribles," line 22) that, figuring "vains desirs" and "concupiscence" (lines 173-74), haunt the subject's dreams. Like the white wolves that inhabit the Wolfman's dreams, these "monstres" (line 21) terrify *because they remain silent*. And in Chanson 10 (84-90), desire drives a lover to kill the beloved. A curiously refracted version of the Actaeon-Diana myth, Chanson 10, echoing a passage from the *Roman de la rose* (15659-15778), tells of a wild boar that came upon Adonis and was smitten with passion for the lovely boy. "Pour apaiser son ardeur" (line 117), the beast sought to kiss Adonis's "cuisse blanche." In the ensuing struggle, the animal's tusk pierced the boy's body. Adonis "cheut / Tout sanglant à la renverse" (lines 131-32), and died.

The (Textual) Body

Eugene Vance notes that in the medieval courtly lyric desire was displaced away from the sphere of sexuality and towards the sphere of language.[22] What this means is that desire, which is always male in the medieval courtly lyric, moves away from the woman in which it was invested and towards language, or representation. The medieval courtly lyric is heavily freighted with a gender ideology that marginalizes woman in favor of what the male has produced, namely, a text on which he has inscribed his name.

There is another, somewhat more psychoanalytic way, of expressing the phenomenon Vance noted. Lacan insists that *being* is above all body.[23] Reworking Freud's idea of primary narcissism (autoeroticism), Lacan argues that the first step in the shaping of the self is what he calls primary identification, by which he means the infant's erotic relationship with its own body, viewed not as a whole but as a collection of discrete, fragmented, dismembered parts. Primary identification is libidinal drive towards objects; the aim of the drive is to compensate for the primordial loss of the mother that occurred at birth. For Lacan libido arises at birth. We are libidinized from the outset.

Originally, libido is a free current. It drifts. Lacan holds that primary identification is a kind of fantasmatic wish in which the infant becomes the fragmented and broken images it perceives around it, primarily its own disarticulated body. Soon, however, libido is channeled, chained up, shifted from the fragmented body of the infant and invested in the "whole" that is perceived in the mirror stage (secondary identification). As the child accedes to the Symbolic, libido moves across the "body" of language, perceived as a whole. The subject gives up fragmented libidinal enjoyment by investing libido in a universal symbol, the phallus. The process of ego-formation entails, then, a shifting of libido from one type of object to another. The self is formed through a succession of identificatory, or narcissistic, gestures. Of course, ego-formation is never complete. Furthermore, early identifications are never really superseded. Libido seeks at every opportunity to slip from the chains imposed on it by the Symbolic and to attach itself once again to objects in which it was formerly invested.

Lacan argues that aggressivity is rooted in primary identification.[24] Aggressive intentions are linked to the earliest images of the fragmented body. The most archaic level of our being is haunted by images of a body that is mutilated, dismembered, torn asunder. Lacan observes that many social practices—from the tattooing rituals of primitive societies to the arbitrary distortions of the bodily form perpetrated by fashion in more advanced societies—are manifestations of our earliest relationship with our own body, which in our primordial fantasy (that is to say, in primary identification), we perceived as being in pieces. For Lacan, then, as Bice Bevenuto and Roger Kennedy put it, "aggressivity is the irreducible accompaniment of narcissism" (59). Aggressivity and narcissism are tightly bound together; both come into play in every process of identification, whether with another person, with an image of oneself, or with fragments of oneself or another. Since our *being* is created through an endless succession of identificatory gestures, our relations with the Other are always marked by aggressive and narcissistic impulses.

Now in the medieval courtly lyric the male subject diverts some of his libidinal energy away from sexuality towards language. He can do this because he is always already firmly fixed in the Symbolic. He has always already given up a fragmented libidinal enjoyment and has invested libido in a universal symbol of power and mastery, the phallus. Images that relate to pre-specular fantasy, that is, to primary identification, do not often figure in the manifest content of the medieval courtly lyric.

Critics who have read the *Rymes* through the traditional, especially neoplatonic, grid have tended to stress the subject's yearning for Oneness. This longing is that of the subject who seeks to compensate for the loss inherent in being itself. The phallus, which the subject in her wish-fulfilling fantasy claims to possess, is powerful precisely because it offers One-ness. The Guilletian text, in its unfolding, narrates the metonymic course of the subject's desire as it shifts from one identificatory project to another, moving always towards the mastery and autonomy that the Symbolic *seems* to offer—*seems* because the most that the ego can attain is an *illusion* of power and autonomy. From a Lacanian perspective, any subject's trajectory is from fragmentation and insufficiency to an illusion of unity.

The traditional lyric (courtly, neoplatonic, petrarchist) depicts a male subject situated unproblematically in the Symbolic; the male subject's position in the Symbolic is unambiguous because the illusory nature of the ego's autonomy is repressed. The Guilletian text, on the other hand, depicts a female subject whose accession to the Symbolic is highly problematic. In fact, the female subject's entry into the Symbolic—an entry that is represented in Elégie 2 by her jubilant appropriation of "puissance"—is cast in the hypothetical mode of a fantasmatic wish that is confined in the inner space of the poem; and we have seen that the conclusion of the poem represses the wish contained in the body of the text.

From the opening poem of the *Rymes*, the Guilletian text thematizes the formation of the female subject by means of identificatory gestures that disclose the aggressive and narcissistic impulses of primary and secondary identification. The penultimate poem in the *Rymes* is called "Pour une anathomie" (118). The poem invites the reader to "look" at the human form, the microcosm, "le petit monde" (line 7). The body figures a whole; it is an entity that contains within its boundaries a universe, in fact, *the* universe. But how can we *see* (and the invitation is precisely to *see:* "venez voir") the various elements that are linked together within the human body and that are analogically related to the "Ciel, et Terre, et Mer" that are contained within the macrocosm? The title tells us how: by "anatomizing" the body, by disarticulating it into its component parts, by dissecting it so as to produce an "anatomie," a term Cotgrave renders as "a carkasse cut up."

The Guilletian text "anatomizes" the texts it inherits from tradition. In the context of the Guilletian project, the appropriation of authoritative male texts, which are dismembered, pulled apart, and torn into pieces that are then reinscribed in a text gendered differently, loses its "innocence" and becomes an expression of the aggressivity that informs every identificatory gesture. Narrating the problematic inscription of the female subject in the Symbolic, the Guilletian text is haunted by recurring images of the ruptured, split, violated body. Arising from the earliest order of ego-formation, that is to say, from primary identification, these images work against the voice that would constitute the subject's self in the Symbolic. By producing the experience of the hallucinatory, pre-specular and imaginary space of dream, of fantasy, of projection, they create an aura that is part of the visuality of the Imaginary. They also translate the frustration of the female subject as she seeks to produce the experience of the lucid and symbolic space of reason, of voice, and of power.

Notes

[1] Pernette du Guillet, *Rymes*, ed. Victor E. Graham, Textes Littéraires Français (Geneva: Droz, 1968) 8. All quotations come from this edition. After Pernette du Guillet's death in 1544, her husband asked the scholar Antoine du Moulin to prepare a selection of his late wife's poems for publication. Twentieth-century readers assume that the order of the poems in the *Rymes* was established by du Moulin and not by Pernette du Guillet. Be that as it may, the text presents its poems in a particular order. My reading seeks to discover the narrative that is inscribed in that order.

[2] For a discussion of *graphie* and *phonè*, see my *"Graphie, Phonè,* and the Desiring Subject in Scève's *Délie," L'Esprit Créateur* (1985) 3-13.

[3] See Graham's footnote, 8.

[4] Ann Rosalind Jones, "Assimilation with a Difference: Renaissance Women Poets and Literary Influence," *Yale French Studies* 62 (1981) 136. Jones discusses du Guillet's poetry further in *The Currency of Eros: Women's Love Lyric in Europe, 1540-1620* (Bloomington: Indiana UP, 1990) 82-103.

[5] Louise Labé, *Œuvres poétiques précédés des Rymes de Pernette du Guillet*, ed. Françoise Charpentier, Collection Poésie (Paris: Gallimard, 1983) 21.

[6] Verdun-L. Saulnier, "Etude sur Pernette du Guillet et ses *Rymes*," *Bibliothèque d'Humanisme et Renaissance* 4 (1944) 67.

[7] Mary Ann Doane, "Film and the Masquerade: Theorising the Female Spectator," *Screen* 23 (1983) 74-87.

[8] *Petrarch's Lyric Poems*, trans. and ed. Robert M. Durling (Cambridge: Harvard UP, 1976) 60.

[9] Ann Rosalind Jones, "Surprising Fame: Renaissance Gender Ideologies and Women's Lyric," in *The Poetics of Gender*, ed. Nancy K. Miller (New York: Columbia UP, 1986) makes a similar point in her discussion of Elégie 2 (83).

[10] Sigmund Freud, "Negation," in *The Standard Edition of the Complete Works of Sigmund Freud*, ed. James Strachey (London: Hogarth Press, 1955) 19: 235-36. Further references to Freud are to *The Standard Edition* (*SE*).

[11] See Nancy J. Vickers, "Diana Described: Scattered Women and Scattered Rhyme," in *Writing and Sexual Difference*, ed. Elizabeth Abel (Chicago: U of Chicago P, 1982) 95-109. See also Vickers, "The Body Re-membered: Petrarchan Lyric and the Strategies of Description," in *Mimesis: From Mirror to Method, Augustine to Descartes*, eds. John D. Lyons and Stephen G. Nichols (Hanover, NH: UP of New England, 1982) 100-09.

[12] On the presence of Daphne in literature and art, see Yves F.-A. Giraud, *La Fable de Daphné* (Geneva: Droz, 1969).

[13] On Scève's use of the Apollo-Daphne myth, see JoAnn DellaNeva, *Song and Counter-Song: Scève's Délie and Petrarch's Rime*, French Forum Monogaphs 49 (Lexington, KY: French Forum, 1983), esp. ch. 4.

[14] For a theoretical discussion of the way a text creates a special lexicon of cognates, see Michael Riffaterre, "Semantic Overdetermination in Poetry," *PTL* 2 (1979) 1-19.

[15] Guy de Tervarent, *Attributs et Symboles dans l'art profane 1450-1600*, Travaux d'Humanisme et Renaissance 29 (Geneva: Droz, 1958) traces the steps by which Danaë "devint . . . un symbole de la chasteté" (308).

[16] Ovid, *Metamorphoses*, trans. Frank Justus Miller, Loeb Classical Library (Cambridge: Harvard UP, 1977) Bk. III, line 141. Further references to the *Metamorphoses* will be to this edition.

[17] Nicolas J. Perella, *Midday in Italian Literature: Variations on an Archetypal Theme* (Princeton: Princeton UP, 1979) 8-9.

[18] Gisèle Mathieu-Castellani, *Mythes de l'éros baroque* (Paris: PUF, 1981) 72.

[19] See JoAnn DellaNeva, "Mutare/Mutatua: Pernette du Guillet's Actaeon Myth and the Silencing of the Poetic Voice," in *Women in French Literature*, ed. Michel Guggenheim (Saratoga, CA: Anma Libri, 1988) 47-55, and Gisèle Mathieu-Castellani, "Parole d'Echo? Pernette au miroir des *Rymes*," *L'Esprit Créateur* 30 (1990) 61-71.

[20] The Actaeon-Diana myth has often been read in terms of the power relationship suggested by the words *cervus/servus, cerf/serf*. See Leonard Barkan, "Diana and Actaeon," *English Literary Renaissance* 10 (1980) 328.

[21] Bice Benvenuto and Roger Kennedy, *The Works of Jacques Lacan* (New York: St. Martin's Press, 1986) 191.

[22] Eugene Vance, "Love's Concordance: The Poetics of Desire and the Joy of the Text," *Diacritics* 5 (1975) 49.

[23] Jacques Lacan, *Séminaire XX: Encore* (Paris: Seuil, 1975) 127.

[24] Lacan, "Aggressivity in Psychoanalysis," in *Ecrits*, trans. Alan Sheridan (New York: Norton, 1977) 8-29. See Ellie Ragland-Sullivan, *Jacques Lacan and the Philosophy of Psycho-analysis* (Urbana: U of Illinois P, 1986) 36.

Robert Griffin

Du Bellay's Wisdom:
Judgment and Desire

The canonical status of "Heureux qui, comme Ulysse" (*Regrets* 31) is assured, if for no other reason than its systematic recurrence, and thus its reconfirmation, in most anthologies of French poetry in this century. Eternal return of this chestnut may justifiably enshrine Du Bellay's elegiac rendition of the fortunate return of Ulysses, "ayant Pallas pour guide," from his nice trip. Yet our anthologizing habit may also have nothing to do with reader response in the Renaissance. The permanent place of this sonnet in the minds of schoolchildren results primarily from rote memorization of a patriotic vignette.[1] Like other sonnets in Du Bellay's sequence, the completed ambit of Ulysses "who learned all the ways of men" is inscribed like a Homeric ring composition as a moment of inimitable poetic insight, derived from a generalized human experience, into the lessons of wisdom.

Regrets 31, however, does not occupy any priority of place in the sequence, as other sonnets do, and it does not appear to strike significant counterpoints with various *Beatus ille* sonnets of the collection (e.g., 38, 48, 94). Indeed, the constant trials of Ulysses (continuing even after the closure of Book 24) made for anything but a "beau voyage," like the anonymous figure in *Regrets* 29 who "S'aquiert en voyageant un sçavoir malheureux"; the "Lyre chrestienne" puts a fine point on the formula: "qui par son peril est sage, / Celuy est sage malheureux" (vv. 103-04). For his part, Jason fits into the comparison as an afterthought ("Ou comme"), perhaps to make the rhyme word *toison* match the cyclic completion in "Et puis est retourné, plein d'usage et raison." Ironic dependence of these two abstractions on the quantifying *plein* underlines the pathetic *nostos* of Ulysses/Du Bellay (cf. *Regrets* 32: "m'enrichir d'ennui," and dedication 1: 42), in contrast to, let us say, Baïf's more programmatic admonition: "C'est estre fol que d'estre sage, / Selon raison contre l'usage."[2] The polarity of inflicted suffering and vengeful attack that defines the epic hero in his first implied mention by Athena in the *Odyssey* (1: 62, *odíno*: to undergo and inflict pain) aligns with the "savoir malheureux" and satire of the melancholy French voyager.

Although "usage et raison," is set off so prominently, can we assign root meanings for this pair, thus sharpening our understanding of the intertextuality of Classical and Renaissance commonplaces, and of the moral tradition(s) against which the ironist makes his judgments? Even Caesar's *Gallic War*, after all, infused a moral tone into his formulaic *usus atque ratio* (2: 20; 3: 8; 4: 1). Laumonier's edition of Ronsard claims that Du Bellay had the nostalgic "Ode au pais de vandomois" in mind when he composed "Heureux qui, comme Ulysse." If so, then we see the significant evolution of *virtus et sapientia* in Horace through *conseil* and *sçavoir* in Ronsard to *plein d' usage et raison* in Du Bellay. This continuity within change suggests a community of values, while it accentuates feelings of virtuous isolation behind the intimate revelations of the *Regrets*. Even in Du Bellay's "love" poetry, a generalized Ulysses, "Sage, ruzé & bienheureux," is cited for perspective on the anonymous lover who can "contempler le paradis en terre!" (*Olive* 80). These terms are illuminated by their close alliance with the complex Renaissance notion of wisdom, ranging in its applications from enlightened statesmanship to errancy of the passions. Drawing mainly on the *exemplum* of Ulysses, this essay will explore the overlap between judgment and desire.

From beginning to end, variations on what Montaigne called the Socratic "exercise de sagesse et de vertu" (I, 11) dominate Du Bellay's sonnet sequence, furnishing more significant properties and subsets of wisdom than could be listed here, let alone examined. These variations allow for extensive pairing of complements, synonyms or antonyms, such that *sage/usage* is the contrast point of Minerva and Venus in *L' Olive* (e.g. 1, 104), and in *Les Amours* where "l'homme est le plus sage, / D'autant qu'en moy decroissoit ce doux feu" (14). Wisdom is the focal point that allows right and reason to be harmonized with divine will in the case of Pope Paul III "que le sens & l'usage /Avoient fait de son temps estimer le plus sage" (6: 148-49). A few remarks here on the genealogy of virtues will set the stage for broader comment later.

The most pertinent is that, like the Cardinal and Theological virtues, systematic philosophy and theology in the Renaissance saw Wisdom as an emanation from the Divine Mind, the way potential creative energy in the *vita contemplativa* is set in motion by the *vita activa*. Hence, Du Bellay's address to Ronsard in his lengthy "Contre les envieux poètes" begins by establishing the origin of poetry, "Les vers sont enfans du ciel. Heureux qui, par un Homere . . ." (vv. 7-8); then comes the prescribed repartition of virtues, as it applies to the dilemma of the poet's desire to forge a "Ferrement de la Memoire" and his need to praise the wisdom of his Maecenus: "Heureux, qui pour guide ont eu / La louange, qui est mere / Et fille de la vertu" (11: 10-12). For Bruno and others, the image of wisdom is not Truth, but is truthful and partakes of Truth. Wisdom is Sophia, not in essence, but by participation.[3]

Just as the narrator's plight in "France, mère des arts" stems from a breach with the nurturing mother, Du Bellay's *désespéré* is beset by severance from divine love: "Heureux, qui a par augures / Preveu les choses obscures! / Et trop plus heureux encor'/ En qui des Dieux la largesse / A respandu la sagesse, / Des cieux le plus beau tresor!" (4: 104). Divine Wisdom is subdivided into lesser virtues—all the while illustrated by Ulysses as the paragon of wisdom and experience—where it is manifest in nature, in the worldly wisdom of statecraft, and in all other arts: ". . . la sage entreprise, / La vertu, la plume, la voix . . . ," "la saige entreprise, / Et la vertu que le ciel favorise" (3: 109, 144). In medieval iconology, Dame Prudence is principal among the seven handmaidens of Lady Sapientia, just as moral philosophy made prudence a subordinate and surrogate of wisdom. When in the *Vers lyriques* Du Bellay defines Ulysses as "un esprit si saige, / Apres long travaulx," his exegate Jean Proust felt obliged to paraphrase: "Ulysses, le plus prudent & ruzé de tous les Grecs, & le plus eloquent" (3: 110).[4] Unlike the Cardinal and Theological virtues, wisdom stands alone as the goal of life's pilgrimage, as in Vives's *Education of a Christian Woman* (1523) where the seventh step brings the initiate to *sapientia*, the composite and summation of partial virtues, including *usus* and *ratio* in the taxonomy.

The initial example of wisdom as the capstone of public virtues in the *Regrets* comes in Du Bellay's dedication to d'Avanson, which concludes with an admonition—a standard feature of Renaissance treatises on education and manuals for the Prince (Rabelais, Erasmus on Proverbs 8, and others)—to pursue the Classical marriage of wisdom with law and justice. His advice culminates in the eternal heroic attributes of "sage & vaillant" (cf. esp. 6: 182-83). Throughout Du Bellay's canon, wisdom paired with valor is epitomized by Ulysses, although at times it is assigned as a collective Greek virtue of "sage vaillance." As an instance of the dominant role of Du Bellay's "exercise de sagesse et de vertu," the epithet "Sage De-l'hospital, qui seul de nostre France" in the first quatrain of *Regrets* 167 makes the future Chancellor of France the diplomatic equivalent of the balanced Horatian satirist; the second quatrain marshalls his virtues: "je voulais louer ton sçavoir, ta prudence, / Ta vertu, ta bonté"; the third crowns him as "Pallas, ornement de nostre aage"; and so forth.

As these values are extrapolated, *puissance* joined with *sagesse* is needed for the perspective of bold satire "Ou, comme en un miroir, l'homme sage contemple" (cf. 5: 408). More than any other virtue, it is wisdom that endears the poet to the muses (e.g., *Regrets* 62, 76, 165).[5] Hence, the derivation and properties of wisdom are intrinsic to the workings of the melancholy poet's mind, to the objects of his praise, and, thus, to the art of writing poetry. Burton's preface to his *Anatomy of Melancholy* sets his theme of *felix idemque sapiens*: "All my joys to this are folly, / None so divine as melancholy."

A glance at several poems from different collections shows the nexus between divine and mundane wisdom, between nature's wisdom and the eloquence of melancholy in the *Regrets*. In the "Hyme de la surdité" Natura assures the transformation from sensory impressions to understanding, as in the appropriate case of the eardrum ("De quel sage artifice & necessaire usage / La nature a basty ce petit cartilage") which allows the mind of the "philosophe sage" to range beyond the body in order to grasp "Les causes de nature et les secrets des cieux." In the closing lines of the hymn, Deafness ("nourrice de sagesse") is surrounded by Imagination, Judgment and other faculties of mind, and is flanked by Melancholy and a mirror (the traditional iconographic attribute of divine Sapientia) which reflects the three dimensions of time.[6] Comparably, the last of the "Sonnets de l'honneste amour" praises the handiwork of nature in fabricating the poet's lodestar of desire, "Puis que la main de la saige nature / Bastit ce corps, des graces le sejour."

Like Petrarch's Laura, the Sapienta figure completes the life cycle by returning to the divine *œuvre*, after passing through the poet's inspiration: "le ciel trassa la protraiture / De cet esprit, qui au ciel faict retour ... Pour se rejoindre à sa vive peincture" (13). In *Olive* 74 the "vivante peinture" contains both "la vive & immortelle image" and "divin savoir." The "vivante peinture" in *Regrets* 159 is the beautiful architecture of the Château d'Anet with its paradisaical garden and "vive fonteine à la source immortelle"; this perfect example of Classical craftsmanship is cited as a (hyperbolic) reflection of Diane de Poitiers's *sagesse*.

As one might expect, the links between wisdom and eloquence are ready-cut in emblem books and heraldic devices (*Sapientiam sequitur eloquentia; Sapienta constans; Sapientia humana, stultitia est apud Deum*, etc.) But due to the narrator's pose in the *Regrets* of casual musings "à l'adventure," these links are so veiled by the refinement of *sprezzatura* as to require Du Bellay's more voluble poems from his full canon in order to educe the connections. Chamard notes that in *Regrets* 47 Du Bellay's allusion to Saint Paul's preaching on wisdom and foolishness is so dim as to be conjectural. In the sequence's (arguably) most masterful understatement—the present to d'Avanson of a "petit hymne," his "Epitaphe d'un chat"—he characteristically promises *not* to invoke "le severe sourcy /De madame Sagesse."[7]

This throwaway gesture takes on greater significance when we consider the multiple roles of Wisdom/Sapientia in Du Bellay's French and Latin elegies. *Amores* 15 invests Faustina with a "numen Amoris,"an emanation of the sacred within the profane, to which all human endeavor is subject, including "Sophiae studium." When we compare this variation on "omnia vincit amor" to another "Heureux qui" elegy (5), it is clear that we are also dealing with a function of wisdom as a primary reflection of ternary values such as the good, the true, and the beautiful, irrespective of any circumscribed philosophical or theological understanding:

> Vere igitur foelix, Diis et numerandus in ipsis,
> Quem Sophia in molli detinet alma sinu.
> Haec te, Morelli, populo subduxit inerti,
> Hac duce, sublimi sidera fronte petis.
> Iussit, et erecta cernere mente Deum.

At the opposite end of the scale from Du Bellay's mask of offhandedness in the *Regrets*, Ronsard's righteous indignation prevents us from knowing whether he decries the misuse of Scriptural citation, or if his aside comment on casual assignment of sources bespeaks so vast a tradition that specific citation serves mainly to establish the narrator's perspective. Ronsard advises his enemies to return to the shelter of the Muses, rather than "reprendre l'Eglise, ou pour estre veu sage, / Amander en sainct Paul je ne sçay quel passage" (11: 43). But in a long poem like Du Bellay's encyclopedic "Discours sur la louange de la vertu & sur les divers erreurs des hommes," the poet clarifies the proportions: the ratio of humble virtue to direct speech is as the hypocritical show of virtue is to idle language. In the final verses, this is the license he provides to himself for his satirical *persona*, where "en raison je me fonde, / Le sage contrefaisant" (4: 156).

Since wisdom is a primeval potential, Du Bellay, like other moralists of his time, often locates its unencumbered qualities prior to world and time. Before the sacrifice that initiated creation, before the Only-Begotten was the son of Mary, and thus before even the existence of the Trinity, the son was both and only the Word (*Logos*) and Wisdom (*Sophia*) of the Creator, i.e., the creative power and reflective pattern by which the world would be formed. As God's companion before creation, Wisdom pre-existed and actively participated in the formation of the world. This dispenser of God's gifts arrays the signs of creation, reflecting yet transcending divine artifice. As Peletier put it, "Voyla commant d'une Idee de sagece e de vertu conçue par le grand esprit Poëtique, se forme le grand e parfet image de la vie."[8] Du Bellay's "Heureux qui" elegy in the *Recueil de poesie* closes with an imagined return to the world's origin, "le monde enclos / Dedans le seing de son premier cahos." There he argues that while the primary elements of fire and water cannot coexist, "un amour saigement entrepris" will endure and reconcile discordant elements in creation, "Car la vertu à la vertu s'assemble." In Christian tradition, the marriage between Creator and consort, Spirit and matter (Genesis 1.1), Logos and Sophia (Proverbs 8) will be complemented by a nuptial song at the end of time. Du Bellay's "Tombeau de Marguerite, Royne de Navarre" closes with the mystic union "De l'Eternel & de l'Ame," "l'Epoux & l'Epousee," drawing on references to the *trisagion* ("Sanctus, sanctus, sanctus") which immediately precedes the Canon in the Mass. His long poem concludes with instructions to the hypothetical audience to sing "Grace, Vertu & Sagessse, / Ainsi qu'elle est au Seigneur, / Estoit, & sera sans cesse" (cf. 2: 262).

As a reenactment of the beloved's inspiriting effect *in illo tempore*, the Mass celebrates beatified form and a desire to restore the paradigm lost. In this sense, Petrarch's *Rime sparse* is a memorial, a re-collection of scattered fragments of time: "Accampa ogni tuo ingegno, ogni tua forza, / Mentre fra noi di vita alberga l'aura . . . memoria eterna" (239). Comparably, after "l'eternel amant / Fist par sa mort vivre sa bien aimée" in the "Easter sonnet" (*Olive* 111), the narrator prays for grace from the Holy Spirit ("L'esprit divin de ton feu vehement") and dedicates his sonnet: "Pleurez, mex yeulx, de sa mort la memoire." Categorical separation between Divine Wisdom and the sensuous effects of Sophia's handiwork in nature is an idea that is shared neither by Church Fathers nor by many Renaissance poets (the etymology of *sapientia* is *sapor*, "taste").[9] The ineffability of love leads to the poet's love for difference, for the ineffability of an Eternally Feminine *persona* who serves as the inaccessible goal of his endlessly savored desire.

In the case of Odysseus/Ulysses, the return to origins invokes the charter myth of the marriage of Thetis and Peleus—the disrupted union which is complemented at the end of the *Odyssey* by the resanctification of marriage laws—and the divisions of power, insight and beauty among society's estates: Ruler, Priestess, and Guarantrix of fruitfulness. Du Bellay's eulogy of Jacques Aubery typifies the way Renaissance poets adapted the famous Homeric contest for the apple of paradise; Du Bellay's Hera appears to usurp the role of Aphrodite in the list of gifts conferred on the Ambassador to England ("Junon sa grace & Pallas sa prudence") for his mission to restore peace following "la Discorde & Mars."

While the course of events punished Paris for choosing Aphrodite in the Trojan beauty contest, the human dilemma remains that wisdom is admonished but beauty is preferred. Late medieval moralists took it upon themselves to jibe at Ulysses for spending so many years under the spell of beautiful Calypso, sitting alone and pensive until Athena was forced to remind him of his goal. Through the epitome of Ulysses *polytropos*, Homer dramatized the potential for chaos among the world's ranked orders, and illustrated the eternal epic tension between virtue and desire. Dating from "Augustine"'s sermons to "Petrarch" in the *Secretum* on lust, greed, and ambition, poets cited these temptations as a backdrop for making refined discriminations between human and divine wisdom, carnal and spiritual love. Inasmuch as early Fathers attributed sinfulness to Lust of the Eyes, of the Flesh, and Pride of Life (Gen. 3), a litany of citations from medieval and Renaissance writing on the distribution of potencies would have an effect of *déjà lu*. In the *Canterbury*

Tales, for example, Dame Prudence queries Melibeus on post-Edenic life: "What is better than wisedoom? Womman!" (B2295-2300). Even edifying historical interpretations like the fourteenth-century *Ovide moralisé* pose comparable questions: "Qui est de greignor vaillance, / Ou bone amours, ou sapience?"[10] The twist given by Ronsard to the distribution of virtues and riches is that Nature gave wisdom and prudence to men, but conferred beauty on women (6: 115).

If Ronsard's trope is read as misogyny, we will miss an important role of wisdom in the relationship beween creator and model. His line "Dieu tout parfait / A tout fait par sapience" (3: 32) is a map to misreading, assigned by Laumonier to the beginning of Hesiod's *Works and Days* and the second *Pythian Ode*; the attribution is arbitrary and dubious. Like painting, Ronsard's and Du Bellay's poetic use of wisdom must be evaluated in perspective in order to see more clearly what values and conventions are at issue.

Indo-European and Semitic traditions alike cast figurations of divine presence in the world, and the impediments to man's apprehensions of divinity, as ineffable feminine form. Myth, theology and art subdivide this dramatic dilemma into sacred action prefiguring human response. In the archaic Mediterranean, Du Bellay's "Berecynthienne" was the generalized mother of the dying and reborn god Attis, whose earthly mother later conceived by placing a ripe almond or a pomegranate seed in her bosom. In personifying the surrogate of the Creator's Wisdom, Catholic iconology features a haloed or crowned Sophia/Sapientia who enigmatically writes all names in her book of the world: "O ludum sapientiae, in libro vitae nomina conscribere!" In allegorizing the wisdom of Ulysses, Jean Dorat put this succinctly: "apud Veteres nondum corrupta Sophia Virginis instar-erat."[11] Liturgy prefigures the Virgin by invoking Sophia ("in gremio matris sedit sapientia patris") who precedes and follows the flicker of worldly appearance with its simulacrum of wisdom. Just as the actual and ideal coexist in a dual relation between preexistence (e.g., the Son of Man) and post-creation (e.g., the Heavenly Jerusalem), Sophia exists before the event and after the fact, and hence circumscribes the life cycle of man ("The first man knew her not perfectly, so also the last will not trace her out," Ecclesiasticus 24.26).

Rabbinical scholars and biblical exegetes note that the first mention of a wise person in Scripture designates a woman (2 Samuel 14), showing traces of a Near-Eastern goddess whose worship was suppressed by Alexandrian scholars and early Fathers (Clement, Tertullian et al.). But it is in Proverbs 8 where wisdom is exalted as the first of God's creations and as the Master Builder's companion—his medium and model—when he encircled the cosmos with his compass, as in the overture to Tasso's *Mondo creato*. Attended by Sophia, the geometer Creator reaching down with his dividers to describe the circle of being is a common image in illustrated medieval French Bibles. As a half-independent figure, Sophia reveals the deity both to himself and to his benighted creatures in nature's reflected splendor. Through the veil of language, these creatures can sustain only the sight and comprehension of simulacra.

Like the Virgin, Sophia is a mediatrix who leads the way to God, restoring the charter of language and knowledge that was broken before the expulsion into time in Genesis 4. She is the Mastercraftsman's surrogate insofar as she realizes God's thought by incarnating and "clothing" it in material form.[12] In Proverbs 8, Wisdom describes herself in this order: as close to God, as playing a role in creation, as dwelling among men, and as bestowing benefits. The same word order opens John's gospel: the Word was God, everything was made by the Word, the Word entered the world, and the *Logos* brought the grace of sonship and truth.[13] After citing Augustine's *Confessions* (8.12), Petrarch declares "L'alma, ch'è sol da Dio fatta gentile, / Ché giá d'altrui non pò venir tal grazia, / Simile al suo fattor stato ritene" (*Rime sparse* 23).

Like many another fragment that could be culled from Petrarch, these verses intimate why it is often idle to establish categorical differences—even between dogmatic Christianity and mystic Platonism—in Renaissance poetry, and they suggest why *L'Olive* does not do so. Petrarch's

> In qual parte del ciel in quale idea
> Era l'essempio, onde Natura tolse
> Quel bel viso leggiadro, in ch'ella volse
> Mostrar qua giú quanto lassú potea?
> (*Rime sparse* 159)

could be cited as a test case to show why specific attribution is misleading, perhaps in conjunction with Du Bellay's comparable universe inscribed within the beloved's eye (*Olive* 73), or his sarcastic

> Son firmament est peinct sur un beau front,
> Tous ses désirs sont balançez en rond,
> Son pole Artiq', ce sont
> Les beaux yeux de sa dame.
> ("Contre les Pétrarquistes")

For this conjunction, critical editions habitually refer readers to *L'Olive*, where Du Bellay does, of course, disembody the features of his Petrarchan *innamorata* by laminating them over the face of nature. As the following brief excursus on Petrarch suggests, St. Bernard of Clairvaux's *Sermones in laudibus virginis matris* might be just as revealing for the Petrarchan connection.[14]

Laura's poetic "assumption" is useful for assessing the Christian substratum in Du Bellay's use of Sapientia as a reflection of the Divine Creator's art. In "Laura," Petrarch remodels the epiphany of Divine Wisdom as a mirror reflection of the scriptural remodeling of Adam through the art and good offices of personified Sophia/Wisdom, as in the culmination of his poem sequence. Adam's *felix culpa* and the pilgrimage to atonement are the prefigural counterparts of the narrator's passion to reconcile sign and referent in the disrepair of post-Adamic speech. The conceit corresponds to the principal section in part 3 of the *Secretum*:

Quia cum creatum omne Creatoris amore diligendum sit, tu contra, creature camptus illecebris, Creatorem non qua decuit amasti, sed miratus artificem fuisti quasi nichil ex omnibus formosius creasset, cum tamen ultima pulcritudinum si forma corporea . . . Verborum queris adminicula; si enim nonnisi quod oculis apparet amare potes, corpus igitur amasti.

Here Augustine uses *form* in the scholastic sense of the organizing principle which gives purpose to matter, and the spiritual principle which gives meaning to human existence.

Rime sparse 366, then, articulates the analogy between the poet's memorial and the Mass. Liturgical language superimposes over the "Laura" figure the *persona* of the Holy Mother as origin and "buon fine," where *persona* is used in the related senses of "person," "mask," and "replica." This final poem plays counterpoint with the overture, where Laura's illuminated features derive from the Creator through the Virgin. The canzone's opening paean to the wisdom of the "Vergine bella, che di sole vestita, / Coronata di stelle," blends imagery from Proverbs, Genesis, the banquet of the "Virgo sapiens" (Matthew 25: the scriptural source of the iconography of enthroned Sapientia), Revelation 12, and the hymn on the Assumption of the Virgin *ad laudes*.

The Assumption is the revelation of the Virgin's eternal reign with Christ, Sophia as the consort of the Logos and matrix of the universe. As the prototype in Catholic liturgy of bodily resurrection, the Assumption is bound up with the feast of the Immaculate Conception which takes its Epistle from Proverbs 8, the "Dominus possedit me." Toward the end of the calendric round in the Great Antiphon of December 17, the Church turns to the world's beginning, and calls on Sophia in order to reform the universe, "mightily and sweetly (*suaviter*) ordering all things." From Bernard Silvestris in the twelfth century to the opening "vive image" of Pierre Lemoyne's *Hymne de la sagesse divine* in the early seventeenth century, Minerva finds common cause with the biblical Sapientia (*Chokamah*) whose capacities remain intact verbatim: "omnium artifex Sapientia, disponit omnia suaviter Sapientia" (Silvestris, *De mundi universitate* 8.1).

Wisdom's preformation of *Homo sapiens*, then, entails formation of primal man and reformation of his successor, so that wisdom becomes his natural potential, implicated both in man's Fall and in his restoration. The origin of the taint on humanity and the paradigm for man's salvation are actually prior to the Fall, causally prior even to Creation, and are therefore inaccessible to post-Adamic language. The imagery of choice used to "flesh out" this complex of ideas, as we have seen, reverts to the Tree in the Garden for its canonical authority, while its referent remains pointedly ineffable and inaccessible. In this respect, figuration of surpassing feminine form in *la poétique de Du Bellay* aligns with the paradoxical search for divine understanding in Cusa's *Layman on Wisdom and the Mind*: "the unattainable is unattainably attained . . . wisdom is higher than all knowledge and at the same time unknowable. It is unutterable in any language . . . Infinite wisdom is the unfailing food of life. Wisdom is the most savory food which, in satisfying, does not diminish the desire to partake of it. Thus the delight of the eternal banquet never ceases."[15] Now that the editing of Du Bellay's full work is nearly complete, two final examples from the *Regrets* and *L'Olive* will underscore: (1) the need and advantage of roaming through his complete canon for a full accounting of sources, and (2) the risk for readers of eliding the richness in the common stock of Renaissance imagery.

(1) *Regrets* 117 continues the *Beatus ille* series: "Celuy vrayement estoit & sage & bien appris, / Qui cognoissant du feu la semence divine . . . ." Chamard's oblique note ("Héraclite") is obviously wide of the mark, since the sonnet elaborates the cyclic return of souls after their purgation by divine fire— a patent reference in its context to Anchises's cosmogonic speech to Aeneas in the Elysian Fields (". . . ordine singula pandit. Principium caelum ac terras . . . ," *Aeneid* 6.724-34), prior to the Jovian succession of gods and rulers. Du Bellay translated this passage twice and used it again in an ode to the Cardinal Du Bellay (4: 133), where the poet's invocation returned once more to the world's cosmogony and to the extraction of form from chaos. But, of course, he tailored Virgil appropriately for the Cardinal. Merely citing this passage in Virgil begs the question of attribution, because the source of Anchises's vision has, in turn, always puzzled Classics scholars. Since Pythagoras is the most commonly proposed "source," the roots of Virgil's embedded vision are shrouded by mysticism of the Fertile Crescent. Against such uncertain parentage, Du Bellay's image shades easily into what could be taken for the effects of Pentecostal fire in the descent of the Holy Spirit. Thus, it is the "petiz feux" of Divine Providence which this time grace the wayward soul with recollection (*anamnesis*) of

> Le lieu de nostre origine.
> Ainsi de raizon l'usage,
> Qui n'est en autre animal,

> Fait que l'homme, qui est sage,
> Discourt le bien & mal.
> (11: 53-56)

Limitations of sight and speech, like the antagonism of fire/water and opposing emotions, are traceable to the fleshly body "Dont nostre esprit est vestu, / Tarde souvent la vertu / De l'ame, qui est celeste" (58-60).

In a letter on the Platonic *furores*, Ficino equates Jove with the *anima mundi* in Anchises's speech, citing the Orphic *Hymn of Jove* as evidence: "Iupiter primus, Iupiter caput, Iupiter masculus et incorruptibilis sponsa, Iupiter indefessi ignis motus," and continuing on to Wisdom the first creator and sweet Love. He quotes it again in full elsewhere, together with commentaries by Porphyry and Proclus which take Jove as the *mens mundi*: "Jovem mundi mentem arbitrantes, quae in se ipsa mundum continens produxit." This interpretation, repeated by Cornelius Agrippa, makes Jupiter into the creative Logos.[16]

(2) The closing section of *L'Olive* contains a mélange of salutations to various gods, Christian and pagan alike. Sonnet 104 begins the series with an apostrophe to Venus and Minerva, and ends by invoking Diana and Apollo. The cameo image of Minerva appears to be common issue ("Toy, qui sortis de la saincte cervelle, / Sage Pallas, Minerve Athenienne"). But in view of the multiple roles assigned to wisdom in the sonnet sequence, and recalling the initial discussion in this essay of Wisdom's origin as "an emanation of the Divine Mind," can we dismiss Du Bellay's metaphor merely as a Renaissance commonplace?

If we keep in mind Ficino's language in portraying Jove as the source of Word and Wisdom, then the explicit parallel between Proverbs 8 and John 1 takes on a new light. Ficino's opening invocation to *Il Magnifico* in his *commentaria Platonis proemium* is close to Francesco Guicciardini's praise of Lorenzo's eloquence, style and wisdom: "Sophia, magnanime Laurenti, quae solo Iovis capite nata, ab initio cum eo erat cuncta componens patrem imitans, ipsa quoque filiam solo peperit, Philosophiam nomine, cuius deliciae forent, esse cum filiis hominum."[17] Aside from the mystery they convey through the language of myth, none of these accretions to the birth of wisdom from godhead could be considered arcane. The Sophia of Mary, for instance, was widely discussed in fifteenth-century devotional writing, and by Jean Gerson at the Council of Constance.

Some classic works of modern scholarship examine such accretions, but without making essential linkage. Jean Seznec's *Survival of the Pagan Gods* discusses a fifteenth-century mythological treatise which attempted to update Fulgentius, through its correspondence of the Gifts of the Holy Spirit to the planetary gods: "Saturn is Prudence, and [since] Prudence is made up of

Memory, Intelligence, and Foresight . . . Jupiter-Benevolencia [,who] sums up Prudentia, Sapientia, and Intelligencia . . . ." Farther on, Seznec uses illustrations from a manuscript of an *Ovide moralisé*, depicting Pallas and the Muses, and Jupiter surrounded by quadrants containing a dozen crowned figures. In a later chapter, he provides illustrations from Mantegna's *Tarocchi*, beginning with Jupiter pictured as *Prima Causa*. These Jupiter figures are enthroned within an almond-shaped *generationis uterus*.[18] The pose of their hands makes them virtually transposable with the sculpted figure common to tympana of Gothic cathedrals, where Christ-Wisdom is surrounded by the four Gospelists—represented by animals from the dozen zodiacal symbols—with his right hand elevated in the "fear not" posture, while his lowered left hand ("gift giving") holds the book of Revelation. Christ, too, is shown coming forth from the *mandorla* of the Virgin Mother, a geometrical figure which became the standard measuring unit in medieval cathedrals.[19]

It would be idle to wonder if many or any of these connections were present in the "beaucoup davantage" to which the Ulyssean Du Bellay aspired. Yet it is clear that the intelllectual and spiritual content of wisdom was not only secularized in precepts and proverbs about the exercise of good judgment, reducible to patent phrases like "plein d'usage et raison," but was also sublimated in European mysticism and love poetry through desire for transcendence.

Notes

[1] An incidental fame which is comparable for its utility to Virgil's "timeo danaos et dona ferentes," known then and now to young Latinists more for a quirky use of *et* (*etiam*) than for any Virgilian poetry in Laocoön's speech. All references to Du Bellay in the text are from *Œuvres poétiques*, ed. Henri Chamard et al., 6 vols. (Paris: Nizet, 1982).

[2] *Euvres en rime de Ian Antoine de Baïf* (Paris: Lemerre, 1881-90) 5: 9.

[3] "E meraviglia, O Sophia, che la Fortuna sappia discorere meglio, e meglio intender gli testi che Minerva, la quale è soprastante a queste intelligenze . . . la dea Bontade non egualmente si dona a tutti; la Sapienza non si communica a tutti con medesima misura" (*Spaccio della bestia trionfante* 2.1). In line with the chain of being between macrocosm and microcosm, Ronsard makes his "Roy tressage & tresbon," "si sage & si prudent," because God is "tout sage & bon," "tout prevoyant & sage." Hence, "c'est le secret de Dieu, lequel sage propose, / Puis le conseil humain execute la chose." *Œuvres complètes*, ed. Paul Laumonier (Paris, 1914-60) 9: 121; 11: 59, 135; 16: 145; 18: 319.

[4] Ronsard's Ulysses: "Estimé le plus sage & facond de son temps" (18: 40).

[5] Ronsard: "Dieu qui est tout prevoyant & sage" (18: 319); "comme prudent & sage . . . une Muse tressaincte / Qui parle sagement" (7: 229); "ces vieux et sages Peres . . . prudent & sage . . . Minerve sage" (8: 16-30). In Christianity, power, goodness and wisdom are the three traditional capacities of God. In *Le Second Curieux* Tyard invites contemplation of artistic excellence: ". . .

estimeras-tu qu'elle soit faicte d'avanture, & non pas par quelque ouvrier doué de très grande puissance & sapience très-excellente, qui n'est d'ailleurs que dedans ce monde, lequel il conduit, engendrant & augmentant ce qui est en luy? Or c'est ce qu'on appelle Dieu," in *The Universe of Pontus de Tyard*, ed. John Lapp (Ithaca: Cornell UP, 1950) 157; cf. Du Bellay: "Carles, des Muses prestre, à qui la vierge sage . . . " (5: 361).

[6] Among the numerous variations that Ronsard worked on the Petrarchan *Solo e pensoso* is "triste, docte, prudent, sage, pensif" (15: 26). After Du Bartas pictures God's self-contained Word and Wisdom in the *Premiere Sepmaine*, "la Sophie grégeoise" is portrayed as a mirror reflection; cf. "La sophie grégeoise orna d'habit romain" (3: 820). As for her names, John Steadman points out that Renaissance commentators slipped easily from one to another: Wisdom, Sapientia, Sophia, Chokamah, . . . Musa, in *Milton's Classical and Biblical Imagery* (Pittsburgh: Duquesne UP, 1984) 102, 105. Du Bellay, however, translates Turnèbe's "sophos sapiensque" with a neologism "saige-sçavant" (6: 117). In the thick of his *Beatus ille* rhetoric (citing Ulysses, Solomon and Olivier along the way) he refers to the "Sages Indiques," which his commentator recognized as the Gymnosophists, the naked philosophers who sought pure truth (6: 214); cf. *Rime sparse* 7 ("Povera e nuda vai, Filosofia") and 278 ("E viva e bella e nuda al ciel salita"). On the title page of his *Traité de la Sagesse*, Pierre Charron explained that "la Sagesse est representée par une belle femme toute nuë."

[7] In the *Enchiridion*, Erasmus admonishes that the Divine Spirit has its own figures of speech: "Balbutit nobis Divina sapientia, & velut mater quaepiam officiosa." *Opera omnia* (Leyden, 1703-06) 5: 8 ff. Cf. *Regrets* 189, Ronsard 10: 320, and Charles d'Orléans, *Ballades* 121.

[8] "Proesme sur le premier livre," *Algèbre* (Lyons, 1554). Following the overture to Christophe de Gamon's "Premier jour de la semaine," for example, an unfettered Wisdom "plays" before God ("Tous jours en sa présence / Sa sagesse luizoit, paroissoit sa Puissance" (11: 35-36: Proverbs 8), whereas the power of the Master Builder is masked, "celant son artifice": *ars est celare artem*. Christ is the fruit from the divine wedding of Logos and Sophia, through whom love entered the world.

[9] Petrarch's contemporary Heinrich Suso described a vision he underwent, following a reading from Proverbs; unlike the Philsophia of Boethius, Wisdom presented herself for his embrace: "now her manner was more that of a wise mistress, then of a beautiful lover." Quoted in *Deutche mystische Schriften*, ed. E. Hofman (Düsseldorf: Patmos, 1966) 166. Cf. Chariteo, *Rime* 157: "Frondosa arbor, gentil, sempre florente, / Sacrata a la celeste, eterna diva, / Di cui la sapïentia alta deriva, / Dove senza pentir *gode* la mente" (emphasis added). A century later, Spenser's *Amoretti* also took the Tree in the Garden as the appropriate metaphor for the imprint of God's artistry: "That is true beautie: that doth argue you / To be divine, and borne of heavenly seed, / Deriv'd from that fayre Spirit from whom al true / And perfect beauty did proceed" (79). See also Marot's "Chant Royal de la Conception de nostre Dame" for the Virgin's *odor suavissimus* (Ecclesiasticus 24) and Laura's paradisal "soave velo." In *Olive* 64, creation is the handiwork of a demiurgic *alma mundi* which separates the elements to form the seeds of the world; this image in the octave sets up the analogy with the effect of the beloved, "O l'ame de ma vie," which "Forma le rond de sa perfection."

[10] Ed. C. de Boer (Amsterdam: Müller, 1914) ll. 3269-70. In the prose version, the author glosses redemption (John 3.16?) from the Fall: "Dieu, par la fleiche d'amours, (dont Cupidon ferit Dané la belle), empannee des pennons de pitié et de charité, ploya et se humilia tant qu'il envoya sapience au monde en fourme humaine d'une humble servante." The bond between love and wisdom is powerfully sanctioned by the Song of Solomon; Louise Labé: "celui qui ha ù le nom de Sage, ha descrit ses plus hautes concepcions en forme d'amourettes" (*Le Débat de l'Amour et de la Folie* 5). Burton's *Anatomy of Melancholy* distinguishes two kinds of "love-melancholy": the first includes those who make God the object of their affection, and the second those who substitute woman (3.3.1.1). Citing the *timor domini* from Proverbs, Belleau's "Discours de la vanité" adheres to the latter: "La Sapience en fin est un gouffre de mer, / Un abysme profond, qu'on ne sauroit sonder . . . plus fiere, plus dure, & plus aigre est la Femme." *Œuvres* (Geneva: Slatkine, 1967) 8: 282.

[11] Dorat, cited by Geneviève Demerson in *Dorat et son temps* (Clermont-Ferrand: Adosa, 1983) 129. Dante frequently draws on this imagery: "Fecemi la divina podestate, / La somma Sapïenza, e 'l primo amore / Dinanzi a me non fur cose create," "O somma Sapïenza, quanta è l'arte che mostri in cielo, in terra e nel mal mondo" (*Inferno* 3.6; 19.10; cf. *Convito* 2.5.8).

[12] As Marguerite phrased it in *Le Triomphe de l'agneau*, "Ce verbe donc toujours victorieux, / Fort, tres puissant, permanent, glorieux, / Par qui le Ciel en toute sa grandeur / Prit ornement, et figure, et rondeur, / Vestu de chair . . . / Verbe divin, sapience profonde, De Deïté plenitude féconde." Cf. Ronsard: "la vertu / Dont le sage est revétu" (1: 124).

[13] Guillaume Postel (1555): "principio Paradisum voluptatis fuisse ante omnia saecula conditum, et qui ANTE ME FACTUS EST, id est in Sapientia creata, sive in mente generali. Nam quod ad generationem tempralem pertinet (Joh. 1)," in *Apologies et rétractions*, ed. François Secret (Nieuwkoop: De Graf, 1972) 199. In Ebreo's *Dialoghi d'amore* Filone explains that the effects of Divine Wisdom radiate through the created universe, along the rivers of virtues emanating from the roots of the Tree of Paradise: "fontana onde emana la prima belleza comme sapienzia." As his canonical authority, he cites Proverbs 8 in full: "con sapienzia creò Dio il cielo e la terra. . . ." Charles de Bovelles's *De sapiente* (1510) also cites Proverbs 8 in connection with Adamic remembrance (*anamnesis*) of the spark of life: "Hoc enim et ipsa Sapientia in sacris litteris de se ipsa attestatur: Pulsitans citansque dormientes, eos, ut se concupiscant, hortatur." Once (a)roused from the sleep of spiritual death, postlapsarian insight into the loss of Paradise contrasts with the original Adam's lack of perspective: "Artis vero Homo, apud se, humanave species Arte progenita dyas est et primi quedam Hominis emanatio, Sapientia, fructus et finis" (ch. 15). Cf. *Le Jeu d'Adam*: Adam—"Jo l'aim e criem." Diabolus—"N'est pas saveir, que poet faire?" Adam—"E bien e mal . . ." Diabolus—"Co est le fruit de sapïence, de tut saveir done scïence . . ." Eva—"D'itel savor est ceste pome."

[14] See Bernard, *In dominica infra octavam Assumptionis sermo*: Mary's face splendidly illuminates the stars wheeling above her head. Castiglione prefaces *Il Cortegiano* by eulogizing Vittoria Colonna: "l'ingegno e prudenzia di quella signora, della quale io sempre ho tenuto in venerazione come cosa divina." In Pallavicino's reckoning, the Fall from unity into multiplicity extends from the most preliminary marriage of form and substance to the perfectibility of the species: "come sapete essere opinion d'omini sapientissimi, l'omo s'assimiglia alla forma, la donna alla materia" (3.15).

[15] *Layman on Wisdom and the Mind*, trans. M. L. Fuhrer (Ottawa: Dovehouse, 1989) 24. Cf. the "Virgo sapiens" of Matthew 25.10. How different is this from Aquinas on the Trinity: "Longing to see that which is not to be seen . . . to eat the forbidden fruit" (cited by Robert Burton 1.2.4.7)? The *Anatomy of Melancholy* begins by ascribing the human condition to eating of the forbidden fruit, "from the day that they go out of their mother's womb, unto that day they return to the mother of all things"; citing Wisdom, Proverbs, and Saint Paul ("no tongue can tell, no heart can conceive it"), Burton attempts to portray God as the object of religious melancholy: "so fair a body, so fair a face, eyes, nose, cheeks, chin, brows, all fair and lovely to behold; besides the beauty of the soul which cannot be discerned" (3.4.1.1).

[16] Ficino, *Opera omnia* (Turin: Bottega d'Erasmo, 1959) 1: 614; Agrippa, *De occ. phil.* 3.7. Cf. La Boderie: "'La Sagesse,' dit-il [King David], 'fut la mere premiere / Avec le dous Amour.' ô Bouche de lumiere!" *Encyclie* (Anvers: Plantin, 1571) 192.

[17] Cf. Ecclesiasticus 24.8: "Then the creator of all things instructed me, 'Pitch your tent in Jacob, make Israel your inheritance'"; John 1.14: "The Word was made flesh, and pitched his tent among us." On the resemblance of son to father, cf. Rabelais's "forme visible" (*Pantagruel*, ch. 8) and Erasmus: "foetum e tuo natum cerebro, quemadmodum Palladem ajunt e cerebro Jovis, vivam parentis imaginem referentem" (1.1022 D). Through her parentage of prudence and foresight, and through the Adamic figure of Prometheus ("foresight"), allegorizing mythographers like Fulgentius related Pallas/Minerva to Divine Providence. The Third Vatican Mythographer (ca. 1157-1217) emphasized the link with Proverbs: "Ego in altissimis habitavi . . . quia secundum fabulam de capite Jovis nata Perhibetur" (10.2).

[18] *The Survival of the Pagan Gods* (New York: Harper, 1961) 94, 110, 138. Cf. Silvestris: "tu, natura, uteri mei beata fecunditas," and the Church's reference to the oceanic Holy Water Font as "uterus ecclesiae." Fray Luis de León's "Noche serena" repeats the relationship of Jupiter and Saturn, while assigning emanations of love to God's wisdom (ll. 41-57). See also Dorothy Gabe Coleman, "Minerve et Olive," in *Du Bellay, Actes du Colloque d'Angers* (Angers: Presses de l'Université d'Angers, 1990) 161-69.

[19] The uniform measure is attributable to the Latin translation of Euclid's *Elements* (1121), of which the *mandorla* is the first illustration (cf. Chamard's note for *Regrets* 189). See Dürer's *Institutio Geometricarum* (Paris, 1535) 2: 55; and Tertullian (one of the Fathers who helped to "sublimate" the Eastern figure of enticing Sophia): "Nos pisciculi secundum *ichthûn* nostrum Jesum Christum in aquâ nascimur," *De baptis.*, ch. 1. Within a few years of Tertullian's equation, we find the identical right-left hand pose of Gautama Buddha, seated beneath the Bo Tree of Enlightenment, who is encompassed by a similar vulva-shaped matrix. This is the first recorded halo form in art history; see Joseph Campbell, *The Way of the Seeded Earth* (New York: Harper, 1988) 95-100.

Glyn P. Norton

Du Bellay and
the Emblematics of Regret

One of the defining modes through which Renaissance views of crisis, periodicity, and time are expressed is that of the Greek figure, *Kairos*, the youngest son of Zeus. Joachim Du Bellay, like many of his contemporaries, was not unaware of the main iconographic features of the *Kairos* myth, transformed sexually by Latin culture into the tableau of the aquatic goddess, *Occasio*, and given new prominence in Renaissance emblem literature. In his *Discours au Roy sur la trefve de l' an M.D.LV.*, Du Bellay invokes the *Kairos/Occasio* figure to define the critical stress of a particular historical moment. With the collapse of the short-lived truce of Vaucelles in 1556 and the continued conflict between Henry II and the Emperor, Charles V, Du Bellay's poetic tribute to the truce, written in the euphoria of the moment, inscribes its own obsolescence. Prior to its publication in 1558, the Poet, thus, feels obliged to add a liminary sonnet which reaffirms the hope of the original truce, deplores the resumption of hostilities ("fureur nouvelle"), and leaves history to contemplate a new opportunity. In the final tercet, the challenge of this moment is linked explicitly to the stock image of Occasion: "Renoüons cest accord d'une plus forte main, / Prenons l'heure aux cheveux: l'homme r'appelle en vain / La sourde Occasion, alors qu'elle est absente."[1]

Though lacking some of the scenic features of the standard emblematic tableau (the marine environment, the razor in outstretched hand, the billowing cloak, the rotating orb or wheel), Du Bellay's summary focuses significantly on the scene's dialogic structure. In this setting, man is defined by his potential enactment of a rhetorical gesture, that of appeal to an unheeding audience, in this case, Occasion. She, in turn, is defined by her immunity to auditory appeal ("sourde") and by her headlong rush into absence. The failing dialogic act thus necessitates a more preemptive gesture eschewing the conventions of rhetorical statement. In grasping Occasion by her protruding forelock,[2] man as a rhetorical agent places his utterance in the gender framework of male domination and female submission. The normal channels of rhetorical appeal are futile against this deaf, temporal virago; the only discourse to which she responds is that of aggression and bondage, the very conditions under which rhetoric transcends its own prescriptive structures.

In the liminary sonnet to his *Discours* on the truce of Vaucelles, Du Bellay strips the *Occasio* emblem of all but its barest essentials. What is left is a situation of largely forensic significance made up of two related events, the one implied by the other: 1) a speaker makes a vain appeal to an audience that has already abandoned him; 2) in the wake of this flight, that speaker is presumed to live on in the anxiety of residual penitence, of opportunity missed and failed eloquence. The scene ventures its own corrective, however, in the form of a tersely worded imperative ("Prenons l'heure aux cheveux"), peremptory in the way it authorizes the speaker's assault on his audience. For purposes of the present essay, what interests us here is not the stock iconographic allusion to Ocasion's forelock, contained in the imperative, but the scene's dramatic, even agonistic, relief concentrated in the phrase "l'homme r'appelle en vain."

This otherwise trivial reference to opportunity missed, to a vocal appeal gone unheeded, leads us, in fact, to a focal poetic gesture whose significance unfolds, as we shall see, in the rhetorical strategy of the preamble to the *Regrets*. The above phrase, not unreminiscent of the Poet's poignant, unheeded call to the homeland in *Regrets* 9 ("Que ne me respons-tu maintenant, ô cruelle?") introduces a human dimension to the myth of Olympian detachment on which the tale of *Kairos* and *Occasio* is traditionally based. In *Gargantua*, Rabelais, alluding to the *Occasio* emblem, had also called attention to this faltering dialogue of humanity and divinity, with the verb "révoquer" incorporating the same vocal gesture as Du Bellay's use of "r'appelle."[3] This presence of a brooding, reactive figure is recorded early on in Latin literature by the Bordeaux poet, Ausonius, writing in the 4th century A.D. In his epigram, *In Simulacrum Occasionis et Paenitentiae*, Ausonius pairs *Occasio* with *Metanoia*, a companion goddess of penitence and regret "who exacts penalties for what is done and what undone, to cause repentance."[4] *Metanoia*, as the vestigial handmaiden of *Occasio*, is a penitential figure who lingers on, absorbed by the spectacle of a rift between the present and a moment falling irretrievably away. What has occurred between the Greek and Latin versions of the *Kairos/Occasio* emblems is a repositioning of the scene's dialogic character.[5] Pathos displaces esthetics, with the sculptor, Lycippos of Sicyon's icy interrogation of *Kairos* described by the Greek writers Posidippus and Callistratus giving way in Ausonius to double divinities, the one Olympian and detached, the other affectively accessible, engaged with humanity ("She [*Metanoia*] is retained by those I [*Occasio*] have passed by"). In other words, *Metanoia* would appear to encode those same concentrated emotions of regret and longing hinted at above in Du Bellay's phrase "r'appelle en vain." If *Metanoia* is all that man retains after the opportunity has passed, then the trick is to turn that absence and its attendant pathos into a creative event, to articulate it rather than wallow in the inertia of melancolia. *Occasio*, otherwise irretrievable in its pure form, thus becomes meaningful only through the opportune expression of its obverse state, the utterance of its own loss.

So conceived, regret is an eminently rhetorical posture, one that was fully integrated into the structure of ancient rhetoric. The Augustan rhetorician, Rutilius Lupus, for instance, classifies *Metanoia* as one of the figures of thought practiced early on by Demosthenes and consisting of a strategy for correcting what has been said previously, for changing the thought.[6] Quintilian latinizes the Greek term as *paenitentia* and incorporates it into his system as a process of rhetorical self-correction (*paenitentia dicti*), a ploy to convince the judge that the speaker's change of heart is evidence of his spontaneity and thus more likely to gain support for his position.[7] Thus, *Metanoia* yields a curious semantic double edge, on the one hand evoking the anxiety of opportunity missed and attendant regret, and on the other, the possibility that such regret take the form of a corrective shift in the text, a means of changing the rhetorical course in midstream to arrest that opportunity.

Renaissance writers, as witnessed in Du Bellay's text, showed great interest in the dialogic format of the *Occasio* myth. The reassuringly human face that *Metanoia* gave to the scene seemed destined, even when the penitential goddess was omitted as a separate deity (as she frequently was; see figures 1-4), to remain encoded in the despairing attempts of an interlocutor to prevail on a departing *Occasio*. In the late fifteenth and early sixteenth centuries, Poliziano, Machiavelli, and Erasmus each gave ample coverage to the Ausonius epigram on *Occasio* and *Paenitentia* and were, thus, responsible for keeping viable the penitential resonance of the myth.[8] In his adage, "Gnosce tempus," Erasmus himself may have stimulated interest in Ausonius's text by citing the epigram in its entirety and by calling explicit attention to the inclusion of *Paenitentia* (Erasmus 253). Erasmus's text would continue to remain the standard locus for the penitential component of the *Occasio* myth, and would find its way into Etienne Dolet's *Commentariorum Linguae Latinae* (1538) and Claude Mignault's important commentary on Alciati (1577). But the early 1540s, however, it had become increasingly clear that *Metanoia* was on the way to being, if not marginalized in the emblematic environment, at least dispersed into the identity of a human subject interacting with the Olympian divinity, Occasion. Gilles Corrozet's *Hécatomgraphie* (1540) (Fig. 5) contains the most graphic evidence of this shift with a wizened Penitence clinging precariously to the stern of Occasion's boat, leaning backward against the onrushing wind, and directing a futile gesture toward the effulgent, Venus-like goddess already at full sail. Unlike the double reference in Ausonius's title, "In Simulacrum Occasionis et Paenitentiae," Corrozet's poem is titled simply "L'ymage d'occasion," omitting any reference to the second goddess. Beneath the picture is an explanatory quatrain that opens with a translation of the ancient caveat "arripe occasionem" ("seize the occasion") and follows this up with a dire warning, addressed to a reading subject, that he himself risks becoming the penitential victim.[9] Thus, the tiny speck of frantic humanity, gesticulating on the distant shore and all but eclipsed by a dominant Occasion in the Wéchel edition of Alciati (1542) (Fig. 1) is no doubt all that remains of Ausonius's second goddess, *Metanoia*. In later French editions of Alciati (Figs. 2-4), the figure is deleted altogether, but still remains conceptually viable as Claude Mignault's 1577 commentary suggests.[10] With Joannes David's scholarly summa, *Occasio Arrepta, Neglecta, huius Commoda: illius Incommoda* (1605) (Fig. 6), however, theology draws on mythology and turns the two deities into extensions of the Christian apocalypse. Secular penitence within the framework of relativistic ethics gives way to a redemptive *Metanoia* that makes contrition not a consequence of opportunity missed, but a strategic shaping of the opportunity itself.[11] Penitence becomes part of a corrective posture through which the Christian meets his transcendent hour of crisis and decision: the Last Judgment.

The useless gesture of appeal to which Du Bellay alludes in his poem on the truce of Vaucelles underscores this humanization of *Metanoia* and constitutes correspondingly one of the most powerful poetic images of the *Regrets*. Just as the liminary sonnet of the 1558 *Discours* could be said to hinge on a strategy for turning loss into opportunity on a political scale—on the need to valorize Penitence, as it were—the sonnets of the *Regrets* emerge against a similar backdrop of contemporaneous political, personal, and, above all, poetic loss. By 1557 and the collapse of the truce, the nascent optimism of the *Discours* must have seemed to Du Bellay significantly out of date, if not the outright embodiment of the *Occasio/Metanoia* disjuncture. At once, a text had become obsolete and a hitherto opportune inscription of hope transformed into a cause for regret.[12] Thus, the sonnet, with its explicit homage to the *Occasio* emblem, attempts to reinscribe that hope and thereby snatch poetic opportunity from the artifact of a dated text. The resonant image of a despondent, human figure calling out to the unheeding goddess, yet enjoined to "take time by the hair," brings us to the very heart of what it means to be a poet. Du Bellay's text is its own best enactment of the emblematic dialogue. It is no doubt telling that the chronological and compositional lag of the *Discours*, spread between 1556 and 1558, encompasses the same span of reintegration leading back from the Poet's Roman "exile" (he leaves Rome in 1557) and culminating in 1558 in the published chronicle of that exile (the *Regrets*). The sonnet cycle of 1558 commemorates, in a sense, the abstract landscape of the emblematic design. Like the lone penitential figure, gesticulating on a distant shore in the Wéchel Alciati, Du Bellay seeks to turn his "exile" into discourse which is quintessentially *ex tempore*, at one with its environmental venue.

Rome, thus, becomes the setting of regret and *Metanoia* through which the Poet's voice carries on a new dialogue with the figure of an ascendant *Occasio* fixed spatially and conceptually in the heartland of a distant France. Through this topographic displacement, the dialogic character of Ausonius's prosopopoeia on Occasion is contextualized into the rift between competing poetics. What certain critics (notably among them, Floyd Gray) have seen as Du Bellay's hidden dialogue with Ronsard in the *Regrets* traces the reinscription of *Metanoia* within the *Occasio* myth as well as its validation as an ascendant poetic response to Ronsard and his environment of favor.[13] One poet (the stand-in for *Occasio*, as it were), celebrated in large measure for his rewriting of an injunction of opportunity (*carpe diem*) stands engaged with another poet (*Metanoia*) whose poetic strategy consists of a parallel injunction (*arripe occasionem*) valorized solely through a discourse of penitence and loss. Seizure, at least in Du Bellay's penitential optics, appears predicated on the poetics of its own disavowal and on a crafted flight from ambition.

The assumption here is that *Occasio* cannot function poetically outside the presence of a conflictual partner (*Metanoia*) challenging its very potentiality. In philosophical and esthetic terms, this means that opportunity as an optimal condition of art and ethics rests on a double motivation. On the one hand, norms and codes are viable only to the extent that they operate in a destabilized present; they dwell on the threshold of their impending obsolescence.[14] Interaction with these norms and codes, on the other hand, presupposes a compound anxiety involving regret for what cannot be stabilized, a longing for the chances missed, and grief at the irreversible loss. In the performative context of discourse, *heterogeneity* thus becomes the embedded consequence of all speech initiatives. For Quintilian, the Orator frames eloquence in a contextualized present, shifting within the hierarchy of styles (high, low, middle) as the occasion demands: "he [the Orator] will use all the styles as necessary . . . altering much to suit persons, places, and times. . . . He will not everywhere be the same."[15] The urge to utter discourse generated out of time (*ex tempore*) contains the built-in premise that such discourse will always emerge from a situational strategy.

It cannot have been lost on Du Bellay that ancient rhetoric viewed eloquence as the supreme enactment of *Kairos* and its agenda of differentiation. On the whole, this judgment has not been well represented in the scholarship on Du Bellay and has tended to remain dormant within the broader, more concerted effort to prove the homogeneity of the *Regrets*, outwardly a work of manifest irregularity.[16] This is not to say that the issue of purposeful disorder has not been well aired in the scholarly record; simply, that the issue needs to be restored to its original philosophical shape and vitality in a program of discourse.

Quintilian's interest in the *circumstances* of the rhetorical event is clearly reflected in the crucial preamble of the *Regrets*. The opening lines of the dedicatory poem "A Monsieur d'Avanson" refer to the central dynamics of a contextualized poetic agenda:

> Si je n'ay plus la faveur de la Muse,
> Et si mes vers se trouvent imparfaits,
> Le lieu, le temps, l'aage ou je les ay faits,
> Et mes ennuis leur serviront d'excuse. (1-4)[17]

Thus, the work begins with the same paradigm of situational discourse attributed above to Quintilian and amply developed by Du Bellay's contemporaries in the fields of rhetoric and dialectic.[18] This situational relief is at once more sharply drawn than in the opening lines of Ovid's *Tristia* (IV), the text on which much of the poem is based. A portion of Ovid's exculpatory plea to his reader expresses the justification that all faults contained in the work are time-specific, present only because they are anchored in a temporal context ("suo tempore," line 2). Du Bellay's rephrasing of Ovid, however, expands the "suo tempore" cliché into something more than a temporal disclaimer. Through the allusion to "le lieu" and "le temps" / "l'aage," the Poet funnels the contextual basis of composition into adjacent spatial and temporal zones. The opportunity on which the poetic event hinges is a function of a localized place marked uniquely along the scale of all possible places and a discrete moment etched along the scale of all possible moments.

This segmentation of opportunity into an *occasio temporis* and an *occasio loci*, illustrated in Joannes David's later treatise on *Occasio* (Fig. 6), forms the backdrop to the poetic event. "Ennuis" constitute an amplification of the Poet's voice, registering the complex melodics of grief (*dolor*), longing (*desiderium*), and regret (*paenitentia*); "lieu" and "temps" form the enclosure in which that voice reverberates. These, then, are the exculpatory consequences of the two opening lines. In the first, the Poet sets himself against the place of favor in which all great art is created. The obligatory Muse is relegated to an inopportune past temporarily and esthetically removed from the Poet's present task. As a result, opportunity and the favored sanctuaries of art are disconnected from the very environment—the seasonal present—in which they are thought to function in the first place. In other words, the figure of a departed Muse comes to have the essential attributes of a departed *Occasio* in the text of Ausonius. She is a figure of the timely consequences of great art, its vitality, its formal perfection, its favored status. Yet, by her restiveness, she also evokes its normative instability, its immunity to a permanent hierarchy of laws. This instability is reflected, in turn, in the impression of compositional flaw, of verse bearing the stigma of imperfection and resistant to structural closure (2).

The first four lines of the preamble to the *Regrets* reduplicate the torsion of the emblematic figure in which *Occasio* becomes meaningful only through the utterance of its own loss. Loss, in turn, manifests itself both on a temporal and esthetic scale. It is the Muse whose favor is of another time and the poetry whose fulfillment as art remains open-ended ("imparfaits"). These initial conditions, however, lay the groundwork for the exculpatory result. Because the Poet's achievement occurs in a differentiated, heterogeneous present ("lieu"-"temps"-"ennuis"), the text turns out to rewrite the balance sheet, transforming deficit into aquisition through the poeticizing of loss itself. What begins in the conventions of artistic loss and deficit is to be revalued poetically through the dynamics of place, time, and feeling, or, as it were, of *Metanoia* and her scenic backdrop.

The introductory poem "A Monsieur d'Avanson" repeats, through a transcription of Ovid's text, the main structures of this scene. If we see France, therefore, as the place of favor, acquisition, and the environment of an ascendant poet, Rome becomes conversely the locus of a marginalized poetics based in a repudiation of fame and favor: "J'estois à Rome au milieu de la guerre, / Sortant desja de l'aage plus dispos, / A mes travaulx cherchant quelque repos, / Non pour louange ou pour faveur acquerre" (5-8). An event—War— predicated on the tactics of gain becomes ironically the setting for an opposing contingency, poetry that capitalizes on estrangement from the very conditions under which it is normally valorized: the acquiring of reputation through constructive effort. Du Bellay's contextual irony, lacking in Ovid's text, gives sharper focus to the series of Ovidian allusions that follows. War and all that it stands for engages its adversaries in agonistic stress; yet, poetry is thought to issue from a pacification of toil in much the same way as *facilitas* emerges in Quintilian's *Institutio* (Book X) from a transcendence of *studium*: "Ainsi voit- on celuy qui sur la plaine / . . . d'un vers fait sans art / S'esvertuer au travail de sa peine" (9-12). This opposition is further developed in references to the galley slave whose "tristes chants" are calibrated to the cadence of his oars (13-16), to Achilles, nursing his anger, whose "triste souvenir" of departed love is relieved "au fredons de sa lyre" (17-20), and to Orpheus whose complaint resonates against an acoustical backdrop of rocks and forest ("Ainsi flattoit le regret de la sienne / Perdue helas pour la seconde fois, / Cil qui jadis aux rochers & aux bois / Faisoit ouir sa harpe Thracienne," 21-24).

In a much tighter restructuring of Ovid's text, Du Bellay groups these examples symmetrically into four quatrains, the first two (9-16) centered on professions of low caste, the last two on mythological heroes. In each of the examples, a lyric performance is framed in a particular set of physical and emotional conditions. Transcending the particularity of these conditions is a common state of loss, embracing, on the one hand, the bondage of serf and galley slave, and on the other, the aspiring movement of desire. The first two examples are, thus, largely about the transfiguration of effort into an art stripped of any performative medium. The artifacts of toil, whether plow or oar, modulate and control the lyrical frequency under which the laborer discovers his poetic voice, but, at the same time, they remain what they are, tools unconnected to any explicit code of instrumentation. Such is not the case, however, with the last two examples in which figures of high epic caste, Achilles and Orpheus, channel their grief into the vibrations and virtuosity of a musical instrument. This is the encoding of poetry as high art and stands in marked contrast to verse whose vehicle of production belongs to a lower order of paraphernalia less visibly lyric than the instruments of Achilles and Orpheus.

In Du Bellay's text, the Ovidian examples take on a resonance they do not have in their Latin form. Their alternation between a poetics of epic virtuosity and one of art in the guise of low-caste negligence embodies the same admixture of high and low styles described in Quintilian's paradigm of *Occasio*. Style, thus, becomes a corollary of timing. Accordingly, the *Regrets* emerge from a notion of rhetorical *aptus* that is based in a heterogeneous poetic voice embracing the genres of elegy, satire, and encomium.

It is clear from this text that Du Bellay problematizes the division of styles in a way that subtly rewrites not only the rhetorical tradition, but the configurations of Ovid's prologue to *Tristia* (IV). In Ovid, there is no initial disjuncture between the Poet and a Muse that has abandoned him. On the contrary, she enjoys the status of a fellow traveler ("Comes") participating fully in the Poet's achievement. Du Bellay's text, however, locates the Muse simultaneously in the opposing frameworks of estrangement and fellowship. At once, she is the figure whose favor the Poet has lost (1) as well as the companion in the seasonal interval of his exile: "La Muse ainsi me fait sur ce rivage, / . . . / Passer l'ennuy de la triste saison, / Seule compagne à mon si long voyage" (25-27). The effect of this double valence is to rework and revitalize the poetic code in which the Muse is thought to operate. If she is a figure of what the Poet once had, but now has lost (the call of inspiration and the lofty style), she is also repatriated into a present that is seasonal, contextualized, and struggling to find a voice consonant with a lower register of production.

For the Muse to remain operative in an environment of "vers imparfaits" and "un vers fait sans art" she is forced to conspire in a new cycle of modulations evoked in the presence of competing emotional values. Traditionally, these values, namely *pathos* and *ethos*, define respectively the affective goals of the high and low styles.[19] While on the upper register, one voice arouses strong emotion (*pathos*), on the lower register, another aims at the pacification of *ethos* and a calmer frame of mind. The preamble to the *Regrets* conflates these interests by reminding us of the Poet's intense emotional investment ("la triste saison," 27; "la douleur," 67, 75; "les larmes," 32, 76; "les soupirs," 76; "le malheur," 66), but at the same time, placing in high lexical relief a term ("douceur" and its attributes) through which *ethos* seems otherwise to attenuate the vigor of that investment.[20] The restive, languishing environment of the exiled Poet, pining on the shores of lost opportunity, remains subtly charged by the very favors he seems initially to have repudiated: "Des le berceau la Muse m'a laissé / Cest aiguillon dedans la fantaisie. / Je suis content qu'on appelle folie / De noz esprits la saincte deité" (59-62). The mechanisms of inspiration, thus, remain viable, but they do so in a context which, far from being liberating, is absorbed in its own torpor and confining pressure. The songs of the galley slave and the plowman are, after all, lyrics of bondage. The precise quality of this bondage, however, becomes clear only as Du Bellay's preamble transforms its cycle of *pathos* and *ethos* into one of seduction as the Poet focuses on what will turn out to be one of the central mythological figures of the *Regrets*: Ulysses.

The culminating section of the preamble opens with the motif of desire given frontal prominence by the words "Je voudrois bien" (41). This clause which seems to announce such a clear optative stance, even a hint of pursuit, does not live up to its promise. Instead, it launches unexpectedly into a disaffirmation of the object of desire, in this case the *Fons medusaeus* as the venue of inspiration and the nine muses: "Je voudrois bien (car pour suivre la Muse / J'ay sur mon doz chargé la pauvreté) / Ne m'estre au trac des neuf sœurs arresté, / Pour aller veoir la source de Meduse" (41-44). Renunciation falls quickly on expectation only to find itself reversed in the following quatrain by an image of bondage and seduction contrived, it would appear, to set the Reader up for one of the most hauntingly familiar episodes of *The Odyssey*, Ulysses's encounter with the Sirens:

> Mais que feray-je à fin d'eschapper d'elles [the Muses]?
> Leur chant flatteur a trompé mes esprits,
> Et les appaz aux quels elles m'ont pris,
> D'un doulx lien ont englué mes aelles (45-48)

Attraction coupled simultaneously with poetic resistance seems to leave the Poet in a state of suspension, doomed to grapple with the treachery of the Muses' lyric appeal and yet, to persevere against this call of the sublime. In a way that the Ovidian source does not, Du Bellay's text plays upon our poetic reflexes, shapes our assumptions, and thereby intensifies the impending reversal. Instead of the familiar tale of Ulysses bound to the mast in order to resist the Sirens' song, our attention is drawn to the episode of the lotus-eaters in which an active Ulysses binds his own men to their rowing benches to help them overcome the amnesia induced by the lotus plant:

> Non autrement que d'une doulce force
> D'Ulysse estoient les compagnons liez,

Et sans penser aux travaulx oubliez
Aymoient le fruict qui leur servoit d'amorce. (49-52)

Du Bellay reworks the elements of Ovid's otherwise unremarkable allusion to
The Odyssey so as to evoke the themes of bondage, seduction, amnesia, and,
above all, the active intervention of Ulysses in helping preserve the luminosity
of memory. This text, perhaps, more than any other in the preamble, valorizes
the central image of the poem, namely, the languishing exile of the Poet on a
strange shore and the effort to sustain the opulence of his regret.

The inverted parallel here with the lotus-eaters is striking. Where Ulysses's
crew "longed to stay forever browsing on that native bloom forgetful of their
homeland,"[21] Du Bellay's strategy is to reverse the structures of this detention.
The obliteration of consciousness together with the open-endedness of exile in
Homer's text marks a venue largely immune to the triple modulation of regret:
grief (*dolor*), desire (*desiderium*), and penitence (*paenitentia*). The horror of
lotusland is that it is pleasure lobotomized, dispersed and protracted over a
boundless temporal horizon. Du Bellay's land of regret and lost opportunity is
a far more ambiguous space. While it impresses on us its capacity to calm the
spirit (*ethos*/'douceur'), to soothe the affective springboard of grief and desire,
it is also the scene of an iterative cycle of emotion (pathos/'*douleur*') rooted in
memory. The homophonous pairing of "aymoient," "amorce," "amer," and
"aymer" in lines 52-55, thus, reveals more than the Petrarchan commonplace
some readers have seen in this text.[22] Desire ("aymer"), seduction ("amorce"),
and spleen ("amer") constitute in the *Regrets* a level of consciousness far more
corrosive than the suspended, frictionless environment of the Petrarchan lover
or the lotus-eater. Du Bellay's Ulysses, rather than the passive spectator of
sirenic appeal, is a figure actively engaged in preserving his companion's sense
of loss much as the Poet of *Metanoia* articulates that yearning moment of
separation when *Occasio* entices him into a pursuit forever doomed to com-
memorate its own failure.

To understand the full resonance of the *Occasio* emblem is to grasp both
its diametric and its dialogic significance. What commentators on the emblem
have rarely stressed is the allusive way the naked figure of Occasion seems
calculated to make us think of Aphrodite and her embodiment of the transcendent appeal of beauty together with its icy aloofness. Like the marine muses of
Du Bellay's preamble, she beckons at the same time that she rebuffs, blurring
temporarily the grief that humanizes and completes this cycle of seduction,
pursuit, and loss:

Elle [la Muse] esblouit les yeulx de la pensée
Pour quelque fois ne veoir nostre malheur,
Et d'un doulx charme enchante la douleur
Dont nuict & jour nostre ame est offensée. (65-68)

The diametric structure of Du Bellay's poem, like the dialogic totality of the emblem, hinges on inverse parameters of mind, the one recollective, aware of its past, its resources of feeling, the other expectant, seduced into the kind of forward propulsion and reach which, much like a vessel edging away from its port of call, seeks to efface the traces of its own history in favor of some new eventuality calibrated to circumstance. These inner spaces form a single integral geography, the meeting place of earth and water, shore and sea, in a dialogue of contiguous poetic hemispheres.

The resonance of the *Occasio* emblem lies, above all, in the recurring image of a distant shoreline, dotted with the faint traces of human habitation and activity (Figs. 1-4), those urban places rife with the collective memories, griefs, and regrets of their inhabitants. It is precisely from such a venue—Rome—that Du Bellay cruelly amd ironically inverts the Ovidian geography. Where Ovid closes his preamble with the exile's desperate plea of estrangement from his homeland, "O Rome forbidden to me!" (IV, i, 107), Du Bellay reminds us at the outset (1-8) that it is in and from Rome that he will poeticize his exile, converting this urban structure into the site of his own *occasio loci* and *occasio temporis*.

Like the emblematic design, the *Regrets* are anchored in a double geo-graphical vantage. Moving shoreward, as it were, toward the contextualized backdrop of cities and people, our vision as readers is made to embrace a cluster of associative elements: Rome, memory, grief, penitence, detention, in short, the creative locus of poetry in which Regret (*Metanoia*), like its ancient prototype, is bound up not only in the mechanisms of *pathos*, but also in the rhetorical ploy of correction and dissembled spontaneity ("vers imparfaits"). On the seaward front, we meet the seductive face of desire, *Occasio* as a catalyst both of propulsion and pursuit, the transcendence of shore-bound context, the contemplation of beauty and sublimity, the exhiliration of the Odyssean journey home, France and the *desiderium patriae*, the prospect of poetic conquest and ultimate reintegration. In a sense, neither of these venues can exist independent of the other, neither the backgrounded shorescape nor the foregrounded seascape. They are the contiguous parts of the ontology which is extemporaneous discourse, a process of expression that encodes and interprets the stress of indeterminism under which all speech naturally occurs. As segments of a single conceptual alignment, they go far in helping us reconsider the significance of Du Bellay's title in light of this indeterminism.

Michael Screech has called attention, not altogether convincingly, both to the banality of the work's title and to its ambiguity, the latter quality evoked presumably in the full, but vague title, *Les Regrets et autres œuvres poëtiques* (Du Bellay 13). Viewed from another angle, however, Screech's remarks could be said to hint at two interests fully congruent with the author's poetic agenda. In the case of banality, once we acknowledge that regret occurs in a constitutive environment of quotidian events, routines, and impressions triggered by contextually familiar stimuli, the commonplace becomes valorized as a poetic attribute in much the same way that Quintilian's *alogos tribe* (X, vii, 11), with its connections to speech based on the wear and tear of the experiental (the *empereia*), comes to define time-centered or extemporaneous discourse.[23] If Du Bellay's title is, indeed, banal, then it is so because it touches the pulse of the Poet's affective dialogue with the surrounding *empereia*. The net result is a work of transcendent heterogeneity embracing not only the admixture of styles (low to high), but also the multiplication of regret as a succession of discrete poetic experiments, hence, "the regrets." As Du Bellay himself points out in his preamble, these experiments seem immune to any generic isolation: "les moiens de plaindre sont divers" (78). Generically ambiguous and rooted in ordinary topicalities, the *Regrets* together with the other unspecified poetic works are fundamentally the vocal half of the *Occasio* emblem. They amplify the appeal, embodying the full rhetorical inflections of the figure, *Metanoia*, as she poeticizes the one-sided exchange with a silent companion she has forever lost.

Du Bellay's title, thus, ceases to be problematic once we view it as its own self-contained poetic statement instead of some half-remembered attempt to give the work a titular identity. Yet, it also does more than simply hint at the pluralities and topicalities to come. Tellingly, Screech calls attention to the discontinuity between Du Bellay's title and that of his Ovidian model, the *Tristia* (Du Bellay 13). Rather than translate the original title by the monochromatic cognate, "Tristes," Du Bellay opts for a word with non-Latin roots ("Regret") and whose semantic field in the vernacular covers three separate Latin terms, *desiderium*, *dolor*, and *paenitentia*. Regret achieves its full semantic potential only when we see it as denoting a complete range of feeling encompassing *desire*, *disappointment*, and *remorse*. Significantly, this triple action corresponds exactly to the narrative played out in the emblem of *Metanoia* and *Occasio*. As the vocal half of the emblem, *Metanoia* is a performative figure whose authenticity, like that of Poet and Orator, derives from her powers of utterance. At the center of that utterance is a disavowal. *Metanoia's* authenticity as performer rests on her subversion of the very mandate she has been called on to fulfill, namely, the order to "seize the occasion" (*arripe occasionem*). Her presence alone shifts our interest away from the primary embodiment of this directive, serene, silent, and unreachable *Occasio*, toward a marginal figure defined largely by a discourse that is expiatory and penitential, absorbed in its account of opportunity lost.

Du Bellay's discourse of regret is, in a real sense, the discourse of an ascendant *Metanoia*. If regret, both emblematically and rhetorically, can only be understood in terms of an injunction annulled, it is equally true that the displacement of opportunity toward the periphery of poetic and human interest leads to substitution of a newly foregrounded, corrective poetics based on those discontinuities that mark the pulse of real time. In fact, this work has little really to do with the triumph of the imperative on which the *Occasio* emblem (and, one is bound to add, the Ronsardian *carpe diem*) is based, but rather privileges an obverse reading of that emblem in the form of an obverse poetics. Where the environment of *Metanoia* differs from these injunctions is in its tendency to see discourse as fully authentic only when engaged in the appearance of reassessment, keeping *Occasio* in a future largely immune to any mandate aimed at seizing the advantage. As one of the ancient figures of thought, *Metanoia* is a way of making the text seem spontaneous through a conscious policy of correcting it as it goes along. This is another way of saying that all ethical and esthetic claims on an erstwhile triumphant *Occasio* remain permanently disabled in favor of ongoing corrective tension. Improvisatory, yet calculatingly so, the poetics of the *Regrets* embrace a strategy embedded in the implicit repudiation of *carpe diem / arripe occasionem*. They enact a text in crisis, or more correctly, in the crisis of context, defining the opposing stresses of a past refracted through its images of remorse and a future deferred by projections of desire.

List of Illustrations

Fig. 1.   *Occasio* in Andrea Alciati, *Emblematum Libellus* (Paris: Wechel, 1542) 20. Folger Shakespeare Library.

Fig. 2.   *Occasio* in Andrea Alciati, *Emblemes d'Alciat*, trans. Barthélemy Aneau (Paris: Hierosme de Marnef et Guillaume Cavellat, 1574). Folger Shakespeare Library.

Fig. 3.   *Occasio* in Andrea Alciati, *Emblemata: Cum commentariis*, ed. Claude Mignault (Antwerp: Plantin, 1577). Pennsylvania State University Library.

Fig. 4.   *Occasio* in Andrea Alciati, *Omnia . . . Emblemata* (Lyons: G. Roville, 1580) 141. Pennsylvania State University Library.

Fig. 5.   *Occasio* and *Metanoia* in Gilles Corrozet, *Hécatomgraphie* (Paris: Denys Janot, 1541). Department of Printing and Graphic Arts, The Houghton Library, Harvard University.

Fig. 6.   Frontispiece of Joannes David's *Occasio Arrepta, Neglecta, huius Commoda: illius Incommoda* (Antwerp: Plantin, 1605). The plate depicts the tripartite division of *Occasio* into an *occasio temporis*, an *occasio rei*, and an *occasio loci*. Pennsylvania State University Library.

Notes

[1] Joachim Du Bellay, *Œuvres poétiques*, ed. Henri Chamard (Paris: Droz, 1931) 6: 4.

[2] Later in the same poem, Du Bellay describes Occasion as "la chauve Deesse, / Qui deux fois aux cheveux empoigner ne se laisse" (lines 169-70), a reference to the goddess's tonsured head and protruding forelock. On the dialogic component of the scene, see Maria Tasinato, *L'Œil du silence: éloge de la lecture*, trans. Jean-Paul Manganaro and Camille Dumoulié (Paris: Verdier, 1986) 99-100. Among the recent relevant discussions of *Kairos*, see especially James L. Kinneavy, "*Kairos*: A Neglected Concept in Classical Rhetoric," in *Rhetoric and Praxis: The Contribution of Classical Rhetoric to Practical Reasoning*, ed. Jean Dietz Moss (Washington, DC: Catholic U of America P, 1986) 79-105; and *Chronos et Kairos: entretiens d'Athènes,* ed. Evanghelos Moutsopoulos, Institut International de Philosophie (Paris: Vrin, 1988).

[3] "Iceulx je suis d'advis que nous poursuyvons cependent que l'heur est pour nous, car l'occasion a tous ses cheveux au front: quand elle est oultre passée, vous ne la povez plus révocquer; elle est chauve par le darrière de la teste et jamais plus ne retourne." François Rabelais, *Œuvres complètes*, ed. Guy Demerson (Paris: Seuil, 1973) 154.

[4] Ausonius, Epigram XXXIII, *Ausonius*, trans. Hugh White (London: Heinemann and New York: Putnam, 1921) 2: 174-77.

[5] For a comprehensive summary of the iconographic and textual transformations of the *Kairos* myth, see Arthur Bernard Cook, *Zeus: A Study in Ancient Religion* (Cambridge: Cambridge UP, 1925) 2 (Part II): 859-68.

[6] "Hoc schema fieri solet, cum ipse se, qui loquitur, reprehendit, et id quod prius dixit, posteriori sententia commutat, ita uti facit Demosthenes." Rutilius, *De Figuris Sententiarum et Elocutionis*, ed. Edward Brooks, Jr. (Leiden: Brill, 1970) 20.

[7] *Institutio Oratoria* (IX, ii, 59-60). See also the *Ad Herennium* on *correctio* (IV, xxvi, 36) and Cicero on *reprehensio* (*De oratore*, III).

[8] Angelo Poliziano, *Miscellaneorum centuriae* (Florence: Autonius Miscomius, 1489), f° hiii^r-hi^v; Niccolò Machiavelli, "Di Fortuna," *Tutte le opere di Niccolò Machiavelli*, eds. Francesco Flora and Carlo Cordie (Milan: Arnoldo Mondadori, 1949-50) 2: 710; Desiderius Erasmus, *Adagiorum opus* (Basle: Froben, 1528) 252-53 (Adage #70).

[9] Haste toy bien tost d'attraper, / L'occasion qu'and el s'avance, / Sy tu la laisses eschapper, / Tu en seras la pénitence." *Hécatomgraphie*, ed. Charles Oulmont (Paris: Champion, 1905) 166.

[10] Andrea Alciati, *Omnia . . . Emblemata: Cum commentariis . . . Per Claudium Minoem* (Antwerp: Plantin, 1577) 416.

[11] Joannes David, *Occasio Arrepta, Neglecta, huius Commoda: illius Incommoda* (Antwerp: Plantin, 1605); see especially the commentary on Figure 11 (227-45).

[12] On this discontinuity, see Chamard's commentary in Du Bellay, *Œuvres complètes* 6: 3n2.

[13] See, for example, Floyd Gray, *La Poétique de Du Bellay* (Paris: Nizet, 1978) 79-95.

[14] On the connection of *Kairos* to relativism in art and ethics, see the important commentary of Jean Cousin in his introduction to Quintilian's Book XI: *Institution Oratoire* (Paris: Belles Lettres, 1979) 6: 152-53.

[15] II, x, 69-71, in *Ancient Literary Criticism*, eds. Donald A. Russell and Michael Winterbottom (Oxford: Clarendon, 1972) 415.

[16] The so-called "macrotextual" or unified approach to the *Regrets* is supported in such standard readings as those of François Rigolot, "Du Bellay et la poésie du refus," *Bibliothèque d'Humanisme et Renaissance* 36 (1974) 489-502; Rosamond J. Bovey, "Joachim Du Bellay's *Regrets* and the Satire of the Poet," *L'Esprit Créateur* 19 (1979) 38-55; Floyd Gray, *La Poétique de Du Bellay* 59-159; and Richard A. Katz, *The Ordered Text: The Sonnet Sequences of Du Bellay* (Berne: Lang, 1985).

[17] Joachim Du Bellay, *Les Regrets et autres œuvres poëtiques*, eds. John W. Jolliffe and Michael A. Screech (Geneva: Droz, 1966). Readings of the prefatory poems of the *Regrets* are rare.

A thoughtful recent study is that of Jeffery C. Persels, "Charting Poetic Identity in Exile: Entering Du Bellay's *Regrets*," *Romance Notes* 28 (1988) 195-202.

[18] See, for example, Barthélemy Latomus, *Summa totius rationis disserendi* (Cologne: P. Quentell, 1527), f° D7ᵛ-D8ʳ; and E1ᵛ-E7ʳ; Philip Melanchthon's *De Rhetorica* (Paris: R. Estienne, 1527), especially the section entitled "De Circumstantiis" (Fo 30ᵛ-33ʳ).

[19] See the treatise on Demosthenes by Dionysius of Halicarnassus, *Ancient Literary Criticism*, eds. Donald A. Russell and Michael Winterbottom 307.

[20] For settings of "doux"/"douceur," see lines 19, 48-49, 54, 57-58, 64, 67, and 81.

[21] Homer, *The Odyssey*, trans. Robert Fitzgerald (Garden City, NY: Anchor Books, 1963) 148 (IX, 82sq).

[22] See, for example, Screech's commentary, *Les Regrets* 49n56.

[23] With its etymological connections to the term *tritus* in Latin, *tribe* in Platonic thought is normally placed in opposition to *techne*. Where *techne* relates to rhetoric as scientific method, *tribe* describes speech as a routine. The term's temporal cast is supported, in turn, by a rich semantic history encompassing notions of experimentation, a wearing away through habit, and the production and consumption of time.

Figure 1

Figure 2

Figure 3

Figure 4

Figure 5

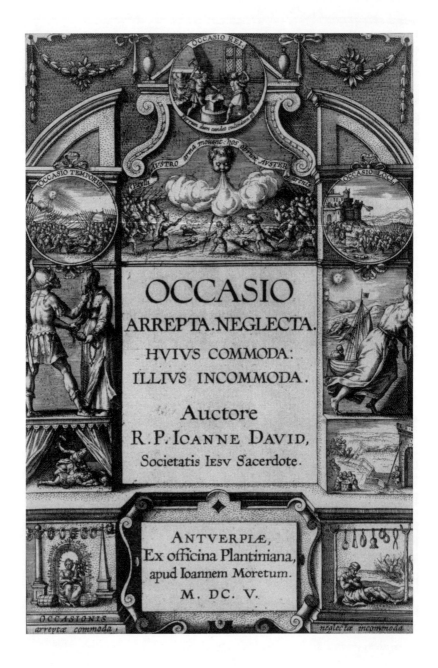

Figure 6

Gregory de Rocher

Ronsard's Dildo Sonnet:
The Scandal of Poissy
and Rasse des Nœux

When Pierre de Ronsard removed one and only one poem, the notorious sonnet xlv, from the 1584 edition of *Les Amours Diverses*, much more was at stake than the mere excision of an embarrassing if not offensive offspring that somehow escaped the poet's otherwise tireless esthetic vigilance.[1] Although the title of this collection might at first glance be incorrectly interpreted as suggesting various types of love, from the heterosexual to the homosexual or Sapphic, even a passing familiarity with Ronsard's work militates against such a convenient reading of the name of the collection. Moreover, while everyone grants that the poet is known to have exploited an extremely libertine vein during his early career in his *Folastries*, it is a simple fact that nowhere else in the poet's entire production—not even in his most violent diatribes against the Protestants or in his collaboration at the Colloquy of Poissy on pamphleteer verse in which he accuses the Sorbonne theologian and dean of the Faculté Nicolas Maillard of sodomy—do we find any mention whatsoever of a dildo or even autoeroticism.[2] It is also a fact that all of the poems of *Les Amours Diverses*, except for sonnet xlv, were eventually placed, starting in 1584, in various other collections: xlviii, for example, was inserted into the *Sonnets à Diverses Personnes*; ii, iii, v, vi, xlix were incorporated into the *Sonnets pour Astrée*; and xxxii was placed in the *Elegies*. But the overwhelming majority of them (viii-xxviii, xxx-xxxi, xxxiii-xxxv, xxxviii-xliv, xlvi, and li) found their way into later editions of his *Sonets pour Helene*.

The question naturally arises, then, as to what could have driven Ronsard to include the dildo poem in the *Amours Diverses* in 1578, only to withdraw it and it alone from the very next collective edition, as well as from all future editions of his lifetime. Indeed, some critics observe the poet's wishes as expressed in 1584 and have no qualms about excluding the poem from their discussion of the *recueil*.[3] But Ronsard specialists have long been aware that historical commentary, although congealing heavily around sonnet xlv, has established little beyond the realm of pure speculation. No facts have been adduced to corroborate, for example, Henri Longnon's claim that Ronsard's masturbator is none other than the aging poet's third literary mistress, Hélène de Fonsèque, demoiselle de Surgères.[4] Nor does Paul Laumonier accept Nicolas Richelet's assertion (followed by Pierre Champion, L. Perceau, Gustave Cohen, and a few others) that the Lucrèce in question is Madeleine Martel, one of the demoiselles de Bacqueville, numbered, along with Hélène de Surgères, among the *filles d'honneur* at the court of Catherine de' Medici.[5]

Hélène de Surgères seems a likely candidate. The *Sonets pour Helene* was the only major collection of poems written by Ronsard in the last years of his life; his energy was divided mostly between the Hélène cycle and the tireless revising of his complete works. This suggests that the collection is less the work of an impetuous young poet-lover than that of a fastidious artisan. In fact, Ronsard's lady seems in this case to have been chosen in terms of the poet's waning sexuality, as I. D. McFarlane reminds us: "The emotional source seems thin enough, Hélène being a rather dreary blue-stocking."[6] But whether or not the historical identity of the woman in sonnet xlv can ever be ascertained interests us far less than the ramifications of the momentary insertion of the dildo poem into the Ronsardian corpus.

We could leap immediately to the most obvious conclusion, finding in the poem the perfect instrument for Ronsard's perpetration of sexual violence in effigy on a woman he is not up to satisfying in the undeviating Priapic manner. Ronsard's will to dominate as well as to humiliate is most apparent in this poem, as a rhetorical analysis of it, not presented here for lack of space, convincingly demonstrates. But what should interest us most, it seems to me, is the significance of this sonnet's *repression*—and therefore its inevitable *return* (*Wiederholungszwang*)—in Ronsard's work. We must have a notion *not only* of how this sonnet was read in the context of the poet's earlier production and in the context of continental European love poetry in vogue in 1578, *but also*— and in particular—in the context of the later work, especially his posthumous sonnets, from which it was barred entry, at least in its *Amours Diverses* guise. Finally, the politico-religious milieu whose part in conserving one of the textual variants of the poem will have to be taken into account, a factor which implicates the historical figure, as well as the collection of, François Rasse des Nœux. Our discussion of this poem's excision must, therefore, take the form of an intertwining account of historical, rhetorical, and textual facts, the whole of which might profit from being informed by psychoanalytic theory, if what we say is to withstand criticism from any one of these camps. Obviously, such a project cannot be aired in the present forum; accordingly, I will limit my discussion to the sonnet's appearance(s) and presentation of hypothetical motive(s) both within Ronsard's corpus and within the reigning religious context.

Readers whose delicate sensibility is highly operative might well ask themselves what there could possibly be in this sonnet that is *not* repressed. All the indecorous aspects of a depiction of female autoeroticism are stated in the text:

> Amour, je ne me plains de l'orgueil endurcy,
> Ny de la cruauté de ma jeune Lucresse,
> Ny comme sans secours languir elle me laisse:
> Je me plains de sa main & de son godmicy.
>   C'est un gros instrument qui se fait pres d'icy,
> Dont chaste elle se corrompt toute nuict sa jeunesse:
> Voila contre l'Amour sa prudente finesse,
> Voila comme elle trompe un amoureux soucy.
>   Aussi pour recompense une haleine puante,
> Une glaire espessie entre les draps gluante,
> Un œil have & battu, un teint palle & desfait,
>   Montrent qu'un faux plaisir toute nuict la possede.
> Il vaut mieux estre Phryne & Laïs tout à fait,
> Que se feindre Portie avec un tel remede.

Among the many readings such a poem activates is the one registering the blow this sonnet deals to the Petrarchan mode so successfully practiced by Ronsard throughout his career. It is as though—unlike Joachim du Bellay who railed at length against the epigonous confections so much in vogue in his *Contre les Petrarquistes*—Ronsard distilled all the yellow bile provoked by distant, hesitant, or otherwise unyielding Egerias and spilled it in one violent access of poetic fury.[7]

1. Hélène

But let us come back to Hélène, both the historical one as recorded in contemporary documents, and especially the poetic one, the young woman constituted by Ronsard in his love poetry. We can justify concentrating our attention on her for at least two reasons: (1) she occupied most of the older Ronsard's poetic efforts; and (2) she proved to have been the most overwhelming presence in the *Amours Diverses* since the two collections Ronsard devoted to her will eventually absorb five times more of this *recueil*'s sonnets than any of those singing the other women in this eclectic gathering. What is perhaps most interesting for our purposes is the *nature* of this presence as portrayed by Ronsard. A scanning of the evolution of Hélène's *Darstellung*, from the poet's first depiction of her until the last words Ronsard utters in the posthumously published eight sonnets of 1609, affords a strikingly new perspective on the generally accepted account of his last mistress's evergrowing standoffishness.[8]

According to Ronsard, the young woman appeared as something of a freshly sprung oasis on his aging poetic and personal landscape. When he first laid eyes on her in 1570, the third of the eight Religious Wars had just run its course, further embroiling the poet who, since their inception, had taken up arms against the Huguenots to defend his curacy at Evaillé; moreover, a long illness in 1568 had taken its toll on Ronsard's health. It was therefore after a long absence that he was greeted at court by a young woman several literary historians have erroneously called a "young widow"; in fact Hélène had only been engaged to a young captain of the guards and former page at court, Jacques de La Rivière, who was killed in a skirmish during the third Religious War. Catherine de' Medici did not fail to take notice of her disconsolate *fille d'honneur*, and asked Ronsard to address some verses to her; the poet responded to the royal will and began composing what was to become his two-volume *Sonets pour Helene*. The sad and ironic part of this love story is that what had started out as a game soon became love in earnest. Ronsard was smitten all the more when the young woman, apparently flattered at first by the attentions of the august poet, seemed to encourage his advances.[9] If we are to believe the poet when he writes of these idyllic early days, she said to him in a fit of passion that she loved him:

> Prenant congé de vous, dont les yeux m'ont donté,
> Vous me distes un soir comme passionnee,
> Je vous aime, Ronsard, par seule destinee,
> Le Ciel à vous aimer force ma volonté.

Hélène also sent him early on tokens of her affection, and when the practice ceased, Ronsard complained:

> Voyez comme tout change (hé, qui l'eust esperé!)
> Vous me souliez donner, maintenant je vous donne
> Des bouquets & des fleurs: amour vous abandonne,
> Qui seul dedans mon cœur est ferme demeuré.

Lest it be thought these gifts were merely imaginary, we recall the fact that on August 8, 1574, Hélène sent from Avignon lemons and green oranges to Ronsard on the occasion of Henry III's return from Poland after the death of Charles IX.

The historical side of this literary liaison resembled many of those lived in fact and in fiction. For a few years there were breaks and reconciliations. Angry at each other in July of 1574, the next month they were apparently on good terms. Together in 1577 for Henry III's victory banquet and in 1578 for the publication of his *Œuvres* in which the *Sonets pour Helene* figured for the first time, they were, however, thereafter separated and Hélène went to the south of France where she remained for two years. This rupture was to mark the beginning of the disintegration of their relationship; Ronsard, suffering from rheumatoid arthritis and gout, came to Paris for only short visits between 1582 and the final one in 1585, whence he returned extremely ill to die on December 27 in Saint-Cosme.

What Ronsard expected from a woman young enough to be his daughter may be at the root of much that later became thinly poetized. After Hélène's early encouragements she seemed to have stood on ceremony, taking far too seriously—at least for Ronsard's taste—her role as one of the minor Muses in the Countess of Retz's *salon vert*, and that of a strictly Platonic *Egeria*.[10] The poet's indomitable turgor ("Ma chair dure à donter me combatoit à force") met head-on with Hélène's unassailable virtue:

> Tes mœurs & ta vertu, ta prudence & ta vie
> Tesmoignent que l'esprit tient de la Deité:
> Tes raisons de Platon, & ta Philosophie,
>   Que le vieil Promethee est une verité,
> Et qu'en ayant la flame à Jupiter ravie,
>   Il maria la Terre à la Divinité.[11]

What is strangely prophetic about the last line of the second tercet is that it captures in miniature the future tragedy of Ronsard's Hélène cycle: his own earthiness is hopelessly joined to a divine, unyielding and uncompromising principle. There can be no doubt about the type of poet-lover Ronsard is portraying in his *Sonets pour Helene*:

> . . . vos dons si precieux
> Me font, en les voyant, devenir furieux,
> Et par le desespoir l'ame prend hardiesse.
>   Pource si quelquefois je vous touche la main,
>   Par courroux vostre teint n'en doit devenir blesme:
> Je suis fol, ma raison n'obeyt plus au frein,
>   Tant je suis agité d'une fureur extreme.
>   (*SpH* I, xxiv)

Hélène's refusals only serve to stir up all the more Ronsard's "flames au cœur," and when the paths to which her constant teasings allude prove to be *sans issue*, the poet claims in his typical fashion that he is unable to bear it: "Comment pourray-je vivre un quart d'heure à mon aise". Indeed, the most salient aspect of Ronsard's despair over Hélène's sexuality pivots upon (1) her disgust for the body ("Vous dites que des corps les amours sont polluës," *SpH* I, xlii) and (2) her idea of love as a bloodless contemplation ("Vous aimez les tableaux qui n'ont point de couleur," *SpH* I, xliii).

With the second book of his *Sonets pour Helene* Ronsard's poetic expression becomes more violent; his anger and frustration begin to stretch beyond the limits of decorum. Hélène is depicted as a monster of her own sex, deformed by an urge which uses laws and customs forbidding heterosexual love as a convenient cover for unspeakable pleasures, desires, and voluptuous activities:

> Vous trompez vostre sexe, & lui faites injure:
> La coustume vous pipe, & du faux vous domtez
> Voz plaisirs, voz desirs, vous & voz voluptez,
> Sous l'ombre d'une sotte & vaine couverture.

We are now but a stylistic breath away from the shocking accusations Ronsard will make in sonnet xlv of the *Amours Diverses*. The discovery, during a palace search, of four dildos among the personal effects of one of Catherine de' Medici's *dames d'honneur* at the very moment Ronsard was composing this collection may have been more than the poet could bear, given his reputation as a poet-lover and acknowledged suitor of the young gentlewoman at court.[12] The dildo sonnet may have afforded the poet the consolation the Spanish name for the instrument suggests if not promises, but full satisfaction was apparently not achieved before Ronsard withdrew the poem from the next edition, for in the very last poem in the entire Ronsardian corpus, sonnet viii of the posthumous additions of the 1609 edition of his works, he once again taxes Hélène for her unnatural sexuality.

Let us consider briefly this final poem of Ronsard's. The last voice to speak in it is Hélène's, and the last thing she says is that she is unable to take pleasure in the heterosexual love Ronsard asks of her. The tone in this last poem, however, is in marked contrast to that which had characterized the dildo sonnet of the *Amours Diverses*. He no longer appears as viciously spiteful about Hélène's "true nature"; in Ronsard's last words, so to speak, he foregoes the use of his own voice in order to let the woman he loved the most desperately tell her own story. This last sonnet can be seen as an effect of *Wiederholungszwang*, the return of the repressed, the reemergence of the excised dildo poem: the dildo sonnet had expressed something that Ronsard's esthetic instincts were unable to silence until 1584. Yet, what was said most brutally in 1578 must have been the truth as Ronsard experienced it in his wounded pride. The embarrassed court poet had had his revenge, but was almost as soon ashamed of his pusillanimity and, perhaps even more, of his lack of critical judgment in allowing the poem to be published in 1578. Sometime before his death in 1585 he had taken the time to redistill his emotions over what he saw as Hélène's peculiar sexuality. He shows her every bit as perplexed as he himself seems to be over a woman who feels no desire for "les presens d'Amour" of the kind he is prepared to offer:

> Ce n'est (ce me dis-tu) le remors de la loy
> Qui me fait t'econduire, ou la honte, ou la crainte,
> Ny la frayeur des Dieux, ou telle autre contrainte,
> C'est qu'en tes passetemps plaisir je ne reçoy.
>   D'une extreme froideur tout mon corps se compose,
> Je n'ayme point Venus, j'abhorre telle chose,
> Et les presens d'Amour me sont une poison:
>   Puis je ne le veus pas. O subtile deffaite!
> Ainsi parlent les Rois, defaillant la raison,
> "Il me plaist, je le veux, ma volonté soit faite."

But should we believe that Ronsard had come to terms with the affront dealt him by Hélène simply because he lets her justify "in her own words" the way she was? It would be naive to think that Ronsard would ever accept the embarrassment of her refusal or listen with sympathy to the reasons she offered to explain it, especially in the light of the poet's last eight unpublished sonnets for Hélène. Moreover, these eight poems are especially interesting because they can be read as a microcosm of the entire two-volume Hélène cycle; they were, we recall, dedicated to her. It is as though Ronsard, in a highly reflective state and in a tightly condensed form, wished to set the record straight on the Hélène affair.

2. The Posthumous Sonnets of 1609

The first opens in one of the poet's most erotic veins, recalling the feverish passion of the Petrarchan *innamoramento*. We are able to imagine in these lines Ronsard poeticizing the moment of their first glance,[13] and the passions attending it, in 1570:

> Maistresse, embrasse moy, baize moy, serre moy,
> Haleine contre haleine, echauffe moy la vie,
> Mille & mille baizers donne moy je te prie,
> Amour veut tout sans nombre, amour n'a point de loy.
>   Baize & rebaize moy . . .

Yet in the very midst of a discourse whose focus seems without ambiguity, Ronsard plants the seed of her unwillingness, and he casts it not so much in the Petrarchan mode of the virtuous lady as in that of neo-Latin *basia* drawing upon a familiar Greek Anthology motif, that of the unfortunate woman who dies a virgin—a variation of the *carpe diem* topos for which he is justly famous:

>   . . . belle bouche pourquoy
> Te gardes tu là bas, quand tu seras blesmie,
> A baiser (de Pluton ou la femme ou l'amie),
> N'ayant plus ny couleur, ny rien semblable à toy?

How Ronsard chooses to finish this sonnet is rather characteristic of "the great Pan of the Renaissance," but it can also be read as a violation of Hélène. In the course of the tercets Ronsard's imperatives ("presse . . . begaye") quickly pass into future tenses ("Je mourray . . . Je resusciteray") accompanied by present and past participles, thus accomplishing virtual possession of this difficult woman who was to be both a source of lasting frustration and, of course, of endless poetic recriminations.

The second sonnet, at first seeming to register a complaint about Hélène's chaperone as an obstacle to the poet's desires, proves to focus more on the old woman's possessiveness of Hélène and, through the metaphor of Argus, on the monstrous nature of this jealous vigilance. Ronsard, who in other *recueils* (*Cassandre, Marie*, and *Astree*, for example) has no trouble assuming protean forms,[14] appears here to be severely hindered by this particular chaperone's fiercely penetrating eyes: ". . . sa rude paupiere, à veiller eternelle, / Te regarde, t'espie & te suit en tous lieux." Although metonymically reduced to an eyelid, a shape more reminiscent of the female genitalia, the chaperone nonetheless fills the masculine role of pursuit and penetration. As though frozen by this distressing scene, Ronsard is unable to metamorphose into the standard mythological figures of male lust (liquid gold = sperm; swan = erect phallus): "Je ne suis pas un dieu pour me changer en pluye: / Dessoubs un cygne blanc mes flames je n'estuye, / C'estoient de Jupiter les jeus malicieux." The poet cast(rate)s himself as out of his depth; to compete for the attention of his mistress in such circumstances would require powers he does not feel in this instance he possesses. Hélène, because of this woman who so effectively replaces his own attentions, is now removed from Ronsard's carnal reach and placed in a space the poet believes she wishes to occupy, that of an idealized icon free from the male grasp: "Je prens de tes beaux yeux ma pasture & ma vie, / Pourquoy de tes regards me portes tu envie? / On voit sur les autels les images des Dieux."

Any synopsis of the Hélène cycle would have to allude to the Petrarchan gifts she sent him from Avignon in August of 1574. The third posthumous sonnet can well be read as an ironic rewriting of sonnet xxvii of the first book of the *Sonets pour Helene*, in which Ronsard amorously dotes over the fruit sent him by Hélène: "Cent & cent fois le jour l'Orange je rebaise, / Et le palle Citron qui viennent de ta main, / Doux present amoureux, que je loge en mon sein. . . ." Orange trees and lemon trees figure also towards the end of the first book of the Hélène cycle in the idyllic landscape evoked in the *chanson* "Plus estroit que la Vigne à l'Ormean se marie" (xlix), where they assume beyond any doubt the power of a fetish. But whereas the earlier sonnet chose to keep alive the hope of finally arresting Hélène, winning her with the fruit that gave Hippomenes final victory in his confrontation with Atalanta ("Oranges & Citrons sont symboles d'Amour: / Ce sont signes muets, que je puis quelque jour / T'arrester, comme fit Hippomene Atalante"), the posthumous sonnet modifies the elements of Hélène's *envoi* and rewrites their signification in terms of his acknowledged posture of despair. The lemons, previously symbolizing bitterness but, at least, also beauty now give way to cypress trees, which can only be read as harbingers of death; moreover, a new signifying element of *flora* is introduced, poppy flowers, which mark Ronsard's final attitude with respect to the Hélène cycle: would that it (could) be forgotten.

From the few sonnets that remain, however, it is clear that Ronsard is not quite ready to fall into the slumber of oblivion. In finishing the third sonnet the poet plays on Hélène's Spanish origins and his self-proclaimed Transylvanian or Moravian ancestry as he engraves an epitaph for himself which manages to paint his distant mistress in her highly "refined" sexuality, that is, at best, her *asexuality* and, at worst, her *perverted sexuality*. He, on the other hand, is brushed quite simply: as a vigorous and straightforward Hercules:

> Une Espagnolle prist un Tudesque en ses mains:
> Ainsi le sot Hercule estoit captif d'Iole,
> La finesse appartient à la race Espagnolle,
> Et la simple Nature appartient aux Germains.

Straightforward, yes, but where, we might ask, is the vigorous Ronsard? In this sonnet he is strangely passive: almost *taken*. He is compared to Hercules in the demigod's less forceful moments. By some sort of *sympathie naturelle*, Ronsard's unvarying sexuality seems in this third sonnet to have been profoundly shaken, if not put under a spell of confusion.

The fourth sonnet is a curious creation whose performative discourse catalogues and immortalizes, in the temple-library it eventually erects, the voluminous correspondence between Hélène and the poet. The messenger-page, whom Ronsard addresses directly in this sonnet, becomes the signifier by means of which the contents of the letter—which the page is watching Ronsard read—will be known. This sonnet must be viewed, because of its morbid insistence on the need for the careful conservation, study, and interpretation of the lovers' innumerable missives, as a monument to their dismal failure to communicate sexually. For all the trips this young Mercury was called upon to make, the commerce between Hélène and Ronsard the poet remained one of a profound and deliberate misreading:

> Mon page que ne suis-je aussi riche qu'un Roy,
> Je feroy de porphyre un beau temple pour toy,
> Tu serois tout semblable à ce Dieu des voyages:
> Je peindrois une table où l'on verroit pourtraits
> Nos sermens, nos accords, nos guerres & nos paix,
> Nos lettres, nos devis, tes tours & tes messages.

It is a silent monument, standing for a dead message whose code has been all but forgotten, whose channel has been closed, and whose illocutionary gestures are no longer recognizable.

Sonnet v offers, in an even more reduced manner, a history of their relationship. It alludes to Hélène's life at court as a young lady lost among countless others, but raised to notoriety because of the poet's enshrinement of her in his verses:

> Quand au commencement j'admiré ton merite,
> Tu vivois à la Court sans louange & sans bruit:
> Maintenant un renom par la France te suit,
> Egallant en grandeur la Royalle Hypolite.

But can we forget that it was Hélène who caused Ronsard to start a new career after the embarrassingly cold reception of his *Franciade*.[15] The poet expresses clearly here that he does not regret the renown she earned them both, but also that her unrequited love was painful to a man who required more than giggles, letters, and glances:

> Je n'en suis pas marry, toutefois je me deux,
> Que tu ne m'aymes pas, qu'ingrate tu ne veux
> Me payer que de ris, de lettres & d'œillades.
> Mon labeur ne se paye en semblables façons,
> Les autres pour parade ont cinq ou six chansons,
> Au front de quelque livre, & toy des Iliades.

The second tercet is of a lucidity that seems to govern all eight of these sonnets: whether in real life or in poetic fiction, all Ronsard's labors proved unsuccessful in gaining him access to his would-be mistress's sexual affections; moreover, Ronsard was keenly aware that the actual product of his evergrowing *Affekt* and Hélène's continuing withdrawal had become a veritable epic in terms of *scripta*. It can be read as a perfect illustration of the notion that writing is born of conflict.

The sixth sonnet calls back to life the period beginning with the Colloquy of Poissy in which Ronsard was in hostile opposition to the Protestants. The allusion is in terms of the miracle metaphor the poet uses to describe the healing effect of Hélène's eyes on his love-sickness. Of the many illnesses that plagued Ronsard during his lifetime, only one qualifies as the one that the young Hélène could possibly be imagined as remedying. From 1568 until 1570 the poet was gravely ill and remained in Saint-Cosme and Croixval; although his return to health was sufficient in 1570 to allow him to return to court, it is not difficult to see that in the eyes of the poet, his healing and his first meeting with Hélène coincide. The quatrains recount this miraculous healing glance:

L'Enfant contre lequel ny targue ny salade
Ne pourroient resister, d'un trait plein de rigueur
M'avoit de telle sorte ulceré tout le cœur
Et brulé tout le sang que j'en devins malade.
    J'avoy dedans le lict un teint jaunement fade,
Quand celle qui pouvoit me remettre en vigueur,
Ayant quelque pitié de ma triste langueur,
Me vint voir, guarissant mon mal de son œillade.

The first tercet of this same sonnet formulates a refutation of the Protestant contention that miracles were no longer possible in the contemporary period. Signs of the validity of the New Religion were, we recall, demanded of the Huguenots by the Sorbonne at the Colloquy of Poissy.[16] The final tercet, however, all the while retaining the Catholic notion that miracles still occur in the present day, returns to the personal side of the metaphor by crediting Hélène with miraculous powers of the type the Protestants were unable to summon:

Encores aujourd'huy les miracles se font:
Les Sainctes & les Saincts les mesmes forces ont
Qu'aux bons siecles passez, car si tost que ma Sainte
    Renversa la vertu de ses rayons luisans
Sur moy qui languissois, ma fievre fut esteinte,
Un mortel medecin ne l'eust fait en dix ans.

There is, nonetheless, an underlying irony in the notion of Hélène as a soothing presence, for she seems to have restored Ronsard to health only to torture the enamored aging poet, reducing him to an even worse state: one in which his reputed hot-blooded nature was again countered by her coldness.

This newly awakened sexuality, which Hélène paradoxically both provoked and resisted, is what was so at odds with the neo-Platonic discourse characterizing the Palace Academy Discussions in general and Hélène's personal views on love. Sonnet vii unleashes, in a blend of rampant hostility and focused anti-Semitism on the person of Leone Ebreo, Ronsard's violent hatred of the platonic doctrine (mis)used by women to spurn carnal delights.[17] This central point is all but lost in the blind fury the poet's agression infuses into the discourse of the sonnet, even down to the tasteless reference to the Jewish rite of circumcision: "Faux trompeur, mensonger, plein de fraude & d'astuce: / Je croy qu'en luy coupant la peau de son prepuce / On luy coupa le cœur & toute affection." We seem to be witnessing once again the level of intensity and lack of esthetic judgment noted in the dildo sonnet. Any disgust we as readers may feel should not blind us to the fact that both sonnets share a common trait: the underscoring of the "unnatural" by Ronsard's *Affekt*. Although sanctioned by the Old Testament, hostile Catholic sentiment with regard to circumcision seems to animate Ronsard as he attacks the Jewish custom in the posthumous sonnet: it was, as the poet saw it, a barbaric and cruel rite.

Contemporary Church doctrine may also help explain Ronsard's belaboring of the depiction of Lucrèce's autoeroticism in the dildo sonnet. Onanism was clearly forbidden in the Old Testament, but only for males. Orthodox moral theology confirmed this view, condemning in addition female masturbation, but left open the possibility of autoeroticism in certain cases for married women when reproduction was the ultimate end.[18] This may explain why the poet went to such lengths to portray his Lucrèce as acting against nature, from the false pleasure motif, to the Phryne and Laïs metaphor, and finally to the inverted Portie figure. Nature rebelled, furnishing the clear symptoms of masturbatory excesses according to the typology promulgated by Renaissance medicine, such as the deep-set eyes, the pallor, and the foul breath.[19] Although no logical link joins Ebreo's promotion of neo-Platonism and the discovery, during a palace search, of four dildos among the personal effects of one of Catherine de' Medici's *dames d'honneur*, the nexus in Ronsard's psyche proves to have been powerful, sending roots into contemporary political, socio-religious, and literary institutions and practices.

These socio-cultural, poetic, and personal realities also inform the final posthumous sonnet, and we can now see how it seems to flow affectively from Ronsard's aversion toward what is not *natural*. Just as it was not natural to remove the foreskin of an infant, it was not natural to deny the carnal side of man; and it was above all not natural to react coldly to the type of love the poet was anxious to offer. Sonnet viii is a recast dildo poem, but one that remains every bit as hostile to Hélène in its dryly mocking rehearsal of that conversation, real or fantasized, in which he *finally* learned that Hélène de Surgères was not *able* to requite his love with hers. Ronsard exorcizes this painful realization *philosophically* in his hostility to Ebreo's diffusion of Platonic love, *sociologically* in the implication in the dildo sonnet that Hélène was a haggard masturbator or perhaps even a lesbian, but above all *poetically* when she herself admits, last and most satisfyingly—for Ronsard—that she is indeed *unnatural* not only in her sexuality but even in the very complexion of her humors. Physical love of the kind Ronsard proposes is held in aversion by her. She knows there is no defense philosophical, sociological, or even physical for such an attitude, and finds herself therefore reduced to invoking the contemporary equivalent for the epitome of *unreasoned* desire, the institution of the monarch's *Begehren*:

> Ce n'est (ce me dis-tu) le remors de la loy
> Qui me fait t'econduire, ou la honte, ou la crainte,
> Ny la frayeur des Dieux, ou telle autre contrainte,
> C'est qu'en tes passetemps plaisir je ne reçoy.
>   D'une extreme froideur tout mon corps se compose,
> Je n'ayme point Venus, j'abhorre telle chose,
> Et les presens d'Amour me sont une poison:

> Puis je ne les veus pas. O subtile deffaite!
> Ainsi parlent les Rois, defaillant la raison,
> "Il me plaist, je le veux, ma volonté soit faite."

Royal will underwrote the overture to the Hélène cycle and presided at its finale; how could Ronsard oppose it? Ronsard was thus exonerated—at least by himself. No man, however young, vigorous, charming or seductive, could have won Hélène. She admits as much herself. Hélène's (Ronsard's) last words on the matter were meant to be conclusive enough.

3. Rasse des Nœux

But the textual history of the dildo sonnet flows also in the opposite direction. By this I mean that another author appropriates—requisitions—the obscene poem for service in the politico-religious altercations of the day. The person is well known by Ronsard specialists: François Rasse des Nœux, *chirurgien ordinaire* of King Charles IX from 1560 until 1573. Like his more renowned fellow surgeon Ambroise Paré, Rasse des Nœux had strong Protestant leanings. As a court surgeon he was in a remarkable position to gather various contemporary manuscripts, and is in fact responsible for the preservation of hundreds of poems by scores of contemporary authors in his *Recueil de Rasse de Neus* (Bibliothèque Nationale, ms. fr. 22560-22565). Rasse des Nœux seems to have taken particular delight in the earthy pamphleteer verse of the times—we mentioned above that he preserved the *Chanson faite par Lancelot Carles*—and many examples could be furnished had we sufficient space. He also enjoyed verse decrying the poetic style in vogue, for he also gives a copy of Du Bellay's *Poete courtisan* (ms. fr. 22561, ff. 9 r°-11 r°). Perhaps, then, it should not surprise us that he preserves in his own hand a "version" of the dildo sonnet which makes the nuns at the Poissy convent sister-users of the type of *godmicy* with which Lucrèce corrupts herself, if not the manufacturers of it: "C'est un gros instrument qui se fait pres d'icy" (Ronsard, 1578); "C'est un gros instrument qu'on practique à Poissy" (Rasse des Nœux).[20] But the most important change this curator turned author made to Ronsard's sonnet was to stretch the tercets into seven lines he was unable to distill back into the two tercets required by the sonnet form. He seems to have had too much to say in connection with the Colloquy of Poissy to have been concerned with the requisite format of the tercets, let alone the *forme marotique* Ronsard nearly always observed in his sonnets:

> Voila le seul jouet dont elle se contente
> Aussi pour recompense une alleine puante
> Le teint pasle & les yeux tous battus et deffaits

Monstrent qu'au lieu du vray tousjours le faux y entre
Et que tels passetemps ne sont que contrefaicts
Car il faut que la ligne aille droit au centre
Ou autrement les ronds demeurent imparfaits.

While we will never know with certainty whether this document records a poem attributable to the poet or to the clerk, it seems highly likely, on grounds of style and personal interest, that Rasse des Nœux was the author of the variants he gives. At any rate, the surgeon-curator allows us to witness a melding of two central notions that characterized Ronsard's suspicious attitude to Hélène's nature and at the same time the hostility between Catholics and Protestants which developed at Poissy. Rasse des Nœux's variant evokes (1) the spectre of the "faux" controlling his mistress's sexuality (as expressed, say, in sonnet xxv of the second book of the *Sonets pour Helene*); (2) the vying between the false and the true religion which a "false" and a "true" sexuality can be seen to figure; and finally (3) the mock Platonic assertions of love in the pamphleteer verse Ronsard helped write.

The scandal of Poissy, so called by historians because it marked the definitive rupture between orthodoxy and Protestantism, was not only the occasion of Ronsard's allusion in pamphleteer verse to the widely-known *unnatural* acts of the theologian Maillard, but also the occasion for Protestants to take revenge, in rewriting Ronsard's dildo sonnet, on the Dominican order in general and on Poissy in particular, the site of sixteenth-century religious irreconcilability. It was no secret that the Dominicans had played a major role in the Council of Trent, both because of the prelates and theologians furnished by the Order and because of the extensive presence of the theology of Thomas Aquinas. With the Protestant revolt in the beginning of the sixteenth century, the Dominicans, because of their role in the teaching and administration of the Church, were called to her defense; all remembered Tetzel's attacks on Luther. Furthermore, Protestant accusations of elitism would have been hard to deflect: the convent at Poissy, like its sister Dominican convents at Aix-en-Provence and at Montfleury, only received women of noble birth.[21] The Protestants must have been jubilant when Ronsard's and Hélène's personal and poetic irreconcilability found such infelicitous expression, for it furnished the man who was to become one of their most prominent if indirect spokesmen a perfect opportunity to take (unnatural) advantage of the scandal of Poissy. In grafting his own scions to Ronsard's excised sonnet, the surgeon-curator fused a privately autoerotic invention onto the commonwealth's politico-religious reality, thus assuring both the poem and the civil strife a much longer moment in the glare of future exegesis. Ronsard's sublime(d) vengeance became both the model and the copy for Rasse des Nœux's Protestant revenge.

Notes

[1] *Les Amours Diverses*, originally made up of fifty poems, was first published in the fifth collective edition (*Les Œuvres de P. de Ronsard*, seven parts in five volumes [Paris: G. Buon, 1578]); it enjoyed the addition of two new poems in 1584 (an elegy and a sonnet), but suffered the removal of sonnet xlv. With the publication of the posthumous edition (Paris, 1587), a new sonnet (LI) appeared. Except where other editions are specifically cited, I am using Henri and Catherine Weber's critical edition of *Les Amours* (Paris: Garnier, 1963). In the Laumonier-Silver edition, this sonnet is numbered LIII.

[2] The complete title of the satirical verse Ronsard helped write while at the Colloquy of Poissy is *Chanson faite par Lancelot Carles, euesque de Riez, contre les ministres estans a Poissy. Ronsard et Bai y ont aussi besongné*, and is preserved in the *Recueil de Rasse de Neus*, Bibliothèque Nationale, ms. fr. 22560-22565.

[3] Fernand Desonay, for example, in his chapter on *Les Amours Diverses*, makes no mention of the sonnet (*Ronsard poète de l'amour*, 3 vols. [Brussels: Publications de l'Académie, 1952-69] 3: 185-99), nor does Donald Stone, Jr., in an otherwise involved discussion of the poet's esthetic concerns (*Ronsard's Sonnet Cycles* [New Haven and London: Yale UP, 1966]).

[4] "Les Déboires de Ronsard à la cour," *Bibliothèque d'Humanisme et Renaissance* 12 (1950) 60-80.

[5] Pierre de Bourdeilles de Brantôme, *Œuvres complètes*, ed. Prosper Mérimée, 13 vols. (Paris, 1858-1905) 10: 103.

[6] *Renaissance France, 1470-1589*, in *A Literary History of France*, ed. P. E. Charvet, 6 vols. (London and Tonbridge, NY: Ernest Benn and Barnes & Noble, 1974) 2: 317.

[7] Du Bellay also speaks briefly of female autoeroticism in his *Divers Jeux Rustiques*, "La Contre-repentie," ed. V.-L. Saulnier (Geneva: Droz, 1965) 147, but stops short of mentioning by name a dildo: "Cherchez, cherchez qui d'un teinct palissant / Trompe l'ardeur de son feu languissant; / Ou qui par art un mary se façonne, / Et son plaisir elle-mesme se donne."

[8] Further corroboration of the demoiselle de Surgère's importance in Ronsard's later years is the fact that the eight posthumous sonnets were, according to Pierre de L'Estoile, dedicated to Hélène: *Journal pour le règne de Henri IV*, 3 vols. (Paris: Gallimard, 1948-1960) 2: 226 and 594.

[9] See Paul Laumonier, *Ronsard poète lyrique: étude historique et littéraire* (Paris: Hachette, 1909) 256-57.

[10] See R. J. Sealy, S.J., *The Palace Academy of Henry III*, Travaux d'Humanisme et Renaissance 134 (Geneva: Droz, 1981) 19.

[11] *Sonets pour Helene* (henceforth *SpH*) I, xlvi.

[12] We recall that Pierre Champion's characterization of Ronsard's reputation as an insatiable poet-lover was "grand Pan de la Renaissance": *Ronsard et son temps* (Paris: Edouard Champion, 1925) 483.

[13] I feel compelled, seeing myself using Ronsard's poetry to divine personal feelings, to cite Laumonier: "Gardons-nous de mesurer à notre aune la sincérité des poètes: il leur arrive d'être de bonne foi, même quand ils déclament, et de cacher sous le voile brillant des métaphores et des jeux d'esprit de vraies souffrances et de vraies joies" (475).

[14] See for example François Rigolot's "Rhétorique de la métamorphose chez Ronsard," in *Textes et Intertextes: études sur le seizième siècle pour Alfred Glauser* (Paris: Nizet, 1979) 147-59.

[15] On this aspect of Ronsard's new creativity, see Laumonier 264.

[16] See V.-L. Saulnier, "Autour du Colloque de Poissy: les avatars d'une chanson de Saint-Gelais à Ronsard et Théophile," *Bibliothèque d'Humanisme et Renaissance* 20 (1958) 44-78.

[17] Leone's *Dialoghi d'Amore* (Rome, 1535) were translated into French several times in the sixteenth century and twice during Ronsard's second love-poetry period: the first was by Denis

Sauvage, published in 1561, and the second by Pontus de Tyard around 1573. See Weber's edition of *Les Amours* 796.

[18] The justification of the self-stimulation of the wife was based on the belief that both the husband's and the wife's sperm were necessary for procreation. The debate starts with the intransigence of Tertullian's *De pudicitia* ("Non sunt delicta, sed monstra"), continues through Thomas Aquinas (*Summa theologica* IIa IIae, q. cliv, a. 11, 12), the Councils of Elvira and Ancyra, Gregory the Great (*Poenitentiale romanum*), the Latran Council, Ronsard's contemporary Pius V (*Horrendum illud scelus*) and well into the eighteenth century when Ligouri gave it in its most distilled form: "[Non peccat mulier] quae seipsam tactibus excitat ad seminationem statim post copulam in qua vir solus seminavit . . . Tactus turpes cum seipso exerciti ex delectatione venerea, absente altero conjuge, suntne veniales vel mortales?—Disputant theologi . . . ."

[19] See, for example, Laurent Joubert's *Erreurs populaires* (Paris, 1578) 192-205. Here are the two final sentences of the chapter: "Et i y a plusieurs hommes ayans les yeus anfoncés, qui neantmoins sont sains, pleins de bon suc, gros et gras, que l'on sait fort bien d'alheurs n'auoir eté angendrés de parens vieus. Dont il faut rapporter la cause de telle anfonçeure a vn'autre raison, que ie reserue a noz ecolles, sur ce que Galen an ha dit an son liure intitulé Art petit, ou Art medicinal." See also Louis Bertrauen's letter in the 1579 edition of the *Erreurs populaires* (5): ". . . ce que font quelques filles, d'un gaudé michi . . . ." Joubert, in his liminal letter (12) claims knowledge of even worse practices among women: "Et pansés vous que i'eusse ecrit tel propos, si ie n'eusse de vray sçeu, qu'il y a des filhes qui font pis que cela?" Finally, we recall Du Bellay's list of symptoms in "La Contre-repentie," cited above in note 7.

[20] The following alternate variant of this line is missing from the Weber edition: "C'est un gros instrument par le bout etrecy. . . ." It is reproduced in the Laumonier edition.

[21] See Donald Nugent, *Ecumenism in the Age of the Reformation: The Colloquy of Poissy* (Cambridge: Harvard UP, 1974); M. D. Chapotin, *Histoire des Dominicains de la province de France: le siècle des fondations* (Rouen, 1898); William A. Hinnebusch, *The History of the Dominican Order* (New York, 1966-73); Pierre F. Mandonnet, *St.-Dominique, l'idée, l'homme et l'œuvre*, rev. ed., 2 vols. (Paris, 1938).

Part III
Montaigne

Richard L. Regosin

Montaigne's Child of the Mind

I

In the closing pages of "De l'affection des peres aux enfans" (II, 8) Montaigne turns from the affection of natural, physical fathers to the love of authors for their writing, and to his own feelings for his *Essais*. Writings are like children, he says, as he works the traditional trope, productions of the mind more worthy than those of the flesh, and more the effect of their progenitor: "ce que nous engendrons par l'ame, les enfantemens de nostre esprit, de nostre courage et suffisance, sont produicts par une plus noble partie que la corporelle, et sont plus nostres; nous sommes pere et mere ensemble en cette generation" (400).[1] To their authors, whom they more vividly represent, these children of the mind bring honor, if they are well formed, and immortality.

The child of the mind is a powerful emblem of the *Essais* whose force we have tended to undervalue, perhaps because the figure is a literary common-place, less original and therefore less revealing than other images which, as Floyd Gray suggested three decades ago in *Le Style de Montaigne*, should be taken as the substance of Montaigne's ideas rather than illustrations or embellishments of it.[2] Montaigne himself claims in "Sur des vers de Virgile" (III, 5) that the best writing of the poets embodies their thought, and our people too, he adds, consider judgment to be language and fine words full conceptions. "Quand je voy ces braves formes de s'expliquer, si vifves, si profondes, je ne dicts pas que c'est bien dire, je dicts que c'est bien penser" (873), Montaigne says speaking of these poets, and we have taken his lead in saying the same about him. The figure of the text as child seems a well-worn and impersonal trope by comparison with this bold, vibrant expression, intimate and revealing.

I fully appreciate the imperative to read the *Essais* as the embodiment of Montaigne's thought because the integrity of his claim to portray himself faithfully, and to be consubstantial with his book, seem to depend on it. But I have never been able to determine whether the essayist's figures are *literally* his thought or whether he writes *as if* they were, practicing that style of writing he describes in "Sur des vers de Virgile" to produce the *effect* of thought through a discourse that resonates with what he calls fullness and natural vigor. The issue may be moot precisely because it is indeterminable, but it can serve to remind us that all literature must be situated *between* the idea of a literal, primary expression of thought and its tangible and figurative, mediated representation and that the richly suggestive reading must refuse the reductionary opposition. I would argue that in order for the *Essais* to approach their own aim of functioning simultaneously as self-portrait and the means to self-knowledge, as memory and as essays of judgment, as personal commentary and as the effort to construct a self, we as readers must read the literal and the figurative—or what might be transposed as the historical and the literary, or the existential and the rhetorical—as interacting and intruding on each other. Only when we consider the terms to overlap without privilege and without priority, when we simultaneously take literal thought to function figuratively and invest the figurative with all the force of literal thought, do we give meaning to Montaigne's claim that he and his book are one, that things and words, life and text may be said to coincide.

We begin to restore its dynamic force to the trope of the child of the mind by remarking that the child itself is a pervasive textual subject that Montaigne treats both as letter and figure. The absence of his own children from the *Essais*—his only surviving child, Léonor, is mentioned once by name in passing—seems to create a space in which textual children proliferate. Children are everywhere: "enfants" is the eighteenth most frequently used noun in the work, 237 times in 56 of the 107 essays; other forms like "enfance," "enfant," "enfanter," "enfantement," and so on, appear another 147 times. [3] Four essays directly address issues in which children are central: "De l'institution des enfans"(I, 26), "De l'affection des peres aux enfans" (II, 8), "D'un enfant monstrueux" (II, 30) and "De la ressemblance des enfans aux peres" (II, 37). Montaigne's children are classical and modern, they appear in essays treating subjects as diverse as affections (I, 3), custom (I, 23), solitude (I, 39), "drunkenness" (II, 2), cowardice (II, 27), and vanity (III, 9) and are evoked 18 times in the "Apologie de Raimond Sebond" (II, 12) alone. They are diversely heroes, victims or fools, models of a natural wisdom or examples of a stupid simplicity, subjects to be educated or to be loved. At times children represent continuity with the past and at other times they allow the essayist to speak about the future. And most strikingly, as we have said, they are both literal, physical children and figurative offspring as well. Léonor and the *Essais*; both progeny are identified in "De l'affection des peres aux enfans"(II, 8).

In this abundant talk of textual offspring—historical and fictional, real and metaphorical—the central irony is that of talk itself. The essayist who could not (or would not) keep his text from spilling over between the lines and into the margins, and onto additional slips of paper, who after the publication of the *Essais* in 1580 and 1588 went back to his writing to amend, to revise, to make additions, this verbose writer speaks repeatedly of the *enfant*, that which by its etymological nature is unable to speak (fr. l. *infans*, [one] unable to speak: *in-*, not +*fans*, pres. part. of *fari*, to speak). Montaigne himself is above all he who speaks, who speaks to speak only of himself ("parler seulement de moy," III, 8, 942), and who seeks to write as he speaks ("je parle au papier comme je parle au premier que je rencontre," III,1,790). More than once he calls the *Essais* the "confession" of his ignorance and his vanity, that is, a form of speaking which is thought to derive from the same root as *fari*. But what does it mean to speak in the *Essais*? What is the significance of these children, literal or figurative, who by their very nature cannot yet speak? What does it mean to say that the *Essais* are Montaigne's child, a child who does indeed speak, and who speaks so copiously? In whose voice and for whom does it speak? And to whom?

These questions might seem inappropriate because they appear to obscure the distinction between what is to be taken literally and what figuratively. The recourse to the etymology of "enfant," for example, resurrects a long-forgotten, perhaps even dead, sense whose own status is not entirely clear (was it to be taken literally that children did not speak or was this a figure for an early stage of physical, moral, or linguistic development?) in order to carry it back with apparent recklessness both to "real" children and to tropes. But isn't that precisely the point? We should seek to upset comfortable distinctions, to open up the literal to its figurative possibilities and the figurative to its literal potential. Under this kind of pressure, and in the dynamic interplay it generates, the letter and the figure (of the child) both produce and reflect the image of writing itself, its construction and its operations, its aspiration to be more (like life) than it is and the limitations which make it less. Within and between Montaigne's narratives and examples of literal children and the functioning of the traditional trope of the child of the mind lie central issues of the acquisition and use of language, of authorship and conception, textuality and representation, reading and interpretation.

II

Referring to his own childhood experience in "De l'institution des enfans" (I, 26), Montaigne implies that the infant is born "tongue-tied" and that the acquisition of language is the equivalent of loosening or unknotting the tongue. In order that he learn Latin as his mother tongue, the essayist tells us, he was placed in the care of Latin speakers "avant le premier desnouement de (sa) langue" (173). (Or perhaps it is language that is tied or bound up in the child that is unleashed.) Once untied, the tongue (or its language) can speak wisely or foolishly depending on how it is educated. There is thus an initial language acquisition in the literal, physical sense and, I would suggest, language learning in the figurative or moral sense; in the *Essais*, until the child learns the second "language" it remains in a sense true to its name, unable to speak. The pedagogical program of the *Essais*—although there is little that is program-matic about it—consists above all in giving the child the right language, in teaching him *how* to speak.

In one of the important paradoxes of the *Essais*, Montaigne turns to the uninstructed masses for the model of proper speaking. They engage in discussion which is spontaneous, forceful, and true to its purpose, he claims in "De l'art de conferer" (III, 8) and in "De la phisionomie" (III, 12) they seem to nourish Socrates's own exemplary speech: "Ainsi dict un paysan, ainsi dict une femme. Il n'a jamais en la bouche que cochers, menuisiers, savetiers et maçons. Ce sont inductions et similitudes tirées des plus vulgaires et cogneues actions des hommes" (1037). This is "natural" speech, the unmediated expression of thought and judgment; "unnatural" language, in Montaigne's terms, is the tutored discourse of rhetoric which dominates the traditional curriculum. But the ideal of untutored speech will not serve the child of the noble Madame Diane de Foix, Contesse de Gurson to whom "De l'institution des enfans" is written, just as it could not serve Montaigne himself. For the bourgeois and aristocratic (male) child, acquiring language is a question of proper schooling. The goal of Montaigne's untraditional curriculum is to anchor language in mind and judgment, to endow words with the truthfulness and sincerity they appear to have in "natural," spoken usage. "Que les mots aillent où va la pensée," he says in "De l'art de conferer"(III, 8, 924), an essay in which he also instructs (adults) how to speak.

The natural is thus also acquired, but the paradox does not end there. "Natural" speech is not only a literal phenomenon in the *Essais* but a figure of the text, a rhetorical trope in a vast fable of nature and the natural which includes not only coachmen and masons, peasants and children, but animals and the cannibals of the New World as well. The essayist figures the natural in order to argue against all forms of cultural and intellectual artifice, and against its hegemonic practices, against all surfaces that might mask and deceive. Rhetoric in particular suffers Montaigne's scathing attack because it shamelessly exploits the "natural" and dangerous disparity between thought and expression and because, as part of the institutional, curricular program, it corrupts the naiveté (and goodness?) of the child learning how to speak. Montaigne's rhetorical discourse thus serves ironically both to show up the facticity of culture and all that is artful—including rhetoric itself—and to affirm positive values such as simplicity, spontaneity and humility.

But this (rhetorical) gesture which turns rhetoric against itself is risky business because it cannot clear a space in which the natural exists absolutely as itself nor can it absolve the writer of complicity. In fact, what rhetoric's "suicidal" strategy announces is its own survival and its persistent presence at the very foundations of discourse itself, both oral and written, and in spite of the *Essais*'s claim of the naturalness of speech and the paradoxical assertion that writing can also speak for the soul. When Montaigne insists on natural language as the proper speech of the child, he suggests, against the powerful Platonic bias for orality which he himself also perpetuates, that writing, too, can be natural. "Le parler que j'ayme," he says in "De l'institution des enfans," "c'est un parler simple et naif, tel sur le papier qu'à la bouche" (I, 26, 171). But the lesson of Montaigne's writing, and the lesson of our reading, is that while he can write *about* a non-rhetorical, natural language he cannot "write" it. As he seeks in his writing literally to express the (alleged) immediacy and authenticity of natural (oral) language he reveals that, at best, he can only represent it, only approximate it, and that to do so he must have recourse to the rich resources of rhetoric, to its forms and figures. In this (mediating) process, he must irresistibly perform the disparity that he seeks most ardently to avoid in teaching the child how to speak, the inevitable gap which separates the soul (judgment, thought) from its expression. Between desire ("le parler que j'ayme") and its fulfillment ("sur le papier") rhetoric repeatedly shows its telltale, and subversive, face.

Montaigne's own writing practice thus confirms the need to bracket the "natural" of language, both because the "natural" shows itself up as a trope and the trope discloses that it is "natural" to language; discourse (even or especially his own) cannot realize itself without enacting the factitious and the artful that it harbors within. When the essayist expresses his desire that "les mots aillent où va la pensée," he reminds his reader that words and thought do not "naturally" coincide and that some effort of will or habit is required, some effect of education. Ideally, then, and in spite of what his writing reveals (or perhaps more correctly, *because* of what it reveals), Montaigne seeks to teach a "natural" language which would overcome language's own "natural" failings, a language which reflects correct judgment, a mimetic language which corresponds faithfully to thought, which is sincere, and which at the same time actively shapes and forms that judgment by its practice. And he teaches not only Mme Diane de Foix and the reader but the child and his tutor as well, speaking both to the tutor and in his place, to demonstrate that proper teaching is most centrally a question of proper speaking. It is a question of speaking and allowing the student to speak, as Socrates did (I, 26, 150); of having the student speak of what has been learned rather than memorized (151); of wisely warning (*advertir*, 155), conversing (*entretenir*, 155), saying (*dire*, 160, 161), communicating (163). The essayist as master tutor instructs how the child is to speak the words of others in quotation and paraphrase, citing his own work as example: "Je ne dis les autres, sinon pour d'autant plus me dire" (148). He teaches how it is to speak the language of self-correction and confession (154-55), how to speak the language of the book of the world (158), and that of philosophy as well (160-61).

III

In all of this talk about language, and in the copious articulation of this essay where the writer, the tutor, and the child all speak, a striking irony of what I am calling "proper language" is that it is as much a question of not speaking as of speaking itself. There is always the danger of saying too much, even when one has something worthwhile to say, as Plutarch knew: "Il sçavoit qu'és choses bonnes mesmes on peut trop dire"(157). There is also the danger of speaking to the wrong people: "On luy apprendra de n'entrer en discours ou contestation que où il verra un champion digne de sa luite" (154). In the school that Montaigne calls "cette eschole du commerce des hommes," children should be learning to listen to others: "Le silence et la modestie sont qualitez tres-commode à la conversation" (154), that is, in both social relationships and in speech. Watching and listening silently, being what the essayist calls a "spectateur(s) de la vie des autres hommes" (158), ideally allows one to judge the life observed and to order one's own. The world, figured in the essay as a mirror, requires (in)sight rather than speech; and the image of the world as book requires reading that by Montaigne's time has become predominantly silent.

Language, then, cannot be expressed in an unbridled, unlimited, manner but must be withheld, denied and negated if it is to function meaningfully, that is, truthfully communicate proper judgment and shape judgment to make it proper. Silence thus functions as a language just as language itself could be said to realize its true "nature" when it functions like silence. Our earlier observations on proper language as untutored and unrhetorical implied that it must be transparent, a window or a mirror of the soul (as one appears to look *through* the mirror at what it reflects). The ideal language shows nothing of itself, or put another way, is nothing in itself. It reveals judgment without revealing itself, expresses thought without itself being expressed. In his desire for pure signifieds, Montaigne demonstrates his distrust of the signifier that must inevitably contaminate truth by its own presence. My own analytical (and rhetorical) vocabulary, drawn from the visual—transparency, showing, revealing—links Montaigne to Ramus, whose misgivings about rhetoric and voice led to the recommendation of a plain, unadorned style whose "perspicuity" or translucency derives from the analogy with visual apprehension.[4] Montaigne too, I would say, longs for discourse—both oral and written—which would function like the invisible, and silent, medium which transmits light.

Montaigne's complex and paradoxical effort to make voice and speech function as if they were not there, or not themselves, prompts his insistence that *dire* become *faire*, that speaking be transmuted into silent, and visible, moral action. In "Du pedantisme" (I, 25, 143), he compares the educational programs of Athens and Lacedaemon with a paradoxically rhetorical flourish which aims at the elimination of rhetoric, and of language itself:

A Athenes on aprenoit à bien dire, et icy, à bien faire; là, à se desmeler d'un argument sophistique, et à rabattre l'imposture des mots captieusement entrelassez; icy, à se desmeler des appats de la volupté, et à rabatre d'un grand courage les menasses de la fortune et de la mort; ceux-là s'embesongnoient apres les parolles; ceux-cy apres les choses; là, c'estoit une continuelle exercitation de la langue; icy, une continuelle exercitation de l'ame.

The comparison operates a series of displacements by which "dire," "mots," "paroles," and "langue" are purged from education. In the parallel structure of the crafted period, Montaigne transmutes verbal action into moral action; the predicates which engage the student in the vacuousness of language in Athens are transformed by the substantial complements of virtue in Lacedaemon. Language, we might say, paradoxically turns against itself, brings the force of both grammar and rhetoric to silence itself. Education is no longer a question of weaning the child in any simple way from its inability to speak, of untying its tongue and giving it voice. The child does not learn how to speak but how to do. In the binary opposition of the comparison, moral action (*faire*) and speaking (*dire*) are mutually exclusive.[5]

IV

It is a supreme irony of the *Essais* that the imperative of *faire* requires the practice of *dire*, that what the essayist *does* is literally "une continuelle exercitation de la langue." He who says in "De la ressemblance des enfans aux peres" that whatever he is, "je le veux estre ailleurs qu'en papier" (II, 37, 784), must admit as he does in "De la vanité" that he is most prominently on paper: "Qui ne voit que j'ay pris une route par laquelle, sans cesse et sans travail, j'iray autant qu'il y aura d'ancre et de papier au monde?" (III, 9, 945). Montaigne himself often claims, as in the closing pages of that earlier essay, that *his* writing is a form of virtuous action, or at least an action that seeks to reflect and shape virtuous judgment. In terms that evoke the educational program of "Du pedantisme" and "De l'institution des enfans," he insists that his study ("mes estudes") has been used "à m'apprendre à faire, non pas à escrire. J'ay mis tous mes efforts à former ma vie. Voylà mon mestier et mon ouvrage. Je suis moins faiseur de livres que de nulle autre besoigne" (784). But the substitution by which the work of life ("ouvrage," "besoigne")—both what he does, the writing, and its product, the book—becomes life itself ("ma vie," "mon mestier") reveals itself as a metonymic structure, a contingent and relational association rather than a necessary identification. And while the rhetorical figure is intended to distinguish Montaigne from the "faiseurs de livres" as he pejoratively calls them, those who make *only* a book, it also implicates him in making a book. Literally speaking, and in the presence of the powerful metonymy we are reminded that the literal cannot simply be dispensed with or ignored, no writing is possible without *dire* and *escrire*. All writers are contaminated by this literal truth, all writers are literally "faiseur(s) de livres."

Because on the face of things Montaigne cannot simply make his language be his thought or his life, because he is drawn in spite of himself into the vacuous realm of "langue," "mots" and "parolles," he insists that speaking/writing be transformed into doing or making and words made into "things." As we might expect, his primary "things" ("choses," "res") are thoughts, ideas, concepts in the mind, the stuff of judgment. But words, he claims, can become secondary "things," they can follow and can gain substance as they express the substantial matter of the mind. This runs counter to what we read earlier as the transparency of "proper" language, the idea that language was most like itself ("natural") when it was nothing in itself, when it let thought shine through. Here language must be transformed from nothing into something, so that it can embody thought; only when it is "improper" is language nothing, and then it is pure vacuity, inanity (l. *inanis*, empty, vain). In "Sur des vers de Virgile" (III, 5, 873), Montaigne describes language that is "non plus de vent, ains de chair et d'os"; he speaks also of words "enflées" by imagination, and in other essays of words that are "remplies," "farcies," "vives." Most prominently, Montaigne's substantial words become corporeal; he seeks to "flesh out" his writing in a literal sense, to incarnate the word of the *Essais*. When language is semantically and morally impoverished, he considers it to be bloodless and fleshless, what we might call the emptiness which is death itself. "J'avois trainé languissant apres des parolles Françoises, si exangues, si descharnées et si vuides de matiere et de sens . . . ," he says, describing his reaction to reading borrowed words in "De l'institution des enfans" (I, 26, 147).

Montaigne's concern to make words into flesh and bone and to conceive the *Essais* as a textual body, and as his own incarnation—they appear as a "skeletos" in "De l'exercitation," a "livre consubstantiel à son autheur" in "Du desmentir," the "excremens d'un vieil esprit" in "De la vanité"—is both a moral and a rhetorical issue that represents yet another effort to transcend contingent and factitious language.[6] As in the case of language that must deny itself in transparency, or of language that negates itself in silence, or language that becomes pure act or substance (*faire*), we once again have language that must be transformed into something other than itself. Our discussion has revealed that these are not consistent strategies, related systematically to each other; rather, they are the diverse and conflicting expressions of Montaigne's desire for unmediated and stable truth. But we have seen that post-lapsarian language resists such stabilizing or transcending gestures; it shifts and turns semantically, disturbing its signifying habits and straining its referential links. The limitations and shortcomings of language cannot be overcome from within, as language itself constantly reminds us.

V

We might argue that the *Essais*'s preoccupation with the child betrays its own concern with learning how to speak, that the writing situates itself anxiously between the initial unloosening of the tongue/language and the mature moral expression (action) toward which it strives. To write is of course literally to "dénouer la langue," to loosen the tongue and to let language loose, and I think it not amiss to speak of the anxiety of writing, even (or especially) in the case of Montaigne, allegedly so settled and secure. What talking about the child has uncovered so far is precisely the presence of elements, both without and within, that disturb, displace, unsettle, and destabilize notions and practices of speaking and writing, and of language itself. What disturbs is not only that Montaigne attacks accepted rhetorical practice or challenges a traditional curriculum where rhetoric has its place but that even in his attack he himself is always implicated in its use, in its excess and artifice. What destabilizes is not that he seeks a direct, immediate moral expression but that to pursue this aim he must force language into paradoxical postures it cannot sustain: silence, invisibility, substantiality. And what is upsetting about silence and invisibility is not that they are intended as the guarantees of truth and the authenticity of being but that they can also be empty or vacuous, as we suggested, non-being which proclaims itself as loudly as if it spoke in its own name. The word made flesh? Montaigne's attempt to transcend language through language itself can only parody incarnation as the impossible (scandalous?) object of his desire, can only temporarily muzzle the irrepressible voice of the trope which pushes forth to speak in the name of its own factitiousness.

If Montaigne *could* have realized the intentions of his writing project, it would have signaled the end of writing, the end of language, for being would have been wholly present in all its plenitude and would no longer have needed to be spoken. Paradoxically these are the terms of Montaigne's ideal friendship with La Boétie whose origin the *Essais* situate before the friends even spoke, and which obviated the need for Montaigne to write at all, as numerous critics have pointed out.[7] But what the complex status of the child reveals, as it strives to be what it cannot be—simultaneously a child and a speaker—is that the writing project cannot entirely "be" either, that the writer must continually write, must continually urge language toward that which *it* can never be or do. "Et quand seray-je à bout de representer une continuelle agitation et mutation de mes pensées, en quelque matiere qu'elles tombent, puisque Diomedes remplit six mille livres du seul subject de la grammaire? Que doit produire le babil, puisque le begaiement et desnouement de la langue estouffa le monde d'une si horrible charge de volumes? Tant de paroles pour des paroles seules!" (III, 9, 946). "What can the child's prattle produce?" Montaigne asks of his own writing. The *Essais* are always in some sense "babil," "begaiement," the not yet fully formed speech of the child of the mind. When the tongue is loosened and language is unleashed in the "desnouement de la langue," the essayist *and* the child, the essayist *as* the child, can only produce empty speech. The pedagogical program of "De l'institution des enfans" seeks to intervene, to form the child and formulate substantial speech, but it can only represent an ideal toward which the child, like the essayist, endlessly strives and which remains endlessly beyond reach. Montaigne imagines his text as a child who does not (will not or cannot) grow up, the very performance of inadequacy, of limitation, the enactment of the shortcomings of language and of the essayist/child coming up short of his own ends.

Given this inevitable situation, one might ask not only "Why the compulsion to write?" but also "Why continue to write?" If the loss of the perfect friendship represented in "De l'amitié," and the consequent loss of the sense of self ("luy seul jouyssoit de ma vraye image, et l'emporta,"III, 9, 983), serve as figures of an alterity that defines Montaigne's relationship to himself and to others, what motivates the writing and makes of Montaigne an essayist is the effort to overcome difference both within himself and between self and other. The desire to know and to possess himself is accompanied by the poignant call to the absent other ("O un amy,"III, 9, 981), by the need for a friend like La Boétie, and by the need to be known by others as he is and for what he is, even or especially in his "childishness." "Je suis affamé de me faire connoistre," Montaigne says in "Sur des vers de Virgile," "et ne me chaut à combien, pourvue que ce soit veritablement; ou, pour mieux dire, je n'ai faim de rien, mais je crains mortellement d'estre pris en eschange par ceux à qui il arrive de connoistre mon nom" (III, 5, 847). The *Essais*, the child of the mind, are conceived to make Montaigne known, and to guarantee that he will not be taken amiss.

All progeny, Montaigne infers in the closing pages of "De l'affection des peres aux enfans," "nous representent et nous rapportent," and the spiritual children "bien plus vivement que les autres"(II, 8, 400). The role of "les enfantemens de notre esprit" is to represent, to be the agent or surrogate for, and also to speak in the father's place, or name, to speak the father ("nous rapporter"). The child speaks in the absence of the father from himself, in the absence of a friend and in the absence of the reader, separated by the physical and psychological distance imposed by the in(ter)vention of printing. And the child will speak after the death of the father, even though Montaigne threatens, in "De la vanité," to come back to speak for himself if he is misread. Given what we already know about the child's problematical speech, what chance does it have to fulfill this speaking role?

VI

In a sense the writing/child is conceived to respond to absence, and absence to some degree always evokes, recalls or represents death. We might say that Montaigne always writes in the face of death, that whatever else he is writing about—friendship, self-knowledge or ignorance, children or writing itself—he is always writing to face up to it and in some way to face it down. I am reminded in this context of Scheherazade for whom speaking alone forestalled death. As long as there were words there was breath, and the teller of tales—both speaker and writer—was able to postpone the inevitable silence and nothingness of the end. In an essay entitled "Language to Infinity," Foucault saw the self-reflexive nature of language itself as the hedge against death: "Headed toward death, language turns back upon itself; it encounters something like a mirror; and to stop this death which would stop it, it possesses but a single power: that of giving birth to its own image in a play of mirrors that has no limits."[8] The figure of language giving birth to a self-reflexive image as the way to defer death strikingly echoes the lexicon of production, of procreation in the *Essais*, of children as "autres nous mesmes" (II, 8, 399), of children of the mind who effectively become "enfans immortels, qui immortalisent leurs peres, voire et les deïfient" (400). This is not the immortality sought after by some, the hollow and superficial glory conferred by public approbation that Montaigne eschews in "De la gloire" (II, 16), what we might call the child of fame or destiny that is always in the keeping of others. Something much more profound and profoundly personal is at stake here than a reputation that might survive on the lips (in the words) of others. Only Montaigne's own voice, his own words, can postpone death, only the self-reflexivity of the essayist speaking about himself and himself speaking, in language turned back upon itself in an endless play of mirrors. Only by that procreation which is the re-creation of the self can the silence and nothingness of death be overcome, only by that bearing witness which is also the bearing of the child of the mind, by the conception of the text that continues to speak in the father's name, in his absence. In the void of the future, even and especially after death, the text endlessly repeats what/that Montaigne (still) is.

But this effort to stave off death by writing, by conceiving the child of the mind, entraps the writer in a double bind. The child is the source of the father's life: in the most literal sense, without the child there is no father, just as figuratively there is no survival without it. But the child is also the source of the father's death, as Montaigne reminds us in "De l'affection des peres aux enfans" (II, 8). Evoking the jealousy of those whose children assume a place in the world just as the parent is about to take his leave, "il nous fache," he says in the first-person plural which includes himself among the envious fathers, "qu'ils [the children] nous marchent sur les talons, comme pour nous solliciter de sortir. Et, si nous avions à craindre cela, puis que l'ordre des choses porte qu'ils ne peuvent, à dire verité, estre ny vivre qu'aux despens de nostre estre et de nostre vie, nous ne devions pas nous mesler d'estre peres" (387). To be a father means to begin to take one's leave, to relinquish one's place, to give up one's authority and one's voice since the child's life and being can *only* occur at the expense of the life and being of the father. This is not some contingency but the very order of things from which there is no escape. The irony here is overwhelming. The father seeks to save himself by becoming a father and he condemns himself; he already begins to absent himself before his death, when the child learns to speak and speaks for the father. Once the child is given language and takes its place in the world, it does not wait around for the father to disappear of his own accord. The child speaks and its voice displaces and replaces that of the father and the father himself. Even though it purports to represent the paternal the child draws attention to its own voice and to itself.

The inevitable replacement of the father by his offspring is not the only irony of conception (writing). The child (as the text) cannot fulfill the ardent desire of its progenitor for protection, it cannot guarantee the father's integrity, no matter what the father does or how hard the child tries. Circulating out in the world in the father's name, inscribed with his signature as author, the child of the mind cannot completely impose its authority. The faithful repetition of the authoritative words of the father, the loyal effort to secure his intention, to assert his meaning, must ultimately fail to guarantee that the father will be taken for what he is once and for all. The child speaks to save the place of the father and opens up the possibility of his violent displacement. And this opening reveals that there is always a gap in the way representation functions, a gap that is the insurmountable difference between the signified and the signifier, and it exposes as well the aporia that lies between intention and interpretation, between what is meant and what is understood.

Montaigne recounts his own concern in "De l'amitié" at the way in which La Boétie's *La Servitude volontaire* has been mis-taken to represent him. Used by the Protestants for political purposes for which it was not intended, the text has communicated a false image of its author. Montaigne knows this because he claims for himself the privileged position of the friend who, like the child, is an "autre nous-mesmes" and thus privy to La Boétie's intention, his will and to his meaning. And also like the child, the friend will speak for the other who is also himself, he will stand in for his friend to maintain him as he was: "Et si à toute force je n'eusse maintenu un amy que j'ay perdu, on me l'eust deschiré en mille contraire visages" (III, 9, 983). The violence of the figure is striking. The voice of La Boétie's child, his writing, does not suffice to safeguard the integrity of its father and the wholeness of his presence which purports to reside within it. A second surrogate is needed, a guardian for the child as well as for the father, one whose own voice supplements that of the child and prevents the father, the model, the original, the signified, from being torn asunder, fragmented into a thousand contrasting appearances. So in "De l'amitié," as a sign of friendship and to fulfill its obligation, Montaigne explains and justifies La Boétie's motives and his meaning: "Et affin que la memoire de l'auteur n'en soit interessée en l'endroit de ceux qui n'ont peu connoistre de pres ses opinions et ses actions, je les advise que . . ." (I, 28, 194). But who will speak for La Boétie after Montaigne is silent? And who for Montaigne himself? "Je reviendrois volontiers de l'autre monde pour démentir celuy qui me formeroit autre que je n'estois, fut ce pour m'honorer" (983), the essayist says to emphasize his concern. The text will be left alone, on its own, to speak the intention of the father, to represent him.[9] But what this dynamic demonstrates is that representation is never self-sufficient, it never can say all that it has to say, or that must be said, once and for all, so that nothing else need be said. The image (of the father) does not have final authority, it cannot speak so as to silence the voices of others who impose upon it, to have the last word. Representation is not closure but the opening to others to speak in its place.

VII

Our own reading, the pressure we have put on both the letter and the figure of the child in Montaigne's *Essais*, demonstrates that the opening that produces reading resides deep within writing, regardless of any specific text's intention to open itself up or to close itself off. But it is also important to emphasize that an opening is not a void but a "between," a space of confrontation and of tension where reading functions between the writer's intention and its textual realization, between the constraints of textual matter and form and reading's inevitable (necessary?) and willful "misreading," between the irreconcilable demands of the historicity of the text and that of the reader. The dynamic that operates among writer, text and reader is announced, reflected, figured in the problematical relationship of father and child, in their connections and disjunctions. As father the writer asks his progeny to accede to his will, to represent him as he is, to be his life in the future; and it could be said that with extraordinary fidelity the writing complies with his wishes and does nothing other than assert insistently the language that it has been given by the father. What in the *Phaedrus* Socrates objects to in writing as its lack of intelligence, its lack of responsiveness to those who ask what it is saying and its repetition of the only words it knows, could here be taken to represent the text carrying out the literal expression of the will and intention of the father. At the same time, since the writing/offspring needs to clear a ground in order to be what *it* is, since to fulfill the natural order of things it needs to free itself from the dictates of the father, it is perhaps not a lack of intelligence that causes it ultimately to betray the father, nor is it simply filial perversity. The son can only be what it is by showing disrespect and speaking in its own voice, that is, only by opening itself up to what is different from the intention of the father. Socrates criticizes writing for drifting all over the place, as he says, getting into the wrong hands, addressing the wrong people and, in what he calls its silence, disclosing both its stupidity and its treachery. But is the text ever really silent, even in the face of unexpected questions, and is it ever entirely in the "wrong hands"? Doesn't it affirm what it is by responding to the different possibilities of what it (or he, the father) is saying, even (and especially) when it responds in ways the father did not anticipate or would not authorize? Even silence can be language, as we saw earlier. Perhaps it is the nature of writing always to be made to speak the words of others, as Socrates feared, words that will be attributed to it as if they were its own, just as I have been doing here. But the problematical and paradoxical figure of the child of the mind allows us to see that this profound failure is also salvation. Only by losing himself in the son can the father save himself; only by opening himself to others can the son be himself; only by producing the unmasterable space of writing and reading and by becoming its products can the text as the child of the mind and the author of whom it speaks master death. And only, we might say, by "fathering" the reader.

Notes

[1] Quotations are from *Les Essais de Michel de Montaigne*, eds. Pierre Villey and V.-L. Saulnier (Paris: PUF, 1965).

[2] Floyd Gray, *Le Style de Montaigne* (Paris: Nizet, 1958) 155. In his magisterial *Montaiqne* (Paris: Gallimard, 1963), which Gray edited, Thibaudet had written, "lorsque Montaigne compare les opérations de son âme à celles de son corps, ce [n'est] pas une métaphore, a peine une image, mais une maniere de penser immédiate et spontanée."

[3] Roy E. Leake, *Concordance des Essais de Montaigne* (Geneva: Droz, 1981) 403-05.

[4] On Ramus and the plain style see Walter J. Ong, *Ramus, Method and the Decay of Dialogue* (Cambridge and London: Harvard UP, 1958, 1983) 283-84.

[5] In *The Matter of My Book: Montaigne's Essais as the Book of the Self* (Berkeley: U of California P, 1977) I explore in some detail the rhetorical and thematic implications of "dire," "écrire," and "faire." See esp. chapters 6 and 9. Paolo Valesio draws attention to this passage from "Du pédantisme" as an example of rhetoric used against itself in *Novantiqua: Rhetorics as a Contemporary Theory* (Bloomington: Indiana UP, 1980) 43.

[6] In *Montaigne: l'écriture de l'essai* (Paris: PUF, 1988), Gisèle Mathieu-Castellani explores the rhetorical and epistemological implications of Montaigne's discourse about the body and of what she calls the body's own discourse, the role it plays in the apprehension and appropriation of reality, and in the activity of writing itself. Cf. especially 135-253, entitled "Ecrire le corps."

[7] Cf., among others, Anthony Wilden, "Par divers moyens on arrive a pareille fin: A Reading of Montaigne," *MLN* 83 (1968) 577-97; Donald M. Frame, *Montaigne's Essais: A Study* (Englewood Cliffs, NJ: Prentice-Hall, 1969) 10; Albert Thibaudet, *Montaigne*, ed. Floyd Gray (Paris: Gallimard, 1963) 143 ff.; Michel Butor, *Essais sur les Essais* (Paris: Gallimard, 1964); Jean Starobinski,

Montaigne en mouvement (Paris: Gallimard, 1982) 52-86; François Rigolot, *Les Métamorphoses de Montaigne* (Paris: PUF, 1988) 61-95; and my *The Matter of My Book* 7-29.

[8] Michel Foucault, "Language to Infinity," in *Language. Counter-memory. Practice: Selected Essays and Interviews*, ed. D. F. Bouchard. trans. D. F. Bouchard and S. Simon (Ithaca, NY: Cornell UP, 1977) 54.

[9] In Montaigne's case, Marie de Gournay, the essayist's "fille d'alliance," spoke for him and for his text, particularly in her prefaces to posthumous editions of the *Essais*. I explore the implications of this "daughter" speaking for the father in "Montaigne's Dutiful Daughter," *Montaigne Studies* 3 (1991) 103-27.

Lawrence D. Kritzman

Montaigne's Fantastic Monsters and the Construction of Gender

> Je n 'ay veu monstre et miracle au monde plus expres que moy-mesme. (III, 11, 1029).[1]
>
> Nostre verité de maintenant, ce n'est pas ce qui est mais ce qui se persuade à autruy. (II, 18, 666)

As early as the chapter "De l'oisiveté" (I, 8) Montaigne informs the reader of the necessity of controlling the movement of his mind. Instead of producing a sense of spiritual tranquility, Montaigne's retirement from public life paradoxically generated intense psychic activity that is transcribed through amorphous images of "chimeres" and "monstres fantasques." The condition of idleness allows the imagination to wander about fortuitously so that the mind's performance, as it is recounted in the text, represents a psychic "reality" whose sheer excessiveness translates the unreal or fantastic qualities of the work. Accordingly, the essayist's apprenticeship to a contemplative existence is characterized by a formlessness of thought; the reflective subject risks becoming like a runaway horse, out of control, and always already beyond itself:

(a) Dernierement que je me retiray chez moy, deliberé autant que je pourroy, ne me mesler d'autre chose que de passer en repos, et à part, ce peu qui me reste de vie: il me sembloit ne pouvoir faire plus grande faveur à mon esprit, que de le laisser en pleine oysiveté, s'entretenir soy mesmes, et s'arrester et rasseoir en soy: ce que j'esperois qu'il peut meshuy faire plus aisément, devenu avec le temps plus poisant, et plus meur. Mais je trouve . . . que au rebours, faisant le cheval eschappé, il se donne cent fois plus d'affaire à soy mesmes, qu'il n'en prenoit pour autruy; et m'enfante tant de chimeres et monstres fantasques les uns sur les autres, sans ordre, et sans propos . . . . (I, 8, 33)

Quite clearly, the essays are about the parenting of the self and the monstrousness of selfhood; they become a *locus* where the act of writing becomes the tool through which the narrating subject can re-present itself to itself. "Encore se faut-il ordonner et renger pour sortir en place. Or je me parle sans cesse, car je me descris sans cesse" (11, 6, 378). In this process of self-portraiture, the text reveals the so-called unnaturalness of the fevered imagination. Montaigne sees language and sees himself in it; and the self that he views risks following its own course uncontrolled as it is by the power of the will. The chimeras—defined as "idle conceits, frivolous thoughts and fruitless imaginations"—reproduce the image of an essentially empty and vain progenitor whose scriptural deformities characterize the unreal or fantastic monster as a difference that resists normative meaning.[2]

For Montaigne, then, writing depends upon a certain kinetic energy, a mobility that is textually represented by an amorphous self capable of undergoing multiple metamorphoses. What began as inactivity becomes a process of self-analysis; the figuration of the ego, in its search for mastery, struggles to make sense of the difference within the self. What is striking here is the way in which the mind usurps the female role of engendering and gives birth to a self representing a monstrous narcissism that is transformed into a spectacle or an object to be seen: "Je ne vis jamais pere, pour teigneux ou bossé que fut son fils, qui laissast de l'avoüer (I, 26, 145).

At the core of Montaigne's scriptural practice is the desire to domesticate the excesses and strangeness of the mind's activities. When the essayist explains the shift from reflection to writing in this chapter he recognizes the need to neutralize what he terms the "monstrousness" within himself. Drawing upon an extended metaphor that comprises images of unplanted fields and infertile women, Montaigne's text discovers the monstrous side of nature as something emanating from what is reproduced without mediation:

(a) Comme nous voyons des terres oysives, si elles sont grasses et fertilles, foisonner en cent mille sortes d'herbes sauvages et inutiles, et que, pour les tenir en office, il les faut assubjectir et employer à certaines semences, pour nostre service; et comme nous voyons que les femmes produisent bien toutes seules, des amas et pieces de chair informes, mais que pour faire une generation bonne et naturelle, il les faut embesoigner d'une autre semence: ainsin est-il des espris. Si on ne les occupe à certain sujet, qui les bride et contreigne, ils se jettent desreiglez, par-cy par là, dans le vague champ des imaginations. (I, 8, 32)

Montaigne's text thus devalues what has not been properly cultivated by *man*. Untamed growth motivates a genetic process that is unequal, irregular and yet thoroughly natural. The paradox of nature lies in the existence of its monstrous imperfections: the disquieting reality of what appears to be unnatural must be submitted to a "different kind of seed" that will *create* and not engender a more perfect nature. Here the use of the maternal metaphor is quite revealing. The biological creation of the mother in the genetic process is represented as inadequate without the intervention of a paternal "artistry" that would enable it to transcend the banality of unmotivated reproduction. When the irregularities of the maternal body submit to the paternal rule, the idea of naturalness loses its role as model and origin of beauty. As it turns out, the figuration of authorship as it is troped on the image of the maternal body, attests to the desire for writing to project a paternal "artistry" that makes art from life.

Montaigne's attempt to give concrete form and order to the mind's amorphous cogitations is but a way to control the possibility of shaping a life and to displace the otherness within the self onto the fantasist narratives constituting text production: ". . . que pour en contempler à mon aise l'ineptie et l'estrangeté, j'ay commancé de les mettre en rolle, esperant avec le temps luy en faire honte à luy mesmes" (I, 8, 33). Montaigne's monster can be seen here as a figure for self-portraiture that renders the text the site of the *unheimlich*, the strange and yet the thoroughly familiar. More than being a mere object of shame as the essayist suggests, the mind's fantastic monsters attest to the omnipotence of thought derived from the fictions that the desiring mind "experiences." By becoming a stranger to himself in the language of the essay Montaigne's text ironically transcribes his most intimate secrets in a process of self-alienation. Nevertheless, if he writes to contemplate the strangeness and ineptness of the mind's activity he does so in order to neutralize it and to seek relief in the concrete realization of the book. "L'ame qui n'a point de but estably, elle se perd: car, comme on dict, c'est n'estre en aucun lieu, que d'estre par tout" (32).

The attempt to curtail the unwieldy nature of the essayist's "fantastic" thought is intertextually rooted in the father's moral imperative to manage the family estate wisely. Throughout the *Essais* we witness numerous references to the law of patrimony as it is exemplified in the father's desire to preserve his household from excessive financial waste and decay by keeping "le registre des negoces du mesnage":

Il ordonnoit à celuy de ses gens qui lui servoit à escrire, un papier journal à inserer toutes les survenances de quelque remarque, et jour par jour les memoires de l'histoire de sa maison . . . . Usage ancien, que je trouve bon à refraichir, chacun en sa chacuniere. Et me trouve un sot d'y avoir failly. (I, 35, 224)

In another context I have discussed Montaigne's ambivalent relation to his father regarding the transmission of property and his feeling of inadequacy concerning the administration of the inheritance.[3] The paternal metaphor in "De l'oisiveté," realized through the writerly act of recording, serves as an antidote to the negative connotations associated with idleness and waste; the act of self-portraiture preserves the proper balance between saving and spending. Etymologically linked to the concept of the rule of law, the essayist's "registre" reformulates this scriptural practice in terms of the son's submission to the paternal metaphor as it is transcribed through the desired entry into the symbolic order. The "register" is also the *regula* or the model of the subject's ideal image of himself that is embodied in another: the father whom he fears he will be unable to live up to. In order to be represented as a totalized and totalizing "self," the Montaignian subject must be positioned in relation to the paternal *phallus* as a kind of reparative gesture for what is later revealed as the son's failure to record the history of patrimony. The dutiful son wishes to establish his legitimacy in the writerly act "qui s'engage à un registre de durée, de toute sa foy, de toute sa force" (II, 18, 665). One might infer, then, that the desiring subject's sought-after "solidity" is an attempt to conform to a standard of what a man should be; it acts as a way to control excessive desire and to limit illegitimate fantasy.[4]

But the enduring account that Montaigne sets forth as the goal of his quest is undone in the writing of the *Essais*; what he terms the "desreglement de nostre esprit" (I, 4, 24) repudiates the image of the father's desire. The monstrous progeny depicted in the text does not reflect a stable identity, but rather a multiplicity of selves that is subject to change: "Je ne puis asseurer mon object. Il va trouble et chancelant, d'une yvresse naturelle" (III, 2, 805). In spite of the idealized patriarchal motivation to impose a unified order on the meanderings of the mind, the "living register" inscribed in the text records the self-division of the writing subject. The question of gender identity is signified through tropic self-consciousness and paradoxes; they assert and disrupt meaning and thereby generate tensions between the irregularities of the natural and the unnaturalness of the culturally coded.

Re-Vising the Monstrous

In the essay "D'un enfant monstrueux" (II, 30) Montaigne records through the trope of the monstrous body an alternative to the rigidity associated with the biologically conceived phallic position; the text allegorizes the possibility of transcending the marginality of the monstrous. The essayist examines the nature of the monstrous and its relation to the concept of difference. The text begins by a concise yet detailed account—described in "objective" terms—of a Siamese twin with one head that the essayist recently viewed being displayed for money. At first the exemplarity of the monstrous stems from the perception of deviation from the normative; difference, portrayed as a visual "effect," attests to the rarity attributed to the object of the gaze:

(a) Ce conte s'en ira tout simple, car je laisse aux medecins d'en discourir. Je vis avant hier un enfant que deux hommes et une nourrisse, qui se disoient estre le pere, l'oncle et la tante, conduisoyent pour tirer quelque sou de le montrer à cause de son estrangeté. . . . Au dessoubs de ses tetins, il estoit pris et collé à un autre enfant sans teste . . . si vous retroussiez cet enfant imparfait, vous voyez au dessoubs le nombril de l'autre. . . . Le nombril de l'imparfaict ne se pouvoit voir. . . . (II, 30, 712-13)

The scopic drive portrayed here draws our attention to the unusual and transforms it into a public spectacle ("de le montrer") of sorts. The identity of the unusual can only be known from the projection of its external features. Representing a composite figure whose boundaries are inadequately differentiated, the monster inscribed in the text calls into question the opposition between self and other. The monster is thus born from the power of the image to evoke what is initially perceived as an abnormal sense of human reality. Vision is presented as a means to reify the sense of the word "monster" by reducing the body to its optical dimensions and by foregrounding the strangeness of its existence.[5]

The representation of the monster in this chapter takes on epistemological consequences based on the perception and experience of the viewer. Recognized as an image that resists classification, the monstrous is depicted as lacking consensual practice as a sign: (c) "Nous apelons contre nature ce qui advient contre la coustume" (713). Even though we attribute value to the monstrous by paying to see it, from the perspective of the divine and natural orders the monstrous can be interpreted as unquestionably normal:[6]

(c) Ce que nous appellons monstres, ne le sont pas à Dieu, qui voit en l'immensité de son ouvrage l'infinité des formes qu'il y a comprinses; et est à croire que cette figure qui nous estonne, se rapporte et tient à quelque autre figure de mesme genre inconnu à l'homme . . . mais nous n'en voyons pas l'assortiment et la relation. (713)

Unlike other Renaissance texts such as Pierre Boaistuau's *Histoire des prodiges* (1560) where monsters are portrayed as supernatural beings produced by miracles, Montaigne's essay domesticates the monstrous and consequently veers toward the erasure of the unnatural. The reduction of the other to the same, first through the emblem of the conjoined body, and then through the text's post-1588 metacommentary, returns the body of the "enfant monstrueux" to itself, in its own image, ironically presented as visually different but still not a shockingly abnormal thing. Difference is just meant to *be* ; the acceptance of diversity neutralizes difference, strips it of its negative connotations, and figuratively represents the possibility of shaping a life free of what is narrowly conceived of as being "natural": (a) "C'est une hardiesse dangereuse et de consequence, outre l'absurde temerité qu'elle traine quant et soy, de mepriser ce que nous ne concevons pas" (I, 27, 181).

Following the description of the child, an interesting anecdote appears in the essay concerning the representation of another type of monster: one who is monstrous within. The text presents in dramatically visual terms a shepherd with the manly feature of a beard but with no sign of genital parts: "Je viens de voir un pastre en Medoc, de trente ans ou environ, qui n'a aucune montre des parties genitales: il a trois trous par où il rend son eau incessamment; il est barbu, a desir, et recherche l'attouchement des femmes" (713). What Montaigne's text portrays is the apparent discrepancy between inside and outside or the gap between the ontological and the biological. In constructing the radical otherness of the shepherd's body, the montaignian text represents a desiring subject whose biological sign of masculinity ("the genitals") is missing. In spite of the presence of the beard, the man's body becomes the *locus* of a lack that leaves no self-determined masculinity in place.

This split in the self demonstrates that the question of gender is not entirely bound up with the question of sexuality alone. If identity does not stem from the biologically given (the natural), then one may infer that sex is clearly not destiny. Here the concept of the monster (derived from the word *monere*, to portend) loses its prognosticating capacities since what we see (that which is visually absent) does not necessarily represent what we get (desire). Suggesting that the equation between the penis and masculinity and the representation of desire is misrecognized, this anecdote teaches us that the only way to read the signs of gender is "à reculons" (713). Montaigne's text thus implies that desire is capable of producing an invisible signifier without the biological means to represent it; the example suggests that even without anything to be seen this absence literally represents the paradoxical presence of the monstrosity of desire.

The shepherd's castration therefore makes him no less a man. Within the chiasmatic logic of the essay, the so-called concept of "normality" is viewed as a consequence of the potency of desire (we are told that he likes to touch women) and not as a biological fact. In this perspective, the absent penis does not foreclose on the functioning of the phallic (an emblem of libidinal [psychic] potency); rather it redefines masculinity as a biologically non-referential version of sexualized thought. Consequently, what makes a man a man is placing him in the position of "being" rather than "having." In other words, the penis does not make the man. If the ontological plenitude of desire displaces the anatomical emptiness of the shepherd, it is because phallic potency is more a psychological than a physical "reality."

Montaigne's Sex-Change Operations

In "De la Force de l'imagination" (I, 21) Montaigne's text focuses on the relationship between psychic activity and sexuality and on how the concept of nature is more a question of mind over matter.[7] The essay is composed of a series of tales each of which carries within it a figural representation of the imagination's power. Attributing anthropomorphic force to the imagination's activity, the essay shows how it is capable of inflicting various forms of violence: "Son impression me perse. . . . Je ne trouve pas estrange qu'elle donne et les fievres et la mort à ceux qui la laissent faire et qui luy applaudissent" (II, 21, 97-98). The imagination, viewed as potentially hostile to the desiring subject, constitutes a threat to its well-being through the illusory force of a destructive drive.

In this essay Montaigne portrays the dangers of the imagination's speculative power as capable of producing fictions comparable to the force of the death instinct. From this perspective the anxiety of anticipation is indeed the cause of the very antagonism inducing the paralysis of the thinking subject. Starting with the Latin quotation "Fortis imaginatio generat casum" (97) ["A strong imagination creates the event"] Montaigne's text presents several case studies in which an overly active and tense imagination submits the ego to an inhibiting and repressive authority. For example, in working too hard to comprehend the nature of madness Gallus Vibius engages his mind in such a state of tension that he quickly becomes the victim of the very object of his reflection: "(a) Gallus Vibius *banda* si bien son ame à comprendre l'essence et les mouvemens de la folie, qu'il emporta son jugement hors de son siege, si qu'onques puis il ne l'y peut remettre" (98). In another tale, a condemned prisoner receives a last minute pardon, but when finally set free to hear his reprieve read aloud he dies out of fear: "Et celuy qu'on debandoit pour luy lire sa grace, se trouva roide mort sur l'eschafaut du seul coup de son imagination" (98). The fear generated by an overactive imagination in each of these cases imprisons the anxious subject in the inner theater of affective quiescence. In both examples, however, Montaigne's text foregrounds the effort required by the imagination to realize the self's extinction. The repeated use of the word "bander"—a term that Cotgrave defines as "to bend, to bind, to tie, and to tighten"—translates the paradoxical result of the imagination's drive to self-expression: the person's subjugation to the omnipotence of thought. However, far from simply limiting the power of the imagination to the paralysis of the subject, Montaigne's text borrows a remarkable example from Ambroise Paré's *Des monstres et des prodiges* to illustrate how the transformative powers of the imagination can enact "sex changes": "Ce n'est pas tant de merveille, que cette sorte d'accident se rencontre frequent: car si l'imagination peut en telles choses, elle est si continuellement et si vigoureusement attacheé à ce subject [sex]" (99). Sexual metamorphoses are realized when conventionally developed gender roles are transgressed. The body, recognized as being anatomically distinct, is nevertheless capable of undergoing transformation through a fashioning of the self that enables one to be perceived as a sexual subject.[8]

In Montaigne's rewriting of Paré's story of Marie-turned-Germain we learn about a twenty-two year old woman who strained herself while jumping, underwent biological metamorphosis by growing a penis, and was finally declared a man:

(b) Passant a Victry le Françoys, je peuz voir un homme que l'Evesque de Soissons avoit nommé Germain en confirmation, lequel tous les habitans de là ont cogneu et veu fille, jusques à l'aage de vingt deux ans, nommée Marie. Il estoit à cett'heure-là fort barbu, et vieil, et point marié. Faisant, dict-il, quelque effort en sautant, ses membres virils se produisirent: et est encore en usage, entre les filles de là, une chanson, par laquelle elles s'entradvertissent de ne faire point de grande enjambées, de peur de devenir garçons, comme Marie Germain. (99)

In this tale of a girl chasing her pig in Vitry we learn that not only is gender variable but so is sex. If gender is a state of mind, then gender construction can miraculously operate sex changes. Although born as Marie, when she acts like a man, the robust activity of her inappropriate behavior, magically inscribes the marks of sexuality on her body. In becoming a man Marie/Germain takes on a particular bodily language that ultimately produces the biological sign of maleness. If gender is actively chosen, then sexuality is passively received as the fatal consequence of thinking difference.

In yet another example that precedes the Marie/Germain story Montaigne quotes a line from Ovid's *Metamorphoses* (IX, 793) that is the conclusion to the tale about a young girl who was born as a female and raised as a boy. Engaged to marry a girl, Iphis, the beneficiary of her mother's prayers, underwent a metamorphosis and eventually got a penis to reflect the man within her: "Vota puer solvit, que foemina voverat Iphis" ["These offerings, vowed by Iphis as a maid, / By Iphis, now a man, are gladly paid"].[9] To become a male thus requires acting like a man. Accordingly, a penis may be the biological mark of masculinity, but it is not the ultimate cause of becoming a man. In this perspective the male member is regarded merely as an appendage, an outward sign, a consequence of habit and the potency generated by the force of the imagination.

Montaigne's "sex change operations" are therefore contingent upon the ways in which we construct ourselves through culturally coded gender roles. As it is represented in the text, gender functions as the variable cultural determinant of sex; it is involved in an ongoing revisionism of corporeal or biological identity. This is perhaps why Montaigne's rewriting of Paré's naturalistic explanation for Marie/Germain's "sex change operation" is so revealing. According to Paré "the reason why women can degenerate into men is because women have as much hidden within the body as men have exposed outside; leaving aside, only, that women don't have so much heat, nor the ability to push out what by the coldness of their temperament is held bound to the interior."[10] Paré's so-called clinical observation is physiologically rooted; sex changes, contingent on the outward movement of the concealed member, depend on bodily heat for their appearance. Of prime importance here is the way in which Paré views sex. Firmly rooted in an androcentric tradition dating back to Greek antiquity, his case study confirms the belief in an archetypal body with men being more capable of realizing perfection.

But Montaigne proceeds otherwise; he adds a moral injunction to the *dénouement* of Paré's story. By treating the man in woman's body as a psychic "reality," the essayist suggests that the only way to control the other within the self is to give women penises as a way to regulate their desire and thereby obliterate the discrepancy between gender and sex:[11] "Pour n'avoir si souvent à rechoir en mesme pensée et aspreté de desir, elle a meilleur compte d'incorporer, une fois pour toutes, cette virile partie aux filles" (99). The consubstantiality that Montaigne seems to be opting for here is merely an allegory of his need to create a more balanced, *natural* self that he conceives as being thoroughly phallocentric in character. Ironically, the gift of the penis undermines women's capacity to think "difference" by biologically reducing the other to the same and discretely establishing the primacy of the male member. Montaigne's representation of the man within the woman ultimately gives birth to a male identity inscribed on a female body only to claim for it the universalizing function of sexual *indifference*.

The centerpiece of Montaigne's essay concerns a discussion of impotence in men and the anxiety associated with sexual performance. In this context, the penis becomes the focal point of the male body, the corporeal *locus* from which manliness might conceivably be "measured" and judged. The fear of inadequacy produces tension in the desiring subject stemming from the inability to conform to a phallic ideal characterized by strength and potency:

> Je suis encore de cette opinion, que ces plaisantes liaisons, dequoy nostre monde se voit si entravé, qu'il ne se parle d'autre chose, ce sont volontiers des impressions de l'apprehension et la crainte. Car je sçay par experience, que tel, de qui je puis respondre, comme de moy mesme, en qui il ne pouvoit choir soupçon aucune de foiblesse, et aussi peu d'enchantement, ayant ouy faire le conte à un sien compagnon, d'une defaillance extraordinaire, en quoy il esoit tombé sur le point, qu'il en avoit le moins de besoin, se trouvant en pareille occasion, l'horreur de ce conte lui vint à coup si rudement frapper l'imagination, qu'il en encourut une fortune pareille. (99-100)

The paradox of impotence is dramatized in the figurative language of the text according to which the "tying" of the imagination corresponds to the idea of a decline or a symbolic fall; stability is depicted as a form of imaginative impotence. The imagination, considered intermittently as the true seat of power, the place where manliness resides, reveals that the phallus (the symbolic) and the penis (the biological) are not always one and the same.[12] Having a penis and being a male is therefore no guarantee of being able to activate the manliness associated with the functioning of the imagination and the generation of libidinal energy.

Within the context of sixteenth-century thought Montaigne's essay seeks to distance itself from the more popularly conceived etiology of impotence.[13] Based on the misogynist traditions associated with superstition, impotence was regarded as having roots in demonology. The ligatures, transcribed by the metaphor of *nouer l'aiguillette*, are defined as that which "empêche[r] le mari ou la femme . . . de se mettre en état d'accomplir, normalement et utilement, les rapprochements sexuels nécessaires à la propagation de l'espèce."[14] However, in Montaigne's essay this symptomology—the impairment of biological functioning—appears to be a consequence of that which is phantasmatically constructed. Through a curious identification with a hypothetical friend, the subject of the narration (the voice representing Montaigne) describes how the fear evoked by the story of another's impotence generates the malady itself: "La veue des angoisses d'autruy m'angoisse materiellement, et a mon sentiment souvent usurpé le sentiment d'un tiers" (97). In constructing the other as a masked version of the same, Montaigne's text reveals how narrative (and language) can move the unsuspecting subject away from the body and paradoxically subjugate it to the effects of a horrific trope of potency that "lui vint à coup si rudement frapper l'imagination, qu'il en encourut une fortune pareille" (100) .

On another level, however, impotence is produced by the conflict between desire and the dangers of intimacy: "(a) Ce malheur [impotence] n'est à craindre qu'aux entreprinses, où nostre ame se trouve outre mesure tandue de desir et respect" (100). If respect is evoked as a hindrance to the realization of desire, it is because respect implies the need to control the excesses of sensuality—the monstrous within the self—and to remain within the boundaries of acceptable behavior. By keeping desire separate from sensuality, Montaigne's text represents the fear of enjoying woman's body and experiencing the pleasures derived from making love. Potency, however, can only be achieved through the relaxation of the imagination ("sa pensée desbrouillée et desbandée, son corps se trouvant en son deu," 100), a phenomenon producing a fluidity of thought that literally "reembodies" the male subject with the "tool" of erectile force. In this context, then, the inflation of the male member operates independently of the biological position of power. Montaigne rewrites male subjectivity here: he brackets tension out of desire and lets the body transcend the masculine paradigm of erotic pursuit for an erotic responsiveness tempered by the moderation of female desire: "Or elles ont tort de nous recueillir de ces contenances mineuses, querelleuses et fuyades, qui nous esteignent en nous allumant" (101).

The "c" version of this essay contains the story of Louis de Foix, count de Guerson who fears impotence but is able to overcome it through a fantasy of empowerment realized by a surrogate object. Montaigne relates the story of a young friend who marries a woman who previously had been courted by someone else. Frightened by the possibility of having his rival cast a spell on him by inflicting him with impotence, the groom expresses great anxiety to Montaigne before the impending wedding. In a gesture of friendship Montaigne offers the friend a gold medal, a valued object, on which "estoient gravées

quelques figures celestes, contre le coup de soleil et oster la douleur de teste"
(100). Beyond having the power to relieve bodily pain, the talisman can also
induce pleasure by miraculously reversing impotence if the proper ceremonial
procedures are adhered to. The gold piece is therefore invested with a surplus
value; the inanity of the trick paradoxically grants it the "poids et reverence"
(101) necessary for generating an inflationary economy of desire. The will may
well be incapable of curing impotence—"on a raison de remarquer l'indocile
liberté de ce membre" (102)—but the power invested by the imagination in the
talisman liberates the paralyzed libido through a cathectic transaction that
temporarily shifts the focus of desire from the body to this mediator of magical
thinking.

On his wedding night, the count believing he is victim of a rival's evil doing
finds himself unable to consummate his marriage: "Il avoit eu l'ame et les
oreilles si battues, qu'il se trouva lié du trouble de son imagination" (101).
Following Montaigne's instructions to tie the gold piece around his waist so
that it lay directly on top of the kidney, the groom "en toute asseurance . . . s'en
retournast à son prix faict" (101). The medal thus enacts a desired effect; and
virility, as represented here, is the consequence of magical thinking motivated
by the psychic investment in a phantasmatic force:

Ces singeries sont le principal de l'effect: nostre pensee ne se pouvant desmesler que moyens si
estranges ne viennent de quelqu'abstruse science. . . . Somme, il fut certain que mes characteres
se trouverent plus Veneriens que Solaires, plus en action qu'en prohibition. (101)

However comic this may appear to be, the realization of potency is nevertheless
the work of the wish itself; the medal takes on a counterfeit value, enabling the
amorous subject to transcend the paralysis of his own non-being. This
identificatory bond takes hold of the subject and engages him in a mimetic
relation whereby the ego temporarily becomes the object of desire. Yet by
displacing the excessive desire for success from the impotent subject to the gold
coin, the text "allows the marital act to regain a beneficial and 'natural'
indifference" (Lyons 141). Ironically, the process of naturalization is realized
through a fiction-making process, represented as a simulacrum of the "real," a
phenomenon that once again blurs the distinction between the biological and
the symbolic.

Montaigne's story thus enacts a dramatic scenario in which the desired
wish is presented as fulfilled by a surrogate object. The subject of the wish—
the bridegroom—has no sense of manliness prior to the enactment of a
mediated fantasy since it is only in fantasy that the desire for potency can be
granted. To be sure, the fantasy attached to the gold medal induces desire and
directs it. Beyond the confines of the patriarchal power structure that depends
on the other for value to be confirmed, the fantasy of potency put forth here

constitutes a simulation of manliness on the part of the desiring subject. Indeed, manliness may be more an illusion and a subterfuge than a "psychic" reality:[15] "Notre discours est capable d'estoffer cent autres mondes et d'en trouver les principes et la contexture. Il ne luy faut ny matiere ny baze; laissez le courre: il bastit aussi bien sur le vuide que sur le plain, et de l'inanité que de matiere, *dare pondus idonea fumo* [Suited to give solidity to smoke]" (III, 11, 1027).

Montaigne's remedy thus naturalizes the artificiality of the cure by giving it potency in the count's imagination: "Il y a des autheurs, desquels la fin c'est dire les evenements. La mienne, si j'y sçavoye advenir, seroit dire sur ce qui peut advenir" (105-06). In recounting this story the essayist seeks to satisfy a potentially "threatened" gender role. If the inadequacies of nature are compensated by the artistry of creative fantasies, it is because manliness is not just a biological issue alone but one of storytelling and narrative verisimilitude. Like the essayist's quest to extract artistry from the disorder of the *monstres fantasques*, the artificially induced cure for impotence represents the attempt to neutralize difference. It acts as a means of controlling nature and paradoxically demonstrates that the "natural" depends as much on the plausibility of fantasy as it does on anything else. We construct nature, then, with imagination, a medium through which reality can assure "being."

The rhetorical acrobatics in Montaigne's text therefore suggest that the self is figured through an Other whose gender differences have their own logic: "Mes fantasies se suyvent, mais par fois c'est de loing, et se regardent, mais d'une veuë oblique" (III, 9, 994). If the penis does not necessarily make the man in the fictions of the *Essais*, it most certainly can reify the image of the man within the woman. To be sure, the workings of nature reveal themselves as much in the unpredictability of the biological as in the consequences generated by the monstrous predictability (from *monere*, the power to portend) of the phantasmatically invested: "Aussi en l'estude que je traitte de noz mœurs et mouvemens, les tesmoignages fabuleux, pourveu qu'ils soient possible, y servent comme les vrais" (105).

Yet, to overcome impotence and the resistances within the self, Montaigne ultimately proposes in a post-1588 annotation to the essay the "talking cure" as a way to moderate tension and give form to the monstrous perception of difference in the spectacle of language: "(c) Il trouva quelque remede à cette resverie par une autre resverie. C'est que, advouant luy mesmes et preschant avant la main cette sienne subjection, la contention de son ame se soulageoit sur ce, qu'apportant ce mal comme attendu, son obligation en amoindrissoit et luy en poisoit moins" (100). By speaking about impotence and incorporating it in the natural order of things, as something to be expected ("ce mal comme attendu"), the desiring subject makes the speaker known for what he is and makes this self-knowledge somehow less monstrous. This "record" of thought embodied in language not only neutralizes difference but it engenders its own set of rules functioning on its own terms: "Les miracles sont selon l'ignorance en quoi nous sommes de la nature, non selon l'etre de la nature. L'asseufaction endort la veuë de nostre jugement" (I, 23, 112). In writing as in speaking the register of thought represents the unevenness of the human condition and suggests that the paralyzing fancies of the imagination can be recuperated and transformed through discursive formations. Only gradually does one come to realize through a series of exemplary narratives that the idealized orderliness that Montaigne sought to impose on his "fantastic monsters" was but a way of transforming what could be perceived as strangeness into a new measure of gender identity: "Je n'ay pas plus faict mon livre que mon livre m'a faict" (II, 18, 648). If the goal of the book was originally to articulate the "natural," the act of essaying has created yet another nature, a more perfect nature, figured in this work of art and destined to tame the monster within: "Me peignant pour autruy, je me suis peint en moi de couleurs plus nettes que n'estoyent les miennes premieres" (665).

Notes

[1] *Les Essais de Montaigne* , édition conforme au texte de l'exemplaire de Bordeaux, préparée par Pierre Villey sous la direction de V.-L. Saulnier (Paris: PUF, 1965).

[2] Randle Cotgrave, *A Dictionarie of the French and English Tongues*, Reproduced from the First Edition, London 1611 (Columbia: U of South Carolina P, 1968), under entry *chimeres* . In *Words in a Corner: Studies in Montaigne's Latin Quotations*, French Forum Monographs 26 (Lexington, KY: French Forum, 1981), Mary B. McKinley discusses the agonistic encounter between Montaigne's essay on idleness and Epistle 2 of Horace's *Ars poetica*. By focusing on the Latin quotation *velut aegri somnia, / vanae Finguntur species*, she suggests that Montaigne violates Horace's warning against trying to combine "the wild with the tame" in a work of art (37-40). Michel Jeanneret's recent commentary concerning the excessive nature of Rabelais's writing is in some ways applicable to Montaigne as well: "il [l'excès] parasite les grilles interprétatives étroites, il déstabilise la lecture et, du même coup la stimule. Se joue ainsi le devenir de l'œuvre. L'excédent des sens possibles fait de la lecture une opération sans fin—recherche d'une totalisation irréalisable, défi permanent qui maintient vivante la productivité du texte." "Débordements rabelaisiens," *Nouvelle Revue de Psychanalyse* 43 (1991) 123.

[3] See Lawrence D. Kritzman, "Montaigne's Family Romance," in *The Rhetoric of Sexuality and the Literature of the French Renaissance* (Cambridge: Cambridge UP, 1991) 73-92 and Glyn P. Norton, *Montaigne and the Introspective Mind* (The Hague: Mouton, 1975) 28-32.

[4] "*Desreglement* is the menace of emasculation, the threat of irresolution that is an ever present danger and that signals the dissolution of the only thing 'really in our power'—our will—and thus, to the extent that being is identified with manliness and steadfastness, the dissolution of being itself." Robert D. Cottrell, *Sexuality/Textuality: A Study of the Fabric of Montaigne's Essais* (Columbus: Ohio State UP, 1981) 25. Cottrell sees in Montaigne's text a binary tension between "the masculine ethics of stiffness and the feminine ethics of laxness" (39).

[5] "We can say . . . that Montaigne's monster is that which is shown and which shows itself, that which shows what it is, that it is." Richard L. Regosin, "Montaigne's Monstrous Confession," *Montaigne Studies* 1 (1989) 77. While Regosin's analysis deals with the "play of language," I have

chosen to focus more on the issue of gender representation. Gisèle Mathieu-Castellani's "L'essai, corps monstrueux," in *Montaigne: l'écriture de l'essai* (Paris: PUF, 1988) 221-40 examines Montaigne's text as an emblem for the multilayered form the essay takes. She pays particular attention to narrative structure and intertextuality and the function of quotation. See also Fausta Garavini, "La Présence des 'monstres' dans l'élaboration des Essais: à propos de I, iii, 'Nos affections s'emportent au-delà de nous,'" in *Le Parcours des Essais: Montaigne 1588-1988*, eds. Marcel Tetel and G. Mallary Masters (Paris: Aux Amateurs de Livres, 1989) 33-46.

⁶ "Difference is here converted into an effect of distance. Life becomes a kind of gigantic anamorphic painting that we can never see from the proper distance." John D. Lyons, *Exemplum: The Rhetoric of Example in Early Modern France and Italy* (Princeton: Princeton UP, 1989) 137.

⁷ For a thematic approach to the imagination see Dora Pollachek, "Montaigne and Imagination: The Dynamics of Power and Control," in *Le Parcours des Essais* 135-45.

⁸ In Foucault's late work sexuality is conceived as a work of art. Michel Foucault, *Le Souci de soi* (Paris: Gallimard, 1984).

⁹ Ovid, *Metamorphoses*, trans. A.D. Melville (Oxford: Oxford UP, 1986) 224.

¹⁰ Ambroise Paré, *On Monsters and Marvels*, trans. Janis L. Pallister (Chicago: U of Chicago P, 1982) 32.

¹¹ My analyses here are different then those found in Thomas Laqueur's *Making Sex: Body and Gender from the Greeks to Freud* (Cambridge: Harvard UP, 1990) which focuses on the concept of the "one-sex model" in early modern texts. Laqueur tends to read Montaigne's allegorical examples in a somewhat literal fashion. In an otherwise remarkable study, I find some indecision in his movement between the real and the representational. Montaigne may well "refuse to come to rest on the question of what is imaginative and what is real (128)" but isn't the representation of the "real" in the essay just another level of the fiction making process or what might be termed an allegory of the essayist's own gender quest?

¹² "For the phallus is a signifier, a signifier whose function in the intra-subjective economy of the analysis, lifts the veil perhaps from the function it performed in the mysteries. For it is the signifier destined to designate as a whole the effects of the signified, in that the signifier conditions them by its presence as a signifier." Jacques Lacan, "The Signification of the Phallus," in *Ecrits: A Selection* , trans. Alan Sheridan (New York: Norton, 1977) 285.

¹³ For a discussion of the impotence topos within the context of cultural history see Lee R. Entin-Bates, "Montaigne's Remarks on Impotence," *Modern Language Notes* 91 (1976) 640-54.

¹⁴ Henri Gelin, "Les Noueries d'aiguillette en Poitou," *Revue des Etudes Rabelaisiennes* 8 (1910) 122. For the physician Ambroise Paré impotence can have demonological roots: "Nouer l'esguillette, et les paroles ne font rien, mais c'est l'austuce du diable. Et ceulx qui la nouent ne le peuvent faire sans avoir eu convention avec le diable, qui est une meschancé damnable." "Des Noueurs d'esguillette," in *Des monstres et des prodiges*, éd. Jean Céard (Geneva: Droz, 1971) 100.

¹⁵ I have discussed other aspects of manliness in Montaigne's *Essais* in "Pedagogical Graffiti and the Rhetoric of Conceit," in *The Rhetoric of Sexuality* 57-72.

François Rigolot

Sur des vers de Montaigne:
La Boétie en Béotie[1]

"Beotia me genuit"
Plutarque[2]

Nuls mieux peut-être qu'Alfred Glauser et Floyd Gray n'ont parlé du style de l'amitié idéale chez Montaigne. On sait que, sous la plume de l'auteur des *Essais*, cette "souveraine et maistresse amitié" (I, 28, 190b) prend des dimensions fabuleuses dont seul un style sublime saurait rendre le caractère proprement "divin" (I, 28, 190a).[3] L'écriture de l'amitié pose donc un problème majeur: "Comment *dire* l'unique," en effet, quand "toute la technique des *Essais* [est] fondée sur le multiple?"[4] Chez le partisan du *distinguo* et des incessantes pesées l'éloge du sentiment parfait ne peut être qu'un paradoxe.[5] Le jugement doit arrêter son balancier devant la "quintessence" indicible, car l'amitié de Montaigne pour La Boétie ne peut se dire que par la tautologie: "par ce que c'estoit luy; parce que c'estoit moy" (I, 28, 188c).[6] La fusion des cœurs emprunte le discours d'une "arithmétique du sublime" (l'idée de deux en un) qui n'est pas sans rapport avec le mythe néoplatonicien de l'origine selon la formule qu'en avait donnée Marsile Ficin dans le *Commentaire sur le Banquet*: "iste in illo, ille in isto vivit."[7]

Cependant on sait que Montaigne a voulu célébrer son défunt ami plus concrètement, conformément à l'engagement qu'il avait pris sur son lit de mort, en se faisant l'exécuteur testamentaire de ses œuvres.[8] Il publia, en particulier, les pièces poétiques françaises de La Boétie en deux fois: d'abord vingt-cinq sonnets d'amour sous le titre de *Vers françois*, en 1571, puis les fameux vingt-neuf sonnets donnés à la suite du chapitre "De l'amitié" (I, 29, 196a).[9] Dans le texte des *Essais* Montaigne ne citera que rarement son ami: on n'y relève en tout que cinq vers latins (I, 14, 56a & II, 12, 493a) et neuf français (I, 10, 39a & III, 13, 1068-9b). La plus longue citation se trouve à la fin du dernier livre, dans le chapitre "De l'experience," au moment où Montaigne parle de la "chasse de cognoissance," des "inquisitions" et des "poursuites sans termes" de l'"esprit genereux"—avec ce va-et-vient typique de Montaigne entre les valences positives et négatives de la *libido sciendi* et de la *libido interpretandi* (III, 13, 1068-69bc).[10] Nous nous interrogerons d'abord ici sur la fonction que jouent ces vers, soudain resurgis, de La Boétie dans l'économie de ce passage si connu des *Essais*.

Le début du dernier chapitre des *Essais* (III, 13) reflète une préoccupation majeure de Montaigne dont il nous avait déjà longuement entretenu dans l'*Apologie de Raimond Sebond* (II, 12). Tout en célébrant les merveilleuses ressources de l'esprit humain, il ne veut pas se leurrer sur les errances où conduit le désir insatiable de connaissance.[11] Le thème humaniste de la *dignitas hominis* se trouve inévitablement mêlé à celui, beaucoup moins optimiste, de la *curiositas hominis* dans un discours dont la duplicité n'a pas manqué de séduire les plus fins lecteurs.[12]

Or il semble qu'au début de son ultime chapitre, Montaigne, après avoir noté l'émiettement des lois et déploré l'opacité des gloses, ait voulu souligner l'importance qu'il accorde au trouble de ce "curieux désir" en citant huit vers de son ami poète. Rappelons ce texte maintes fois glosé, dans la dernière version revue et corrigée par l'auteur:

Nul esprit genereux ne s'arreste en soy: il pretend tousjours et va outre ses forces; il a des eslans au delà de ses effects; s'il ne s'avance et ne se presse et ne s'accule et ne se choque, il n'est vif qu'à demy; ses poursuites sont sans terme, et sans forme; son aliment c'est admiration, chasse, ambiguïté. Ce que declaroit assez Apollo, parlant tousjours à nous doublement, obscurement et obliquement, ne nous repaissant pas, mais nous amusant et embesongnant. C'est un mouvement irregulier, perpetuel, sans patron, et sans but. Ses inventions s'eschauffent, se suyvent, et s'entreproduisent l'une l'autre.

> *Ainsi voit l'on, en un ruisseau coulant,*
> *Sans fin l'une eau après l'autre roulant,*
> *Et tout de rang, d'un eternel conduict,*
> *L'une suit l'autre, et l'une l'autre fuyt.*
> *Par cette-cy celle-là est poussée,*
> *Et cette-cy par l'autre est devancée:*
> *Tousjours l'eau va dans l'eau, et tousjours est-ce*
> *Mesme ruisseau, et tousjours eau diverse.*
> (III, 13, 1068-69)

La citation de La Boétie, empruntée avec quelques retouches à l'édition que Montaigne avait donnée des *Vers françois* de son ami en 1571, mérite d'être relevée par son apparition inattendue en ce dernier chapitre du dernier livre. L'ombre de La Boétie devait d'ailleurs resurgir encore dans un "allongeail" au dernier chapitre du second livre des *Essais* (II, 37). Mais ici Montaigne ne se contente pas d'évoquer le souvenir de l'ami disparu ([les médecins] "me tuarent un amy qui valoit mieux que tous, tant qu'ils sont," 754c); il cite les vers mêmes de celui dont il appréciait tant la poésie qu'il en avait assuré la publication posthume. Qu'on se rapporte à la dédicace des *Vers françois* de La Boétie à Paul de Foix:

De ma part, Monsieur, ce n'est pas mon gibbier de juger de telles choses, mais j'ay ouy dire à personnes qui s'entendent en sçavoir, que ces vers sont non seulement dignes de se presenter en place marchande: mais d'avantage, qui s'arrestera à la beauté & richesse des inventions, qu'ils sont pour le subject, autant charnus, pleins & moëlleux qu'il en soit encore veu en nostre langue. . . . En gentillesse d'imaginations, en nombre de saillies, pointes et traicts, je ne pense point que nuls autres leur passent devant.[13]

Sans doute pouvait-on s'attendre à ce que, dans le contexte juridique du début du chapitre "De l'experience," Montaigne pensât à La Boétie, magistrat comme lui et avec qui il s'était sans doute longuement entretenu du problème de la multiplicité des lois. C'est d'ailleurs en tant qu'ancien "Conseiller du Roy en sa Court de Parlement à Bordeaux" qu'il avait présenté son ami poète à ses lecteurs en 1571.[14] Cependant ces vers prennent un sens très différent lorsqu'on les replace dans leur contexte original. Dans l'édition des *Vers françois* procurée par Montaigne, en effet, la thématique héracliteenne de l'écoulement n'est nullement mise au service du caractère indécidable de l'interprétation. Le "doubte" n'a pas de place dans le mouvement toujours renouvelé de l'"eternel conduict." Dans la lignée des poètes de la Pléiade, qu'il admirait, La Boétie s'adresse en fait au problème de la création littéraire en termes essentiellement positifs: avec une promesse de renouveau en la moderne saison.

Voyons le contexte. Les vers que cite Montaigne appartiennent à un long poème d'escorte dans lequel La Boétie présentait à Marguerite de Carle, sa future épouse, la traduction qu'il avait faite des "Plaintes de Bradamante" de l'Arioste.[15] Connaissant la satire acerbe que Joachim du Bellay avait lancée contre les traducteurs dans la *Deffense et Illustration de la langue françoyse*, le présentateur devait s'entourer de précautions.[16] Il commence par répéter les propos malveillants du célèbre manifeste. Les premiers vers donnent le ton:

> Jamais plaisir je n'ay prins à changer
> En nostre langue aucun œuvre estranger:
> Car à tourner d'une langue estrangere,
> La peine est grande et la gloire est legere.[17]

Cependant, en dépit du lourd passif qui grève le travail du traducteur, notre poète va se mettre à la tâche pour répondre au vœu de sa bien aimée; ce qui nous vaut un joli compliment:

> Mais à ce coup, par ton commandement,
> Je t'ay tourné le dueil de Bradamant:
> Bien qu'à tourner ma Muse soit craintive,
> Quand tu le veus, si faut il qu'elle suive.
>   (vv. 136-39)

Ce travail de "tourneur" (v. 26), c'est-à-dire de traducteur, n'est donc qu'un pis-aller, habilement exploité à des fins amoureuses. En revanche, ce qui domine le discours préfaciel de La Boétie c'est l'insistance sur la qualité d'*autheur* avec la promesse de "gloire" qui lui est associé ("Tousjours l'*autheur* vers soy la gloire ameine, / Et le *tourneur* n'en retient que la peine," vv. 25-26). Etre *autheur*, au sens fort, c'est être créateur dans toute sa plénitude. Ici encore la préférence avouée pour le poète au détriment du "tourneur" suit les prescriptions de du Bellay. Dans le *Discours de la Servitude volontaire* La Boétie manifestait son enthousiasme pour l'entreprise de la nouvelle école, célébrant "nostre poësie françoise . . . faite tout à neuf par nostre Ronsard, nostre Baïf, nostre du Bellay, qui en cela avancent bien tant nostre langue que j'ose esperer que bien tost les Grecs ni les Latins n'auront gueres pour ce regard devant nous, sinon possible le droit d'aisnesse."[18]

La revendication d'une identité poétique se profile donc sur une toile de fond de préoccupations d'époque: "J'ayme trop mieux de *moymesmes* escrire / Quelque escript *mien*, encore qu'il soit pire."[19] On croit entendre déjà Montaigne quand il nous dira vouloir peindre "non un visage parfaict, mais le mien" (I, 26, 148a). Jalouse déclaration d'autonomie qui se double d'un défi à la critique: "Si mal *j*'escris n'ayant prins de personne / A nul qu'à *moy* le blasme *je* n'en donne" (vv. 7-8). Ce fier aveu de responsabilité se retrouvera aussi, amplifié, dans les *Essais* lorsque Montaigne désignera les défauts de son ouvrage sous le nom d'"escrivaillerie" (III, 9, 946b)—avec tout un cortège de synonymes pittoresques: "fagottage" (II, 37, 758a), "fricassée" (III, 13, 1079b), "galimafrée" (I, 46, 276a), ou quelque "marqueterie mal jointe" (III, 9, 964c). Quoi qu'il en soit, sous la plume du poète "Honneur" et "Gloire" sont associés à la recherche d'une invention individuelle, qui ne doive rien à d'éventuels prédécesseurs, si illustres soient-ils: "Donc qu'à *trouver de soymesme* on se range, / Si l'on a faim de la belle louange" (vv. 47-48). Seul compte véritablement le jugement de la postérité; et l'on aura l'ambition d'écrire "Quelque œuvre grand qui defende sa vie / Maugré la dent du temps et de l'envie" (vv. 51-52).

Dans un second mouvement La Boétie s'en prend alors aux théories poétiques de l'invention qui privilégient les Anciens par rapport aux Modernes et retirent à ces derniers tout espoir de rivaliser avec "ces vieux champions-là" (I, 26, 147c). Prêtant la parole à des adversaires imaginaires, il dénonce le tableau que voudraient nous peindre ceux-ci de la défaite des modernes. A cette fin il commence par recourir ironiquement à l'image de la course olympique dont avaient tant usé et abusé les poètes de l'Antiquité:

> L'un dit qu'il faut qu'on quitte l'avantage
> D'inventer bien à ceux du premier aage;
> Que les premiers bienheureux s'avancerent,
> Et que du jeu le pris ils emporterent:
> Si que par eulx la palme jà gaignée

> A nul meshuy ne peult estre donnée,
> Et desormais que sa peine on doit plaindre,
> A suivre ceux que l'on ne peut attaindre.
> (vv. 55-62)

Ronsard avait déjà répondu à cet argument dans la préface aux *Odes* de 1550 et dans le "Vœu" placé en tête des *Amours* de 1552. Si La Boétie rouvre la polémique de l'antériorité c'est pour se moquer du poncif éculé dont osent encore se servir les adulateurs des Anciens. Ceux-ci auraient-ils gagné la palme? Qu'on ne vienne pas nous en rebattre les oreilles; que nos poètes modernes essaient plutôt de les rejoindre, sinon de les dépasser!

Changeant de registre d'images, La Boétie répond ensuite à l'argument selon lequel la source de l'inspiration poétique aurait été finalement tarie. Là encore le thème est loin d'être nouveau. Des générations de poètes ont fait jaillir la fontaine des Muses du sabot de Pégase. Mais c'est justement pour prendre à revers la position insoutenable des "révérents de l'antiquaille," comme les appelait Rabelais, que La Boétie choisit de traiter sur le mode burlesque une mythologie dûment autorisée:

> L'autre se plaint qu'en la *source tarie*
> Ores on tire à grand'peine la lie,
> Et ne croit pas que grand profit on face
> A *labourer* une terre si lasse:
> Quand *tout est prins*, qu'il se faut contenter,
> Si l'on n'en a, d'en pouvoir *emprunter*;
> Que les *premiers* en la saison meilleure
> Feirent soigneux la *moisson de bonne heure*,
> Et à l'envy prinrent la *cruche pleine*
> Dans le *surjon* de la *neufve fontaine*:
> Nous, tard venus en ce temps mal-heureux,
> Faisons en *vain* la *recherche* apres eulx.
> (vv. 63-74)

Le topos de la source était bien connu en France depuis les tapageuses sorties polémiques de la Pléiade.[20] Ronsard, dans l'*Ode à Michel de L'Hospital*, avait magnifiquement recréé le mythe antique dans un discours d'apparat qui décrétait le retour des Muses sur terre. La Boétie fait écho aux détracteurs du somptueux geste ronsardien; en mimant leurs objections il s'amuse à entasser des métaphores hétéroclites: source tarie, emprunts forcés, moisson prématurée. Le lecteur ne peut que sourire devant l'évocation de ces anciens munis d'une cruche et armés d'une faux, qui se transforment en redoutables moissonneurs-puisatiers. Qui eût cru qu'après leur passage l'herbe ne dût repousser sous leurs pieds?

A cette double formulation burlesque d'une propagande défaitiste de l'invention—celle de la course perdue et de la source tarie—La Boétie entend offrir une solution de rechange. Avec assurance, il repousse énergiquement les soupirs inutiles, appelant ses contemporains au travail poétique. On admirera la vigueur du coup d'envoi:

> *Mais je croy* que ceste plainte vaine
> Ne vient pour vray que de craindre la peine:
> (Car *pour certain jamais* aux siens la Muse
> Quelque chanson nouvelle ne refuse).
>
> (vv. 75-78)

Sur un ton résolu il dénonce les Cassandre de l'épuisement ("Or est ce bien un grand abus, s'on cuide / Que d'inventer [c'est-à-dire qu'*à force* d'inventer] la *fontaine soit vuide*," vv. 99-100). L'esprit humain est en perpétuel ressourcement (c'est ce que Montaigne appellera un "esprit genereux," 1068c). Recourant à la figure hyperbolique de l'*adunaton*, La Boétie déclare qu'on ne saurait épuiser la créativité humaine pas plus qu'on ne peut atteindre les bas-fonds des océans ("De voir le *fond* on ne doit presumer / De nostre esprit, ny le *fond* de la mer," vv. 101-02). On assiste alors à la réaffirmation solennelle de principes en accord avec l'élan optimiste de l'humanisme triomphant:

> Des grands discours la *semence infinie*
> D'œuvre nouveau pour jamais est fournie.
> Nostre esprit prend en sa *source eternelle*
> Or une chose, or une autre nouvelle:
> Or ceste cy, or ceste là il treuve,
> Et puis encor une autre toute neufve.
>
> (vv. 103-08)

Montaigne parlera un langage semblable à propos de son propre ouvrage dans un *allongeail* au chapitre "Considération sur Cicéron": "Qui voudra esplucher un peu ingenieusement [mes histoires], en produira *infinis* Essais . . . Elles portent souvent, hors de mon propos, la *semence* d'une matiere plus riche et plus hardie" (I, 40, 251c). Mais ici c'est l'auteur même qui se place en position de source originelle: en lui réside la semence infinie, de lui découle la source éternelle. On pense, avec l'arrogance en moins, au Ronsard de la *Responce aux predicans* dont les fameux vers réaffirment une plénitude dont tous les autres poètes français sont tributaires: "Car de ma plenitude / Vous estes tous remplis . . . / Vous estes mes ruisseaux, je suis vostre fonteine / Et plus vous m'espuisés, plus ma fertile veine / Repoussant le sablon, jette une source d'eaux / D'un surjon eternel pour vous autres ruisseaux."[21]

C'est alors que se placent les vers de La Boétie cités par Montaigne au chapitre "De l'experience." Nous les reproduisons ici d'après l'édition originale de 1571 en notant entre crochets les modifications apportées par Montaigne au texte de son ami:

> Ainsi voit l'on en un ruisseau coulant,
> Sans fin l'une eau après l'autre coulant, [*roulant*]
> Et tout de rang, d'un eternel conduit, [*conduict*]
> L'une suit l'autre, et l'une l'autre fuit. [*fuyt*]
> Par ceste cy celle là est poussée,
> Et ceste cy par une autre avancée: [*par l'autre est devancée*]
> Tousjours l'eau va dans l'eau, et tousjours est-ce
> Mesme ruisseau, et tousjours eau diverse.
> (vv. 109-16)

On peut se demander pourquoi Montaigne a choisi de citer ici ces huit vers sur la source perpétuelle de l'inspiration. Dans le contexte du chapitre "De l'experience" où il place ce passage c'est le problème de l'interprétation qui le préoccupe. La prolifération des lois et des gloses l'inquiète: non seulement elle ne parviendra jamais à rendre compte de la variété des cas possibles, mais elle ne fait que disséminer le sens, le pluraliser, l'éloigner donc de la plénitude de la source originelle: "Je ne sçay qu'en dire, mais il se sent par experience que tant d'interpretations dissipent la verité et la rompent" (III, 13, 1067b). Montaigne en vient alors à parler de sa propre expérience en tant qu'écrivain. Il établit un rapport entre ses essais et les gloses proliférantes, reconnaissant non sans effroi que son écriture ne saurait se contenir, qu'elle est toujours à la fois en deçà et au delà de ce qu'elle cherche à représenter.[22]

Or, comme nous l'avons vu, si l'on replace les vers de La Boétie dans leur contexte originel, il est bien évident qu'ils ne font pas référence à quelque indétermination angoissante du sens liée aux incertitudes de l'interprétation. Au contraire, ils témoignent d'une conviction optimiste en l'intarrissable source de l'invention: la plénitude des origines est là à notre portée; l'eau ne manque pas; allons puiser gaiement à l'inspiration. Ce que retient, en revanche, Montaigne des vers de son ami c'est que cette hereuse croyance des modernes est elle-même formulée par le biais de la métaphore ambiguë de l'écoulement. Pour lui il y a quelque chose d'inquiétant dans cet infini "rhéisme" héraclitéen. Les mots de La Boétie ont changé de sens: "ruisseau coulant sans fin," "l'une eau après l'autre," "eternel conduict," "l'une suit l'autre," "l'une l'autre fuyt," etc: la répétition et la circularité des expressions donnent le vertige. C'est le règne de la tautologie: "l'eau va dans l'eau." Et le paradoxe veut que toute altérité et toute diversité se résorbe dans le gouffre du "tousjours" et du "mesme" ("mesme ruisseau et tousjours eau diverse," v. 116).

Pour satisfaire à son parti pris Montaigne va jusqu'à supprimer la conclusion logique de l'original. Aux vers 127-28 du poème de La Boétie on lisait: "*Doncques* je croy qu'il ne faut jamais craindre / Que d'inventer le fond on puisse attaindre" (vv. 127-28). Le "Nolite timere" rassurant du poète est remplacé par un propos désabusé sur les glossateurs: "Il y a plus affaire à interpreter les interpretations qu'à interpreter les choses, et plus de livres sur les livres que sur autre subject: nous ne faisons que nous entregloser" (III, 13, 1069b). Montaigne semble avoir détourné les vers de La Boétie de leur sens pour les plier aux besoins de son propre discours. A l'encontre des espérances fallacieuses d'un progressisme béat, l'auteur des *Essais* se sert ironiquement des vers de son ami pour faire état de son profond scepticisme. *Cave curiositatem!* L'injonction moralisante avait sa place dans l'"Apologie de Raimond Sebond" (II, 12). Le paradoxe veut ici que l'euphorie du savoir soit mise en cause dans les vers mêmes où elle se déploie. Au delà de l'hommage au poète et à l'ami disparu, la citation apparaît désormais, sous sa forme pervertie, comme l'exemple même de l'indétermination du sens.[23]

Cette appropriation perverse des vers de La Boétie ne prend pourtant tout son sens que par rapport à un autre intertexte. En effet Montaigne ne cite son ami qu'après une allusion aux oracles ambigus d'Apollon. Rappelons le passage:

[c] Nul esprit genereux ne s'arreste en soy; . . . [b] ses poursuites sont sans terme, et sans forme; son aliment c'est [c] admiration, chasse, [b] ambiguïté. Ce que declaroit assez Apollo, parlant à nous tousjours doublement, obscurement et obliquement, ne nous repaissant pas, mais nous amusant et embesongnant. (1068)

Or deux textes de Plutarque éclairent singulièrement le rôle et la fonction de cette référence aux vaticinations du fameux "Apollo *Loxias*" ou "oblique" des Anciens: un opuscule moral, le *De Garrulitate*, traduit par Amyot sous le titre "Du trop parler," et un dialogue pythique, le *De Pythiae Oraculis*, qui a pour thème le problème de l'évolution des modes d'expression oraculaires et dont Amyot traduit le titre complet: "Pourquoy la Prophetisse Pythie ne rend plus ses oracles en vers."[24]

Dans le *De Garrulitate* Plutarque fait une satire mordante des "babillards" dont les intempérances de langage sont à la fois dangereuses, odieuses et ridicules.[25] Nous avons la preuve que Montaigne avait cet opuscule en tête, dans la traduction d'Amyot, lorsqu'il écrivit son dernier chapitre: l'anecdote de Carnéade, qui parlait trop et trop fort (1066b), en est directement tirée (96C, 233-34). Voici le texte d'Amyot:

Aussi estoient ceux qui parloient peu jadis en grande estime emprès les anciens. [De là] sur les portes du temple d'Apollo Pythien . . . ces briefves sentences: "Cognoy toy-mesmes" . . . tant ils ont prisé un parler simple et rond, contenant soubs peu de paroles une sentence bonne et bien tournée. Mais Apollo luy-mesmes n'est-il pas grand amateur de briefveté et succint en ses oracles? C'est pourquoi on l'appelle *Loxias*, qui est à dire oblique, pourautant qu'il aime mieulx parler peu que clairement." (94H-95A, 222-23).

On comprend pourquoi Montaigne a pu s'intéresser à l'exemplarité des cas cités par Plutarque dans cet opuscule. Au début de son chapitre il a lui aussi pour sujet d'"'arrester le babil," de limiter le nombre des lois, de mettre un terme aux commentaires, aux gloses et aux interprétations, même si cette infinie diversité reflète parfois un noble désir intellectuel, la "chasse de cognoissance" (1068b).

L'autre intertexte plutarquien est d'un intérêt encore plus considérable pour notre propos. Dans le *De Pythiae Oraculis* on nous propose une théorie qui explique "pourquoy la Prophetisse Pythie ne rend plus ses oracles en vers." (XXIII-XXIV).[26] Notons que, dès le début du chapitre "De l'experience," Montaigne avait fait mention de l'exemple de Delphes à propos des similitudes (1065b).[27] Mais c'est surtout la fin du dialogue pythique qui nous intéressera ici, parce qu'on y trouve une théorie de l'évolution parallèle des oracles et de la société. Il fut un temps à Delphes, nous dit Plutarque, où l'on ne connaissait que les vers, la musique et les chants et où Apollon favorisait la poésie dans les oracles de la Pythie:

Luy mesme [Apollon] leur donnoit des imaginations & conceptions de poësie, & aidoit à poulser en avant ce qu'il y avoit de braverie & de doctrine, comme chose bien seante alors, & qui estoit grandement prisée et estimée.[28]

Mais le cours des choses allait changer. Et Plutarque retrace en l'approuvant l'évolution d'une société qui devait peu à peu bannir tout ce qu'elle considérait comme superflu dans ses usages et ses rituels. On supprima les coiffures richement ornées et les longues tuniques luxueusement fourrées. On prit l'habitude de considérer l'absence de recherche et d'affectation comme un ornement supérieur au faste et au raffinement. Le langage devait subir une transformation identique vers le dépouillement. La poésie fut finalement "bannie du trépied" et l'on rendit désormais les oracles en toute clarté. La conclusion de Plutarque est significative:

Ostant aux oracles les vers, les mots estranges, les circunlocutions [périphrases], & l'obscurité, [Apollon] apprit [à la Pythie] à parler à ceux qui venoient à l'oracle, *comme les lois devisent aux citez* [un langage analogue à celui que les lois tiennent aux cités], . . . en sorte qu'elle fust pleine de sens et persuasifve. (Amyot 634v C.)

Or que se passe-t-il dans la France de Montaigne? Celui-ci nous parle justement de la situation des lois au début de son chapitre (III, 13). La multiplicité des lois a fait perdre au langage juridique sa transparence et son efficacité:

Nous avons en France plus de loix que tout le reste du monde ensemble, et plus qu'il n'en faudroit à reigler tous les mondes d'Epicurus.. . . Qu'ont gaigné nos legislateurs à choisir cent mille espèces et faicts particuliers, et y attacher cent mille loix? (1066b)

Une fois encore, comme on le lisait dans le *De Garrulitate*, "il faut ficher le pied et arrester le babil" (cf. Aulotte 233 [96B]). La multiplication des lois et leur subdivision croissante—outre le fait qu'elles ne peuvent rendre compte de l'infinie variété des actions humaines—n'ont fait que rendre le langage "obscur et non intelligible" (1066b). Il est nécessaire de revenir à des lois "simples et generales." Abandonnons ces divisions maniaques de peur d'être "enfrasquez et embrouillez en l'infinité des figures" (1067b). Nous en sommes arrivés à une situation paradoxale: par un souci de trop grande clarté, nos législateurs en sont arrivés à "subdiviser les subtilités" et à rendre tout confus. Sénèque avait bien vu le problème, ajoutera Montaigne en se relisant: "*Confusum* est quidquid usque in pulverem sectum est" (1067c).

Il y a donc eu une véritable perversion de la logigue du *distinguo*. En cherchant systématiquement à rendre clair le langage, on en a finalement renforcé l'obscurité. L'évolution a conduit à un état de choses que ne pouvait prévoir Plutarque. Pour vouloir trop en dire (en oubliant l'avertissement du *De Garrulitate*) on a abouti à une situation pire que celle que l'on voulait éviter. Un nouvel "*Apollo Loxias*" est né paradoxalement du désir d'en finir avec l'obscurité prétendue des lois. Relisons donc le *De Pythiae Oraculis*: nous nous apercevrons que nous en sommes revenus à la Delphes des premiers temps.

Il convient dès lors de se demander quel type de rapport entretiennent ces réminiscences plutarquiennes, par le biais de la traduction d'Amyot, avec la citation de La Boétie et quelle importance a cette conjonction d'intertextes pour notre lecture de Montaigne. Notons d'abord que le problème que posent les vers de La Boétie (la source de l'inspiration est-elle tarie?) se trouve déjà clairement exposé par Plutarque dans son dialogue pythique. Par deux fois, en effet, Diogénianos, le jeune étranger, interroge son maître sur l'évolution des oracles de Delphes (Amyot 629r C et 631v H). Si la Pythie a cessé de prophétiser en vers, demande-t-il, n'est-ce pas "que le vent qui l'inspiroit est estaint, & la force & puissance faillie?"[29] Autrement dit, ne sommes-nous pas arrivés au seuil d'une époque de stérilité?

Dans leur contexte original les vers de La Boétie, nous l'avons vu, devaient être lus dans le sens d'une réaffirmation du pouvoir de la poésie moderne. Comme les membres de la Pléiade, ses devanciers, l'ami poète était convaincu que la source de l'inspiration continuait à couler; et ses propres vers s'en voulaient la preuve: "Des grands discours pour la semence *infinie* / D'œuvre nouveau *pour jamais* est fournie" (vv.103-04). Or, relus à la lumière des *Œuvres morales* de Plutarque, ces vers doivent maintenant s'interpréter différemment. C'est du moins ce que veut nous faire entendre le Montaigne de la fin des *Essais*. A Delphes comme à Bordeaux, semble-t-il nous dire, la Pythie ne rend plus ses oracles en vers. C'est que les temps ont changé: les hommes et la société aussi. La Boétie est mort, les "troubles" et les "nouvelletez" ont fait oublier l'euphorie confiante des années d'amitié. Aux œuvres de jeunesse ont succédé les essais de l'âge mûr. A "l'art de conférer" des vivants a fait place l'entre-glose momifiante des textes.[30] Montaigne en est réduit à constater, comme Diogénianos, le jeune étranger de Plutarque, l'évolution historique qui problématise la "resurgence de l'écoulement" et jette le doute sur le "surjon de la neufve fontaine" (v. 72). L'eau tonifiante de la source des Muses est devenue cet océan fatal où se noient les chiens d'Esope:

Non guiere autrement qu'il advint aux chiens d'Esope, lesquels, descouvrant quelque apparence de corps mort floter en mer, et ne le pouvant approcher, entreprindrent de boire cette eau, d'assecher le passage, et s'y estouffarent. (1068b)[31]

Ainsi la double référence, boétienne à la "fontaine non tarie" et béotienne à la fin des "oracles en vers," éclaire-t-elle singulièrement le propos montaignien. Elle permet de mettre en évidence une tension dans la conscience de l'écrivain. Comme toujours Montaigne ne peut se dire "autheur" directement et positivement. Il lui faut un détour—c'est par là qu'il se singularise—et il trouve ce détour en plaçant la citation de son ami dans un double contexte ancien qui lui permet d'admettre ce qu'autrement il n'aurait pu reconnaître ouvertement, dans la pleine clarté d'un discours univoque. Montaigne arrive ainsi à s'inscrire, via La Boétie et Plutarque, dans une histoire de la création littéraire: celle qui célèbre l'inspiration poétique tout en prenant acte du passage historique de la poésie à la prose—passage qu'accomplit le prosateur Montaigne en acceptant d'être le "successeur" du poète La Boétie. On comprend alors pourquoi l'itinéraire du chapitre "De l'experience" se termine par une prière à Apollon:

> *Frui paratis et valido mihi*
> *Latoe, dones, et, precor, integra*
> *Cum mente, nec turpem senectam*
> *Degere, nec cythara carentem.*[32]

Comme dans le parcours suivi par les visiteurs de Delphes dans le dialogue de Plutarque, le dernier chapitre—et avec lui l'ensemble des *Essais*—doit aboutir au temple du dieu pythien: Montaigne ne peut se reconnaître "autheur," qu'en transportant, pour ainsi dire, La Boétie en Béotie.[33]

Notes

[1] Une première version de ce travail a été communiquée oralement à une session du congrès annuel de la Modern Language Association qu'avait organisée Mary McKinley en 1985 à Chicago. Je remercie celle-ci ainsi que Barbara Bowen, Jules Brody, Edwin Duval et André Tournon de leurs utiles suggestions.

[2] *Les Vies des hommes illustres*, trad. Jacques Amyot, éd. Gérard Walter (Paris: Gallimard, 1958) 1: viii (Introduction).

[3] Toutes les références aux *Essais* de Montaigne que nous donnons entre parenthèses dans les texte se rapportent à l'édition procurée par Pierre Villey et rééditée sous la direction de V.-L. Saulnier (Paris: PUF, 1978). Le chiffre romain indique le livre et les deux chiffres arabes donnent le chapitre et la page. Les lettres a, b, et c indiquent, selon la tradition, les éditions de 1580 (a), 1588 (b) et les additions manuscrites postérieures à l'édition de 1588 sur l'exemplaire de Bordeaux.

[4] Floyd Gray, *La Balance de Montaigne: exagium/essai* (Paris: Nizet, 1982) 122.

[5] "La présence est remplacée par les mots" au point où l'on en arrive paradoxalement à une "Amitié détachée de tout ami." Alfred Glauser, *Montaigne paradoxal* (Paris: Nizet, 1972) 138.

[6] Comme le remarquait déjà Pierre Villey, "l'examen de l'exemplaire de Bordeaux révèle que cette addition manuscrite n'a pas été écrite en une fois: Montaigne a d'abord écrit "parce que c'était [sic] luy." Une autre fois il a ajouté "parce que c'était [sic] moy." Edition des *Essais* citée 188n7.

[7] *Commentaire sur le Banquet de Platon*, éd. Raymond Marcel (Paris: Belles Lettres, 1978) II, viii, 20r, 156. Pour caractériser "cette divine liaison" Montaigne parle de "confusion" (190a) au sens originel du mot (mélange intime), comme s'il s'agissait d'une "ame en deux corps" (190c): "(a) c'est je ne sçay quelle quinte essence de tout ce meslange, qui, ayant saisi toute ma volonté, l'amena se plonger et se perdre en la sienne; (c) qui, ayant saisi toute sa volonté, l'amena se plonger et se perdre en la mienne, d'une faim, d'une concurrence pareille" (189a, c).

[8] "Il [me] laissa . . . heritier de sa bibliotheque et de ses papiers" (I, 28, 184c). "Lettre de Montaigne à son père sur la mort de La Boétie," *Œuvres complètes*, éd. Albert Thibaudet et Maurice Rat, Bibliothèque de la Pléiade (Gallimard: 1962) 1352.

[9] On sait que ces sonnets devaient être supprimés par Montaigne sur l'exemplaire de Bordeaux. Pour une interprétation de cette suppression nous renvoyons à nos *Métamorphoses de Montaigne* (Paris: PUF, 1989), "Avatars de l'amitié: la lettre et l'essai," 61 sq. Pour une étude de la poésie française de La Boétie on consultera la thèse de J. Florack, *Untersuchungen zu den französischen Dichtungen und Übersetzungen E. de la Boéties* (Cologne, 1972).

[10] Voir à ce sujet les pages très neuves de la *Balance de Montaigne* 169-86.

[11] Voir en particulier à ce sujet les articles de Constance Jordan, "Montaigne's 'Chasse de cognoissance': Language and Play in the *Essais*," *Romanic Review* 71 (1980): 265-80, et d'André Tournon, "'J'ordonne mon ame . . .': structure d'*essai* dans le chapitre 'De l'Experience,'" *L'Information Littéraire* (mars-avril 1986) 54-60.

[12] Sur cette double postulation voir, en particulier, l'ouvrage de Gérard Defaux, *Le Curieux, le glorieux et la sagesse du monde dans la première moitié du XVIe siècle: l'exemple de Panurge (Ulysse, Démosthène, Empédocle)*, French Forum Monographs 34 (Lexington, KY: French Forum, 1982). "Parallèlement à l'éloge du savoir et de la raison se déploie à l'époque un autre type de discours rhétorique, antithétique du premier, et dans lequel l'Humanisme prêche à l'homme les vertus de l'inscience et de la soumission" (97). Cependant ce "parallèle" se trouve ensuite démenti chez Defaux par l'affirmation d'une "condamnation sans appel" du premier discours (l'éloge du savoir) par le second (le sermon de l'inscience).

[13] Lettre "A Monsieur, Monsieur de Foix," *Œuvres complètes*, éd. Thibaudet/Rat 1369-70.

[14] Vers françois / de feu E. de La Boëtie / Conseiller du Roy en sa Cour de Parlement / A BORDEAUX. *Œuvres complètes d'Etienne de La Boétie*, éd. Paul Bonnefon (Bordeaux: G. Gounouilhou; Paris: J. Rouam & Cie, 1892) 251.

¹⁵ Il s'agit du chant XXXII du *Roland furieux* de l'Arioste. Pour une analyse de ce poème d'escorte, voir Léon Feugère, *Etienne de La Boëtie, ami de Montaigne: étude sur sa vie et ses ouvrages* (Paris: Labitte, 1845) 138 sq.

¹⁶ Voir *La Deffense et Illustration de la langue françoyse*, éd. Henri Chamard (Paris: Didier, 1948), Livre I, chapitres 5 ("Que les Traductions ne sont suffisantes pour donner perfection à la Langue Francoyse") et 6 ("Des mauvais Traducteurs, & de ne traduyre les Poëtes") 32 sq.

¹⁷ A Marguerite de Carle / sur la traduction des plaintes de Bradamant / au XXXIIe chant de LOYS ARIOSTE. Edition citée 251, vers 1-4. Ces vers sont répétés presque textuellement plus loin: "Ainsi je n'ay onc aymé de changer / En nostre langue aucun œuvre estranger" (vv. 128-29). Nous mettrons désormais le numéro des vers de La Boétie entre parenthèse dans le texte.

¹⁸ Ed. Malcolm Smith (Genève: Droz, 1987) 64. Citant ce passage de la *Servitude*, Michel Magnien écrit: "La Boétie avait fait sien les principes de la nouvelle école et s'était joint à la foule des émules de Ronsard, qu'il a sans doute personnellement approché, tout comme il a connu Baïf et Dorat." "De l'hyperbole à l'ellipse: Montaigne face aux sonnets de La Boétie," *Montaigne Studies* 2 (1990) 9.

¹⁹ Edition citée, vers 5-6, repris aux vers 131-32. Voir aussi les expressions "tout mien" (v.10); "toute mienne" (v.12).

²⁰ Sur ce topos de la source, voir la thèse de David Quint, *Origin and Originality in Renaissance Literature: Versions of the Source* (New Haven: Yale UP, 1983).

²¹ *Discours des misères de ce temps*, éd. Malcolm Smith (Genève: Droz, 1979) vv. 1035-42. L'expression "le surjon de la neufve fontaine" se trouve dans les vers de La Boétie (v. 72).

²² Dans l'analyse brillante qu'il donne de ce même passage Terence Cave insiste sur la "vue péjorative" qu'a Montaigne de l'interprétation. Il remarque néanmoins qu'il y a une contre-partie positive à ce jugement négatif dans la mesure où le lecteur se trouve investi d'un droit au sens au moins aussi valable que celui des gloses érudites. *The Cornucopian Text: Problems of Writing in the French Renaissance* (Oxford: Clarendon Press, 1979) 315n48.

²³ Il ressort aussi de cette analyse que Montaigne semble citer La Boétie à la fois pour revendiquer à sa suite sa place d'"autheur" (la source n'est pas tarie) et pour signifier sa différence (la course continue). Sans doute est-ce toujours le "mesme ruisseau" de l'inspiration qui coule, mais l'eau est "tousjours diverse": changement dans la continuité. Montaigne "entreglose" La Boétie au moment même où il définit ses *Essais* comme une entreglose: "Nous ne faisons [ici] que nous entregloser" (1069b). Sur la conscience qu'avait Montaigne d'être l'inventeur d'un nouveau genre, voir le chapitre "Du repentir" (III,2).

²⁴ Sur ces sources de Montaigne, nous renvoyons à l'étude d'Isabelle Konstantinovic, *Montaigne et Plutarque* (Genève: Droz, 1989) 506. Celle-ci ne cite pas le *De Garrulitate* qui joue pourtant, comme nous allons le voir, un rôle considérable dans l'interprétation du début du chapitre "De l'experience."

²⁵ Plutarque, "De Garrulitate," traduit par Jacques Amyot et présenté par Robert Aulotte dans *Plutarque en France au 16e siècle* (Paris: Klincksieck, 1971) 189.

²⁶ *Les Œuvres morales & meslées de Plutarque*, translatées du Grec en François par Jacques Amyot (Paris: Michel de Vascosan, 1572), réimpr. Classiques de la Renaissance en France (La Haye: Mouton, 1971) 2: 627-36.

²⁷ Montaigne avait d'ailleurs commis un *lapsus*: Cicéron disait "Delos" et non "Delphes" (*Académiques* II, 18).

²⁸ Traduction d'Amyot 634r C (éditions modernes: 406C-D).

²⁹ Le texte grec est encore plus explicite comme on en jugera par la traduction moderne: "Car ce qui discrédite surtout l'oracle, c'est que l'on pose cette alternative: si la Pythie ne prophétise plus en vers, c'est ou bien qu'elle ne s'approche pas de la demeure du dieu, *ou bien que l'exhalation inspiratrice s'est complètement tarie et que son efficacité a cessé*" (402B-C).

³⁰ Les "nouvelles questes" dans lesquelles s'engage l'esprit ne sont qu'"apparence de clarté et verité imaginaire"; en fait "elles l'*esgarent* et l'*envvrent*" (1068b). Le langage de Montaigne est symptomatique: il met en évidence un doublet révélateur dont les paronymes sont trompeurs.

Séduction par le vertige de la *libido sciendi* et mise en garde contre les travers où elle conduit. Parallèlement on note la prise de conscience d'une tension entre l'*égarement* des gloses et l'*enivrement* de la quête de la vérité. Les essais devront négocier un discours qui, tout en courtisant le commentaire, évitera l'écueil du labyrinthe infini.

[31] L'eau de la fontaine est aussi devenue la poix du piège à rat: *Mus in pice* (1068b). Voir à ce sujet: Steven Rendall, "*Mus in pice*: Montaigne and Interpretation," *MLN* 94 (1979): 1056-71; Barbara Bowen, "La Souris dans le goudron," *Kwartalnik Neofilologiczny* 34.2 (1987) 123-30..

[32] "Permets que je jouisse, ô Latonien [Apollon, fils de Latone], de mes biens et d'un corps sain, de facultés saines, et que j'obtienne, avec une bonne vieillesse, le pouvoir de toucher encore ma lyre!" Horace, *Odes* I, XXXI, 17-20.

[33] Resterait à savoir comment la rencontre entre La Boétie et Plutarque a pu se faire si naturellement dans le texte du dernier essai. Il serait tentant de penser que les intertextes ont été suggérés à Montaigne par un souvenir personnel. Dans le chapitre "De l'institution des enfans" nous apprenons en effet que c'est à la lecture d'un traité de Plutarque, *De la mauvaise honte* (*De immodica verecundia*) que La Boétie aurait eu l'idée d'écrire la *Servitude Volontaire* (I, 26, 156b). A cette époque-là, apprend-on, il avait une "familiarité déjà longue avec Plutarque" (cf. Aulotte 64). On sait que La Boétie devait traduire les *Règles de Mariage* et la *Lettre de Consolation de Plutarque à sa femme*, publiées d'ailleurs par les soins de Montaigne. A ces rapports biographiques, historiques et thématiques il faut peut-être ajouter la médiation des signifiants. Plutarque, l'archante éponyme de Chéronée, est le dernier fleuron de la Béotie. "Boetus quidem est Plutarchus" lit-on sous la plume d'Erasme (Dédicace du *De Colubenda Ira*, 1525). L'équivoque Béotie/Boétie a pu suggérer à Montaigne un rapprochement onomastique d'autant plus probable que les équivalents latins étaient pratiquement des homonymes.

Gisèle Mathieu-Castellani

Crise dans les *Essais*

Si l'on se donnait pour objet de repérer les effets de la crise dans les *Essais* de Montaigne, crise multiforme, politique et religieuse, crise de culture et de civilisation, on aurait à évaluer la place occupée dans l'œuvre par l'instance du social; il conviendrait alors de discerner dans la pensée de Montaigne, mais aussi dans son écriture, dans cette écriture sceptique, toujours suspendue, interrogative plus qu'assertive, les traces d'une mentalité maniériste qui saisit un univers éclaté, comme en morceaux, et tient un discours fait de *lopins*, fragmenté en éclats tranchants comme l'acier. Sans doute devrait-on également analyser la crise comme cela même que les *Essais* se sont donné à penser, en tant qu'ils sont essais du jugement et des facultés naturelles, exercice de cette *crisis* qui est faculté de discerner et de cribler.

En proposant *Crise dans les Essais*, comme *Tempête sous un crâne* ou *Cyclone sur la Jamaïque*, on veut signaler d'abord par l'absence d'article défini le statut figural du mot "Crise," et ensuite le caractère dramatique de ce qui se joue non pas à côté du texte, hors de lui, ou dans ses marges, mais dans la mise en scène de l'écriture, d'une écriture mise en question, mise à la question. On considérera les *Essais* comme un corps, un corps en péril, entre maladie et santé, un corps guetté comme celui du scripteur par le démembrement, *un corps en crise*, pris en ce moment périlleux et décisif où précisément l'urgence du péril appelle une décision.

Les *Essais* comme corps, comme corps monstrueux, comme corps non embesogné, comme excrément: la métaphore corporelle insiste trop souvent dans la représentation que l'essai donne de lui-même pour qu'il faille justifier le propos. Les *Essais* comme *corps fragile* aussi, imprudemment confié à un langage, le français, qui manque de fermeté (III, 5, 982), les *Essais* comme *corps solide* pourtant; et nous retiendra un moment ce curieux liminaire, inclus dans le chapitre "De la ressemblance des enfans aux peres" (II, 37) au lieu de se situer sur ses bords:

Madame, vous me trouvates sur ce pas dernierement que vous me vintes voir. Par ce qu'il pourra estre que ces inepties se rencontreront quelque fois entre vos mains, je veux aussi qu'elles portent tesmoignage que l'autheur se sent bien fort honoré de la faveur que vous leur ferez. Vous y reconnoistrez ce mesme port et ce mesme air que vous avez veu en sa conversation. Quand j'eusse peu prendre quelque autre façon que la mienne ordinaire et quelque autre forme plus honorable et meilleure, je ne l'eusse pas faict; car je ne veux tirer de ces escrits sinon qu'ils me representent à vostre memoire au naturel. Ces mesmes conditions et facultez, que vous avez pratiquées et receuillies, Madame, avec beaucoup plus d'honneur et de courtoisie qu'elles ne meritent, je les veux loger (mais sans alteration et changement) en un corps solide qui puisse durer quelques années ou quelques jours apres moy, où vous les retrouverez, quand il vous plaira vous en refreschir la memoire, sans prendre autrement la peine de vous en souvenir: aussi ne le valent elles pas. Je desire que vous continuez en moy la faveur de votre amitié, par ces mesmes qualitez par le moyen desquelles elle a esté produite. (II, 37, 783)[1]

Etrange petit texte, où une orgueilleuse ambition feint de se masquer sous les formules de modestie! La dialectique du même et de l'autre (*même* port et *même* air, *mêmes* conditions et facultés, *mêmes* qualités, *sans altération et changement*, *vs* quelque *autre* façon, *autrement*, quelque *autre* forme) s'inscrit dans la problématique d'une représentation "au naturel," d'une *vive représentation*, dont l'objet-modèle serait *moi* et ses synecdoques. Est-il aussi aisé que Montaigne le dit de composer une "mémoire de papier"?

A ce livre, à ces écrits, se voit confiée la représentation du corps du sujet, air et port, conditions et facultés: les *Essais* seraient le tombeau du corps du sujet. Le livre serait la métamorphose d'un corps encore vivant, mais mortel, en corps solide immortel (car nul n'est dupe de l'apparente dépréciation des "inepties," ni de la modeste correction "quelques années ou quelques jours apres moy").

Ces assertions catégoriques posent en fait double question. Celle de la re-présentation, qui serait présence d'une absence, présentification d'un absent— et l'on note l'insistance du préfixe re-:reconnoistrez, *re*presentent, *re*trouverez, *re*freschir; et celle de l'identité idéale postulée ici entre sujet représentant et objet représenté. Question vite, trop vite, réglée par le scripteur ici, où "en moy" a pour référent "mon livre," comme ailleurs: "Me represente-je pas vivement? suffit!" (III, 5, 875). Voire…

Ce que suggère cette séquence programmatique, c'est que s'articulent dans le projet lui-même problématique de la représentation et problématique du sujet; que s'il y a une crise de la représentation, c'est qu'il y a une crise du sujet aux deux sens du terme: "Et puis, me trovant entierement despourveu et vuide de toute autre matiere, je me suis presenté moi-mesmes à moy, pour argument et pour subject" (II, 8, 385). Dans cette auto-analyse où l'on croit percevoir, à tort, la trace d'une humeur mélancolique—car dans la mélancolie, le moi se vide!—Montaigne semble régler le problème de l'objet—*que* représenter?— en le confondant avec le sujet: *je/me* représenterai. Mais entre *je* présentant et *moi* représenté, quel rapport au juste?

La crise et sa double polarité

"Crise? Qu'est-ce donc qu'une crise? Décidons de ce terme!" s'écrie Paul
Valéry dans ses *Essais quasi-politiques*. Et il ajoute: "Une crise est le passage
d'un certain régime de fonctionnement à quelque autre; passage que des signes
ou des symptômes rendent sensible. . . . Toute crise implique l'intervention de
'causes' naturelles qui troublent un équilibre mobile ou immobile qui existait."[2]
Une telle définition rend compte des mutations qui affectent le régime de la
représentation à l'âge baroque, lorsque la mimésis, se détournant de la
reproduction des modèles littéraires et de l'imitation de la nature, s'oriente vers
la mise en scène de la subjectivité, vers le questionnement du sujet. N'est-ce
point le moment où dans le brouhaha d'un étrange banquet, Béroalde de
Verville promeut au rang d'acteurs *Quelqu'un, L'Autre,* et *Le Premier Venu*?
    Dans la notion de crise se nouent en effet deux figures contrastées. *La
figure du péril, du* trouble (de l'indécis, de l'incertain) ou *des* troubles: des
phénomènes perturbateurs de l'ordre, soudain compromis, en voie de
désorganisation; *du suspens* devant des signes, ou des symptômes, à déchiffrer
comme indices, comme indicateurs d'un mal ou d'une maladie. *La figure du
décisif*, car *crisis* désigne, comme on sait, dans la littérature médicale la phase
décisive d'une maladie, qui évoluera ensuite vers la guérison ou l'issue fatale;
et plus généralement tout moment "périlleux et décisif" (Littré) qui détermine
une évolution heureuse ou malheureuse; la crise alors est ce qui met fin au
trouble et au suspens, ce qui dénoue une situation confuse portée à son
paroxysme. La notion de moment *critique* fait référence à une situation
dangereuse d'équilibre précaire, comme sur le fil du rasoir.
    Dans sa double polarité, la notion de crise "convient" aux *Essais*. D'abord
en tant qu'ils sont le chef-d'œuvre de la littérature critique aux deux sens du
terme; ils pratiquent l'activité de *crisis* (action de distinguer, de cribler, de
séparer) et Montaigne le dit fort bien: "DISTINGO est le plus universel membre
de ma Logique" (II, 1, 335), et ils ne cessent de contester les codes du savoir,
du pouvoir, du devoir. Mais aussi en tant qu'ils partent de la suspension,
du suspens: 'Επεχω, *je retiens, je suspends* (mon jugement), la devise de
Sextus Empiricus, est inscrite sur la travée de la célèbre Librairie. Les *Essais*
marquent de surcroît la phase décisive d'une histoire qui orientera autrement
la littérature. Enfin la notion de crise convient tout particulièrement à la
démarche des *Essais*, une démarche titubante et tâtonnante, mais s'assurant
progressivement des prises, mimant le trouble et l'incertain—mots-clés de
l'analyse phénoménologique de la conscience—ainsi que le décisif, ce geste
gros de conséquence par lequel l'essayiste, sans se résoudre à résoudre—"Si
mon ame pouvoit prendre pied, je ne m'essaierois pas, je me resoudrois: elle

est tousjours en apprentissage et en espreuve" (III, 2, 805)—substitue à la métaphysique la physique, et au discours le vrai sentiment. "Je ne puis asseurer mon object. Il va trouble et chancelant, d'une yvresse naturelle. Je le prends en ce point, comme il est, en l'instant que je m'amuse à luy. Je ne peints pas l'estre. Je peints le passage" (ibid.): une telle séquence, oscillant du négatif au positif, du positif au négatif, dans un mouvement pendulaire, figure les deux pôles de la crise suspens/décision, noeud de difficultés/dénouement. Comme ces philosophes dont il se défie, Montaigne, "par cette varieté et instabilité d'opinions," nous mène "comme par la main, tacitement, à cette resolution de [son] irresolution" (II, 12, 545).

En même temps cette séquence, en écho au "liminaire" précédent, définit le projet: "me représenter," et la décision de mettre en scène le trouble et l'incertain, sans les évacuer. Mais la représentation d'un "particulier" - "Les autres forment l'homme; je le recite et en represente un particulier bien mal formé" (III, 2, 804)—met en question la représentation de l'in-forme...

La crise de la représentation

Qu'est-ce que représenter? *Imiter*, *reproduire* un modèle, *peindre* ("c'est moy que je peins"), et la référence est d'abord picturale. Mais aussi *mettre en scène*, *donner à voir*, *monter un spectacle*, et la référence est alors théâtrale; les récents traducteurs de la *Poétique* d'Aristote en français, Dupont-Roc et Lallot, ont choisi de traduire systématiquement (ce qui est sans doute contestable) *mimésis* par *représentation* et *mimeisthaï* par *représenter*, rappelant que "la famille de mimesis s'enracine dans une fonction de représentation au sens théâtral du mot."[3] En enfin *substituer une personne à une autre* dans un acte officiel de la vie publique, et la référence est en ce cas juridique.

Remplaçant un objet (ou une personne) par un simulacre, la représentation met en jeu une dialectique de la présence et de l'absence: "Portrait porte absence et présence," dit Pascal.[4] Mais aussi une dialectique de la vie et de la mort; Alberti disait que "la peinture rend présent l'absent et vivant le mort":[5] l'inverse est vrai aussi! La représentation absente le modèle, et ce trait vaut pour la peinture, l'art théâtral, le domaine de la loi. Représenter, mettre sous les yeux, présenter à nouveau ou de nouveau, répéter, reproduire, c'est figurer, quel que soit le mode de figuration, un objet qui *tient lieu* d'un autre, c'est jouer sur des signes, des valant-pour. La figure moulée qui dans les obsèques solennelles "représentait" le défunt nous rappelle opportunément que la représentation occupe toujours la place d'un mort. Elle restitue, du modèle qui est là sans être là, une fiction. Une feinte. Et juridiquement la représentation, qui désigne la qualité d'une personne qui tient la place d'une autre, et notamment, "le droit que l'on a de recueillir une succession comme représentant d'une personne prédécédée" (Littré), s'autorise d'un(e) mort. Représenter, c'est en effet rendre par art, par artifice, présent un absent, vivant un mort, c'est simuler vie et présence en jouant du "comme si…" Commentant son ouvrage, Les *Simulachres de la Mort*, le poète Jean de Vauzelles le dit fort bien: "Simulacres les dis-je vraiment, pource que simulacre vient de *simuler* et feindre ce qui n'est point."[6] En ces simulacres est peinte la feinte… Le langage ordinaire éclaire aussi cette insistante présence de l'absence dans la représentation. Si je dis: "*Je vous présente M.X.*," M. X est là, devant nous. Si je dis "*Je représente ici M.X.*" c'est que M. X est absent; et les "représentants" du peuple évacuent le peuple de la salle des Assemblées: la représentation légitime l'absence.

Cette dialectique de la présence et de l'absence, de la mort et de la vie, supporte la représentation de ce particulier que les *Essais* se sont donné pour argument et pour sujet: présence au lieu d'absence, disent le "liminaire" à Madame de Duras et l'avis *au lecteur* ("… à ce que *m'ayant perdu* … ils y puissent *retrouver* aucuns traits de mes conditions et humeurs …"), corps vivant au lieu de corps mort. Mais Montaigne, en général si défiant, ne montre-t-il point ici une excessive confiance en assurant que l'essai restitue *au naturel* l'air et le port du causeur? Les *Essais* auraient-ils, comme il se plaît à le dire, le statut d'une conversation? Non, bien sûr. Et ce corps qu'ils nous restitueraient idéalement préservé, ne se rebelle-t-il pas au statut d'objet? "Je me presente debout et couché, le devant et le derriere, à droite et à gauche, et en tous mes naturels plis" (III, 8, 943): le corps réel, comment se mettrait-il en mots? La représentation du corps propre, indissolublement objet-sujet, du corps vécu dans l'imaginaire du sujet, construit un simulacre, comme le corps *supposé* de Descartes, à l'ouverture de son *Traité de l'homme*.[7] Simulacre-similitude: "ce mesme port et ce mesme air," simulacre-image: "retrouver au naturel," simulacre-imitation parfaite: "ces mesmes conditions … sans alteration," simulacre-fiction "vous les retrouverez … quand il vous plaira" (II, 37, 783), "et que par ce moyen ils [parents et amis] nourrissent plus entiere et plus vifve, la connoissance qu'ils ont eu de moy" ("Au lecteur," 3). La crise prend alors la figure d'une aporie. Le corps ne devient intelligible que s'il accède à la représentation par le régime des métaphores et des analogies, mais toute comparaison aliène le corps et l'"étrange":

Il n'y a pas plus de retrogradation, trepidation, accession, reculement, ravissement, aux astres et corps celestes, qu'ils en ont forgé en ce pauvre petit corps humain. Vrayement ils ont eu par là raison de l'appeler le petit monde, tant ils ont employé de pieces et de visages à le maçonner et bastir. (II, 12, 537)

Si la voie des similitudes est barrée, quel chemin prendre en ce labyrinthe? Le corps récuse le statut d'objet—c'est l'échec de l'*Apologie*—et il échappe à la mise en mots, à l'"algébrose."[8] Au discours sur le corps, se substituera alors le discours du corps, ultime tentative pour restituer son langage au corps, pour restituer le corps au langage. Et le corps sort de la représentation, pour affirmer sa présence par ses rythmes, par ses images. Par ses métamorphoses, et non par ses métaphores.

La crise du sujet

A l'échec de la représentation lorsqu'elle prend pour objet ce qui ne saurait être objet, le corps-sujet, répond une écriture "corporéisée": le sujet élabore son identité dans l'acte même d'écrire, "de minute en minute," prenant alors le risque de s'y trouver ou de s'y perdre. Car au cri triomphal: "Je n'ay pas plus faict mon livre que mon livre m'a faict, livre consubstantiel à son autheur" (II. 18, 665)—notons bien *à son autheur*, non *à l'homme*—, répond, sinon l'angoisse, au moins l'inquiétude: "Quand tout est conté [à la fois calculé et conté], on ne parle jamais de soy sans perte" (III, 8, 922).

La dialectique de la présence et de l'absence marque encore le rapport de la matière à la manière. La matière: un être de fuite! "Je fons et eschape à moy" (III, 13, 1101). La manière: un être de fuite aussi! Comme le songe, les "resveries, plus folles et qui [lui] plaisent le mieux" (III, 5, 876) échappent au scripteur, ne laissant qu'une vaine image... Dans l'analyse qu'il tente de ses échecs, Montaigne ne distingue pas, ne sépare pas, l'indigence du sujet et celle de son écriture:

J'ay tousjours une idée en l'ame et certaine image trouble, qui me presente comme en songe une meilleure forme que celle que j'ay mis en besongne, mais je ne la puis saisir et exploiter. Et cette idée mesme n'est que du moyen estage. (II, 17, 637)

Un sujet en crise: *je*, seul point de référence, est mobile et métamorphique, "chaque piece, chaque momant, faict son jeu" (II, 1, 337); ce "particulier" que *je* récite se définit par le système de ses différences autant que par celui des ressemblances: "La ressemblance ne faict pas tant un comme la difference faict autre" (III, 13, 1065). *Moi* n'est qu'une mosaïque mal assemblée, irréductible au *cogito*, un conflit d'instances: "Moy à cette heure et moy tantost sommes bien deux" (III, 9, 964).

Distinguant l'individu, notion juridique ou scientifique (individu *vs* société ou Etat, individu *vs* espèce), du sujet, catégorie philosophique mettant en jeu une épistémologie, Montaigne articule et noue trois postulats qui sont les points forts de son analyse.

Du sujet il souligne *la dualité interne*, le clivage des instances, dans la lignée d'un Saint-Paul ou d'un Saint-Augustin:

... nous sommes, je ne sçay comment, doubles en nous mesmes, qui faict que ce que nous croyons, nous ne le croyons pas, et ne nous pouvons deffaire de ce que nous condamnons. (II, 16, 619)

Mais aussi *son altérité radicale*:

... ce qui souffre mutation ne demeure pas un mesme, et, s'il n'est pas un mesme, il n'est donc pas aussi. Ains, quant et l'estre tout un, change aussi l'estre simplement, *devenant tousjours autre d'un autre*. (II, 12, 603)

Enfin il situe *la différence au cœur du même*:

Et se trouve autant de difference de nous à nous mesmes, que de nous à autruy (II, 1, 337).

Et, au rebours du commun, reçoy plus facilement la difference que la ressemblance en nous. (II, 37, 229)

Ce sont là de considérables avancées, dont il convient de ne pas mésestimer la radicale nouveauté. Dualité, altérité, différence, trois concepts soutiennent désormais la représentation du sujet. Et Montaigne ne se borne pas à dévoiler les moi successifs, mourant l'un après l'autre, qui altèrent la stabilité et la cohérence du sujet—"combien de fois ce n'est plus moy! (III, 13, 1102)—, ni même à mettre en évidence, comme le reconnaissait Lacan, que le moi n'est ni synthétique ni exempt de contradictions, il découvre différents *étages* dans l'âme-labyrinthe, différents niveaux dans la "conscience," et un inconscient producteur d'images troubles que l'écrivain tente—en vain!—de fixer dans leur évanescence.

S'il manifeste devant les ruines de Rome sédimentées en couches de divers âges à la fois stupeur, déception, et vive émotion, c'est que cette Rome-là est l'image du sujet, sédimenté comme elle, et de ses archives secrètes.

Crise de la représentation, crise du sujet, les *Essais* disent l'une et l'autre, lient l'une à l'autre, mettant ainsi en question l'écriture. Chaque découverte d'une partie du continent inconnu, de ces nouveaux territoires dont ils mettent à jour les couches sédimentées, profondes comme celles de Rome,"jusques aux antipodes" (III, 9, 997), chaque annexion de ces domaines jusqu'alors exclus du champ de la représentation, les folles rêveries, les songes, les chimères fantasques, amènent l'écriture à essayer ses possibles, à tester aussi ses limites. Car c'est bien de limites qu'il s'agit, lorsque Montaigne, en des "petites phrases" riches de suggestions, commente son ambition… et son échec. En écho au texte cité plus haut, évoquant l'amertume de l'écrivain devant son impuissance à retenir *certaine image trouble*, aperçue *comme en songe*, cet aveu: "Et, quand je suis allé le plus avant que je puis, si ne me suis-je aucunement satisfaict: je voy encore du païs au delà, mais d'une veüe *trouble* et en nuage.*" (I, 26, 146). Et cette consolation douce-amère: "Tant y a qu'en ces memoires, si on y regarde, on trouvera que j'ay tout dict, ou tout designé. Ce que je ne puis exprimer, je le montre au doigt" (III, 9, 983). C'est précisément, me semble-t-il, cette défaillance, cette béance, qui ouvre l'espace du texte et conduit l'écrivain à écrire "autant qu'il y aura d'ancre et de papier au monde" (III, 9, 945).

Si une crise se définit par le contraste de deux figures, le trouble et le décisif, les *Essais* sont en effet un corps en crise. Fragile et solide. Solide de sa fragilité mesurée, acceptée. Offrant au sémiologue tous les symptômes de ce moment périlleux et décisif où naît, avec un nouveau modèle de subjectivité, une écriture ouverte à "ce qui peut advenir": "Il y a des autheurs, desquels la fin c'est dire les evenements. La mienne, si j'y sçavoye advenir, serait dire sur ce qui peut advenir" (I, 21, 105-06). Où l'essai, se détournant du modèle de la *Vie* et des mémoires, rêve d'être poésie...

Notes

[1] Les références renvoient aux *Essais de Michel de Montaigne*, éd. Pierre Villey et V.-L. Saulnier, 2 vols. (Paris: PUF, 1965). Pour des analyses plus détaillées de certains points avancés ici, je renvoie à mon livre *Montaigne: l'écriture de l'essai* (Paris: PUF, 1988), et à quelques articles récents, "Discours sur le corps, discours du corps dans le troisième livre des *Essais*," in *Le Parcours des Essais: Montaigne 1588-1988*, éd. Marcel Tetel et G. Mallary Masters (Paris: Aux Amateurs de Livres, 1989) 125-34; "L'Essai et ses représentations," *Europe* No. 729-30 (janvier-février 1990) 49-56; "L'Ecriture du moi et la problématique du sujet," *Saggi e Ricerche di Letteratura Francese* 28 (1989) 11-25; et "Rome, l'enfance et la mort dans les *Essais* et le *Journal de voyage en Italie*," in *Montaigne e l'Italia*, à paraître (Actes du Colloque de Milan-Lecco 1988).

[2] Paul Valéry, *Essais quasi-politiques*, in *Œuvres*, Bibliothèque de la Pléiade, 2 vols. (Paris: Gallimard, 1957-60) 1: 1091.

[3] Aristote, *La Poétique*, éd. Roselyne Dupont-Roc et Jean Lallot (Paris: Seuil, 1980) 20.

[4] Pascal, *Pensées*, éd. Louis Lafuma (Paris: Seuil, 1962) 137.

[5] Alberti, *De Pictura*, éd. Cecil Grayson (Bari: Laterza, 1975) 69.

[6] Jean de Vauzelles, *Les Simulachres et Historiées faces de la Mort . . .* (Lyon: Trechsel, 1538) 3.

[7] Descartes, *L'Homme*, in *Œuvres philosophiques*, éd. F. Alquié (Paris: Garnier, 1963) 1: 379.

[8] Marcel Jousse, *L'Anthropologie du geste* (Paris: Gallimard, 1974) 108-12.

André Tournon

"Un langage coupé . . ."

Sainte-Beuve, Auerbach, Thibaudet avaient déjà parlé, et admirablement, du "style de Montaigne." Pourtant, lorsqu'il s'est attaqué à ce sujet toujours périlleux, en 1957, Floyd Gray a su innover presque en tous points; ou, pour mieux dire, il a su modifier radicalement les conditions et la portée de l'étude, en l'ordonnant par rapport à des données présumées alors extra-stylistiques: "la structure des *Essais*" et "la composition des *Essais*" (titres, respectivement, de la première et de la troisième partie de son ouvrage). A l'époque, ce choix a pu surprendre: parler de structure et de composition à propos de style, c'était conduire des investigations d'ordre logique dans le domaine aux contours flous où triomphaient déjà les thématiciens, sur les décombres de l'esthétique du bien-dire; ou encore, rappeler aux analystes des idées que le style est organisation des signifiés et discipline intellectuelle, autant que jeu des signifiants. Le projet avait quelque chance d'irriter tout le monde. ll s'est imposé cependant: la visée était juste, et conjuguait les exigences légitimes du stylisticien et de l'exégète de manière à dévoiler, par croisement de leurs deux perspectives, la complexité réelle du texte, et ses raisons; à faire surgir des problèmes de sens là où, faute de les soupçonner, on avait raffiné sur les appréciations esthétiques; mieux, à montrer que le style, pour Montaigne, est un problème permanent, qui met en cause la relation au lecteur et à la vérité autant qu'au langage.

Dès ses premières analyses, à l'échelle de la phrase, Floyd Gray montre ainsi que l'écriture des *Essais* se cherche et s'invente à l'aide des recettes disponibles, mais à leur détriment—par combinaisons insolites de formes qui normalement s'excluent entre elles. Les rhétoriciens se plaisaient à y reconnaître les modèles répertoriés: tantôt la phrase longue et équilibrée, imitée de la période cicéronienne, tantôt la sentence brève, incisive, à la manière de Sénèque. Floyd Gray saisit jusque dans les plus anciens chapitres, comme caractéristique de leur style, la contamination des deux formules; au lieu de simplement repérer des modèles, il décèle les tensions que produit leur confrontation. Cela le conduit d'emblée au cœur du mobilisme de Montaigne. Si la sentence "vient se juxtaposer" à la phrase oratoire traditionnelle, "trancher brutalement la continuité du mouvement périodique," cet assemblage insolite rend saisissable le "passage," le mouvement de la pensée et de la vie que l'essayiste veut enregistrer sans le fixer;[1] et ses éléments, à terme, changent de nature: "Dans le style mûr du IIIème livre, la phrase coupée . . . se transforme en phrase à *lopins*, et la phrase oratoire du XVIème siècle devient une phrase qui cherche des rythmes souples, brisés ou fluides, qui n'a plus rien des lignes régulières et de l'ordonnance logique de celle de Jean Lemaire, de Calvin" (31). Un pas de plus, et c'est la phrase "pointilliste," qui "trace le courant de la pensée qui cherche. Le mot s'y trouve comme en suspens, isolé, libéré de son groupe syntaxique" (32). D'où il suit que les modèles rhétoriques permettent de repérer, par différences, les structures de la prose inventée par Montaigne, mais non d'en rendre compte, parce que ces structures s'élaborent en perturbant presque systématiquement leurs agencements.

C'était une gageure sans doute que de vouloir décrire et situer le style des *Essais* en privilégiant cette propension de Montaigne à écrire "en dépit des règles de la rhétorique et de la bonne composition," anomalie qui le place "en marge du courant de la prose française régulière" (38), comme sa pratique de l'*essai* le place en marge des courants philosophiques classiques et de leurs modes d'investigations. Et de nos jours encore, à voir des poéticiens, à l'affût de sèmes erratiques et de signifiants embusqués sous les mots, rester parfaitement indifférents aux singularités syntaxiques et logiques du texte, on se prend à douter que l'enseignement de Floyd Gray ait été totalement reçu et assimilé. Il était pourtant cautionné par Montaigne lui-même, qui enjoint à l'écrivain de travailler sur les structures de la langue plutôt que sur le lexique, de la "plier" et "contourner outre son alleure commune," en "l'estirant et ployant" pour lui "appren[dre] des alleures non accoustumées."[2] Peut-être cette citation, en dépit de la réussite exemplaire du critique qui s'en prévalait, n'était-elle pas suffisante pour venir à bout des routines. Le présent article tentera d'apporter, en guise de contribution à la même entreprise sans fin, des indices d'un autre ordre, dûs également à la plume de Montaigne, mais à la fois plus discrets et plus insistants: discrets sans doute, puisque tous les éditeurs des *Essais*, qui depuis quatre cents ans ont préféré les ignorer, ont pu se persuader que leur élimination systématique ne falsifiait pas le texte; insistants, parce qu'ils sont disséminés par milliers d'un bout à l'autre de l'Exemplaire de Bordeaux.

Il s'agit des retouches apportées par Montaigne à la ponctuation et à l'emploi des majuscules dans l'édition de 1588. Décisions du scripteur, à chaque fois, mais aussi, et peut-être surtout, traces d'une lecture attentive aux structures latentes des énoncés, aux articulations propres à leur donner leur relief et leur poids exact, sans avoir besoin de la magie ou des truquages du verbe, connotations et paronomases. Avant 1588, à l'en croire, Montaigne ne s'en souciait guère. Il écrit dans le chapitre "De la vanité" (à propos des coquilles, et de sa nonchalance envers celles qui n'altèrent pas les sens du texte): "Je ne me mesle, ny d'ortografe, & ordonne seulement qu'ils [= les imprimeurs] suivent l'ancienne, ny de la punctuation: je suis peu expert en l'un et en l'autre."[3] Cette indifférence s'est sans doute prolongée au-delà de 1588. Un grand nombre d'additions manuscrites de l'Exemplaire de Bordeaux sont ponctuées de façon très lacunaire—par exemple, en marge du passage cité ici:

(C) Antiochus avoit vigoureusement escrit en faveur de l'Academie il print sur ses vieux ans un autre party: lequel des deux je suivisse seroit pas tousjours suivre Antiochus. Apres avoir establi le doubte vouloir establir la certitude des opinions humaines, estoit ce pas establir le doubte non la certitude. Et promettre qui luy eust doné encores un eage à durer qu'il estoit tousjours en terme de nouvelle agitation: non tant meilleure qu'autre.

Mais lorsque les ajouts, accumulés, ont donné matière à une nouvelle édition, avant la remise du texte à l'imprimeur (ou plus probablement à un copiste chargé de le mettre au net), Montaigne se met à réviser minutieusement la ponctuation de son exemplaire: sur la seule page dont sont extraites les citations ci-dessus, pas moins de onze retouches jalonnent le texte imprimé;[4] j'en ai compté près de deux mille dans le premier livre; qui aura le courage de continuer le dénombrement ne sera pas déçu par les deux suivants. Et lorsque Montaigne inscrit enfin, sur la page de garde, ses consignes au futur imprimeur, il est formel:

[Ou]tre les corrections qui sont en cet exemplaire il y a infinies autres a faire de quoi [l'i]mprimur se pourra aviser, mais *regardez de pres aus pouints qui sont en ce [sti]le de grande importance.* [C'e]st un langage coupé / q*u' il n' y espargne les poincts & lettres majuscules.* Moimesme ai failli [souv]ant à les oster & à mettre des comma où il faloit un poinct.[5]

Il ne peut vraiment plus dire qu'il ne se mêle pas de la ponctuation. Quant à savoir s'il y est devenu "expert," c'est une des questions auxquelles le présent article essaiera de répondre; encore faut-il en exposer les données—car celles-ci ont été réservées jusqu'à présent aux lecteurs qui disposaient d'une photocopie de l'Exemplaire de Bordeaux.

Prenons la phrase célèbre par laquelle Montaigne donne une définition du style qu'il aime. En voici d'abord la version de l'édition de 1588:

Le parler que j'ayme, c'est un parler simple & naif, tel sur le papier qu'à la bouche: un parler succulent & nerveux, court & serré, plustost difficile que ennuieux, esloigné d'affectation & d'artifice, desreglé, descousu, & hardy: chaque lopin y face son corps: non pedantesque, non fratesque, non pleideresque, mais plustost soldatesque, comme Suetone appelle celuy de Julius Caesar. (I, 26, 171-72; Ex. de B., f° 64)

Elle a été ainsi retouchée dans l'Exemplaire de Bordeaux:

Le parler que j'ayme, c'est un parler simple & naif, tel sur le papier qu'à la bouche: Un parler succulent & nerveux, court & serré, non tant delicat et peigné que vehement et brusque

Haec demum sapiet dictio, quae feriet
Plutost difficile qu'ennuieux. Esloingné d'affectation; Desreglé, descousu, & hardy: Chaque lopin
y face son corps: Non pedantesque, non fratesque, non pleideresque, mais plustost soldatesque,
comme Suetone appelle celuy de Julius Caesar: et si ne sens pas bien pour quoy il l'en appelle.

L'intervention affecte assez peu la ponctuation proprement dite: à la
quatrième ligne, un point et un point virgule, fortement tracés, sont substitués
à des virgules. L'effet est déjà sensible: est détaché et comme mis en exergue,
dans la série des adjectifs qui qualifient le "parler," le syntagme "esloigné
d'affectation," propre à transposer sur le plan éthique (où l'"affectation"
connote le mensonge) le refus d'apprêt que dénotaient les qualificatifs stylistiques
"desréglé" et "descousu." Mais en outre le texte est scandé énergiquement par
la répartition des majuscules, qui se combinent avec la ponctuation et la syntaxe
sans coïncider exactement avec elles. C'est là le trait le plus caractéristique du
"langage coupé" des *Essais* parvenu à son ultime état. Pour le passage qui nous
occupe, le résultat est flagrant. Dans la précédente version, la phrase se
présentait globalement comme une série de qualificatifs déterminant "parler,"
simplement diversifiée par groupements en syntagmes variés: un couple
d'adjectifs coordonnés par "&," puis un syntagme comparatif ("tel . . . qu'à
. . ."); encore deux couples coordonnées par &, suivis d'un couple articulé en
comparaison ("plustost. . .que. . ."); un syntagme de participe avec complément;
trois adjectifs en énumération; une indépendante isolée par ponctuation plus
forte (deux-points); enfin un groupe de trois adjectifs juxtaposés et opposés
ensemble, par la négation qui les précède, à un quatrième que développe une
proposition de comparaison ("comme Suétone . . ."). Muni de ses retouches et
de l'addition qui s'y insère, le passage prend un relief plus accusé, et différent.
On distingue un premier mouvement ponctué par des virgules, avec, à sa
relance par reprise du substantif "parler," un deux-points (d'origine) accentué
maintenant par une majuscule de scansion ("*U*n parler . . ."); le schéma
énumératif reste ici prépondérant, sans vraie rupture. Mais après le vers latin
cité à la fin de l'addition, la série de qualifications se poursuit de manière toute
autre. Le premier groupe reçoit une majuscule qui le détache du contexte
précédent et un point qui le sépare de la suite. Le second, abrégé et isolé par sa
nouvelle ponctuation, est un syntagme qui désormais se lit d'un trait (alors qu'il
portait auparavant deux accents, comme les énoncés décomposables qui
l'encadrent); il constitue ainsi une sorte de bloc, placé à peu près au centre de
l'ensemble du passage. Vient ensuite une configuration d'allure symétrique:
trois adjectifs liés par allitération, puis trois autres liés par anaphore et
homéotéleute, de part et d'autre d'une proposition indépendante, chaque sous-
groupe étant marqué par une majuscule initiale; mais faute de ponctuation forte
et de majuscule on ne peut séparer les trois derniers adjectifs du quatrième, en
opposition ("mais plustost soldatesque"), auquel se rattache la comparative

LIVRE PREMIER.   64

tions de l'autre. Voire mais, que fera-il, si on le presse de la subtilité sophistique de quelque syllogisme? Le iambon fait boire, le boire desaltere, parquoy le iambon desaltere. Si ces sottes infiies, luy doiuent persuader vne mensonge, cela est dangereux: mais si elles demeurent sans effect, & ne l'esmeuuent qu'à rire, ie ne voy pas pourquoy il s'en doiue dóner garde. Il en est de si sots, qui se destournent de leur voye vn quart de lieuë, pour courir apres vn beau mot, ou rebours, c'est aux paroles à seruir & à suyure, & que le Gascon y arriue, si le François n'y peut aller. ie veux que les choses surmótent, & qu'el-les remplissent, de façon l'imagination de celuy qui escoute, qu'il n'aye aucune souuenance des mots. Le parler que i'ay-me, c'est vn parler simple & naif, tel sur le papier qu'à la bouche: Vn parler succulent & nerueux, court & serré, pluftost difficile qu'ennuieux, Esloingné d'affectation, & d'artifice, desreglé, descousu, & hardy: Chaque lopin y face son corps: Non pedantesque, non fratesque, non pleideresque, mais plustost soldatesque, comme Suetone appelle celuy de Iulius Cæsar. I'ay volontiers imité cette desbauche qui se voit en noftre ieunesse, au port de leurs vestemens, de laisser pendre son teistre, de porter la cappe en escharpe, & vn bas mal tendu, qui represente vne fierté desdaigneuse de ces paremens estrágers, & nonchalante de l'art. Mais ie la trouue encore mieux employée en la forme du parler. Ie n'ayme point de tissure ou les liaisons & les coutures paroissent. Tout ainsi qu'en vn corps, il ne faut qu'on y puisse compter les os & les veines. Les Atheniens (dict Platon) ont pour leur part, le soing de l'abondance & elegance du parler, les Lacedemoniens de la briefueté, & ceux de Crete, de la fecundité des cóceptions, plus que du langage: Ceux-cy sont les miens. Zenon disoit qu'il auoit deux sortes de disciples: les vns qu'il nommoit φιλολόγȣς, curieux d'apprendre les choses, qui estoyent ses mi-

"comme Suétone . . . ," puis la réserve ajoutée en marge, "et si . . . ," qui ralentit et stabilise la fin de phrase. Au terme de ce remodelage, le passage se scinde en trois séquences d'allures différentes, la première et la troisième, aux enchaînements assez souples, encadrant les expressions vigoureusement détachées au centre, dont trois mettent en jeu le mode de communication déterminé par le style ("Plustost *difficile* que *ennuieux*. Esloingné d'*affectation*; Desreglé, descousu, & *hardy*")—la quatrième, excentrée, donnant sa formule technique qu'illustre précisément la scansion surajoutée. Il est clair qu'en procédant ainsi Montaigne a trouvé le moyen de conjuguer la continuité logique des énoncés (déterminée par la syntaxe d'ensemble et par la rhétorique de l'énumération) et leur fragmentation expressive en "lopins" dont chacun marque péremptoirement une décision, sinon un défi.

Les deux agencements doivent jouer concurremment pour que le texte prenne sa physionomie et son énergie propre. On a vu plus haut la version ponctuée selon les normes de l'éditeur de 1588, qui correspondent, à peu de choses près, à celles de 1595; on pourra examiner à loisir les libertés que prennent les éditeurs modernes pour l'assagir encore, selon les prescriptions de leurs manuels de typographie; il est facile de constater que la netteté et la nervosité dues aux retouches manuscrites sont affaiblies jusqu'à exténuation lorsqu'on cherche ainsi à les réassujettir aux normes. Les aurait-on sauvegardées en choisissant de renforcer les signes de ponctuation pour les assortir aux majuscules surajoutées? Cela aurait donné la version suivante, pour les dernières lignes:

*. . . Plustost difficile que ennuieux. Esloingné d'affectation. Desreglé, descousu, & hardy. Chaque lopin y face son corps. Non pedantesque, non fratesque, non plaideresque, mais plustost soldatesque, comme Suétone appelle celuy de Julius Caesar; et si ne sens pas bien pour quoy il l'en appelle.

Le relief subsiste, semble-t-il, mais non la hiérarchie des coupures qui l'accusent; en particulier, le privilège conféré à la formule qui définit le principe éthique de ce style, seule à être encadrée de deux ponctuations fortes, n'est plus perceptible. Dans une fragmentation presque uniforme, où les "lopins" ne se détachent plus sur des séquences plus faiblement segmentées, le rythme et l'articulation logique deviennent moins distincts, et moins efficaces.

Nous rejoignons ainsi les conclusions des analyses proprement stylistiques de Floyd Gray: la force du style de Montaigne provient de la combinaison de schémas antagonistes, qui détermineraient, chacun à part, des agencements anodins, mais, conjoints ou superposés, animent le texte de tensions virtuelles; ce sont de telles tensions que décèlent ou avivent les retouches des dernières années.

Ces retouches sont très nombreuses; mais leur efficacité ne se mesure pas à leur fréquence: telle intervention minime peut suffire à remodeler une phrase de grande ampleur. Un passage du chapitre "De l'amitié," lu dans la version de 1588, paraît à peu près conforme au modèle cicéronien: une sentence pour palier d'élan, suivie d'une très brève formule explicative, en pierre d'attente; puis, à titre de justification, une longue période régie par un schéma comparatif qui marque la symétrie entre la protase, répartie en deux propositions parallèles séparées par une brève incise, et l'apodose, dont les deux principaux groupes syntaxiques, parallèles et contigus, sont précédés d'une participiale de cause et suivis d'une énumération:

> En ce noble commerce, les offices & les bienfaits nourrissiers des autres amitiez, ne meritent pas seulement d'estre mis en compte: cette confusion si pleine de nos volontez en est cause, car tout ainsi que l'amitié, que je me porte, ne reçoit point augmentation, pour le secours que je me donne au besoin, quoy que dient les Stoïciens, & comme je ne me sçay aucun gré du service que je me fay: aussi l'union de tels amis estant veritablement parfaicte, elle leur faict perdre le sentiment de tels devoirs, & haïr et chasser d'entre eux, ces mots de division & de difference comme, bien faict, obligation, reconnoissance, priere, remerciement, & leurs pareils. (I, 28, 190; Ex. de B., f° 72)

Sur l'Exemplaire de Bordeaux, Montaigne marque par deux majuscules de scansion et un point-virgule le découpage du début de la phrase (". . . *C*ette confusion si pleine de nos volontez en est cause*; C*ar . . ."); ce qui ne fait qu'en souligner la structure. Mais il introduit aussi une majuscule au début du dernier groupe syntaxique. ("*E*t haïr et chasser. . ."), auquel il donne en outre une allure plus heurtée en remplaçant "comme" par un deux-points. L'ordonnance rhétorique en est fortement perturbée, au bénéfice de l'expressivité: au lieu de se ranger à sa place dans l'organisation générale, le dernier segment est détaché, en dépit de la syntaxe, pour que prenne tout sa force l'oxymore qu'il énonce, en réplique à la formule encore modérée sur laquelle se greffait l'ensemble. Le déséquilibre est brutal, entre la tranquille explication de la sentence initiale qui se bornait à déprécier les "offices et bienfaits nourriciers des autres amitiés" (idée qui se retrouve dans l'avant-dernière proposition, "elle leur fait perdre le sentiment de tels devoirs"), et le paradoxe final, qui dévoile des "mots de division & de difference" dans le vocabulaire usuel de la solidarité; cet effet pouvait passer inaperçu dans la version de 1588; marqué par la segmentation nouvelle, il saute aux yeux.

   Ce traitement de choc n'est pas réservé aux périodes. Il peut donner du relief, sans vraiment infléchir le sens, à des phrases moins régulièrement composées, au prix d'infimes anomalies syntaxiques. Tel est l'effet d'une majuscule ajoutée après une virgule, à la fin de la version imprimée du chapitre trois du premier livre, sur les funérailles et tombeaux:

> Si j'avais à m'en empescher plus avant, je trouverois plus galand, d'imiter ceux, qui entreprennent, vivans & respirans, jouyr de l'ordre & honneur de leur sepulture, Et qui se plaisent de voir en marbre, leur morte contenance. (I, 3, 20; Ex. de B., f° 6)

·LIVRE PREMIER.   71

de celle d'vn tel amy. Il n'eſt pas en la puiſſance de tous les diſ-
cours du monde, de me deſloger de la certitude, que i'ay des
intentions & iugemens du mien. Aucune de ſes actions ne me
ſçauroit eſtre preſentée, quelque viſage qu'elle eut, que ie n'en
trouuaſſe incontinent le vray reſſort. Nos ames ont charrié ſi
long temps enſemble, elles ſe ſont conſiderées d'vne ſi ardan-
te affection, & de pareille affection deſcouuertes iuſques au
fin fond des entrailles l'vne à l'autre: que non ſeulement ie cō-
noiſſoy la ſienne comme la mienne, mais ie me fuſſe certainement plus volontiers fié à luy de moy, qu'à moy meſme.
Qu'on ne me mette pas en ce reng, ces autres amitiez cōmu-
nes: iē i'en ay autant de connoiſſance qu'vn autre, & des plus
parfaictes de leur genre; mais ie ne conſeille pas qu'on con-
fonde leurs regles; on ſ'y tromperoit. Il faut marcher en ces
autres amitiez, la bride à la main, auec prudence & precautiō:
la liaiſon n'eſt pas nouée en maniere, qu'on n'ait aucunemēt
à ſ'en deffier. Aymés le (diſoit Chilon) comme ayant quelque
iour à le haïr; haïſſez le, cōme ayant à l'aymer. Ce precepte, eſt
ſi abominable en cette ſouueraine & maiſtreſſe amitié, il eſt
ſalubre en l'vſage ordinaire. En ce noble commerce; les offices
& les bienfaits nourriſſiers des autres amitiez, ne meritent pas
ſeulement d'eſtre mis en compte : Cette confuſion ſi pleine
de nos volōtez en eſt cauſe: car tout ainſi que l'amitié, que ie
me porte, ne reçoit point augmentation, pour le ſecours que
ie me dōne au beſoin, quoy que dient les Stoiciens, & comme ie ne me ſçay aucū gré du ſeruice que ie me fay: auſſi l'vniō
de tels amis eſtant veritablement parfaicte, elle leur faict perdre le ſentiment de tels deuoirs, & haïr & chaſſer d'entre eux,
ces mots de diuiſion & de difference; comme bien faict, obligation, reconnoiſſance, priere, remerciement, & leurs pareils.
Tout eſtant par effect commun entre eux, volontez, penſe-
mens, iugemens, biens, femmes, enfans, honneur & vie, ils ne

La ponctuation, conforme à la syntaxe, sépare à peine les deux relatives; la majuscule tend à les dissocier, pour mettre en valeur le face-à-face du vivant et de son effigie funèbre (détachée par la virgule, elle aussi ajoutée à la main). Encore une fois l'effet stylistique est produit par tension entre deux modes d'organisation de l'énoncé.

La scansion du texte peut aussi avoir un rôle plus humble, d'élucidation. Quelques lignes au-dessus de la dernière phrase citée, on trouvait dans l'édition:

> Cette autre curiosité contraire, en laquelle je n'ay point aussi faute d'exemple domestique, me semble germaine à ceste-cy, d'aller se soignant & passionnant à ce dernier poinct à régler son convoy, à quelque particuliere & inusitée parsimonie, à un serviteur & une lanterne.

Le tour est équivoque: on ne sait si l'infinitive "d'aller se soignant . . ." est apposée à la première locution démonstrative ("cette autre curiosité . . .") ou à la seconde ("ceste-cy"); et la contiguïté, comme d'ailleurs la fonction usuelle des démonstratifs déterminés par "-ci," incite à préférer la seconde construction—ce qui provoque un contresens. Après 1588, par une simple majuscule ("*D*'aller . . ."), Montaigne supprime l'effet fallacieux de la contiguïté; mais il laisse la virgule, en dépit des usages de ponctuation, pour ne pas disloquer la phrase de transition. Notons en passant que les éditeurs modernes ont laissé la virgule, mais ôté la majuscule, maintenant ainsi l'équivoque.

D'autres segmentations presque aussi discrètes agissent à l'échelle de l'ensemble du discours. Tel est le cas de quelques majuscules ajoutées dans le chapitre "Du jeune Caton." Montaigne vient de s'en prendre aux détracteurs des "belles et généreuses actions anciennes," et explique: ils font ainsi

> soit par malice, ou par ce vice de ramener leur creance à leur portée, dequoy je viens de parler: soit, comme je pense plustost, pour n'avoir pas la veuë assez forte & assez nette pour imaginer & concevoir la splendeur de la vertu en sa pureté naifve: comme Plutarque dict, que de son temps, il y en avoit qui attribuoient la cause de la mort de jeune Caton, à la crainte qu'il avoit eu de Caesar: dequoy il se picque avecques raison: & peut on juger par là, combien il se fut encore plus offencé de ceux qui l'ont attribuée à l'ambition. (I, 37, 231; Ex. de B., f° 96 v°)

L'allégation, prise dans le fil du propos, paraît simplement destinée à confirmer les hypothèses précédentes sur les causes des dénigrements: et l'on pourrait déplorer un certain relâchement dans l'articulation logique du texte, puisqu'en fait Plutarque, ni dans l'original ni dans le résumé qu'en donne Montaigne, ne traite des motifs de la malveillance.[6] Dans l'Exemplaire de Bordeaux, les propos de Plutarque sur "le jeune Caton" sont détachés et scandés fortement par des majuscules initiales: "*Comme* Plutarque dict . . . ," "*Dequoy* il se picque . . . ," "*Et* peut on juger . . ." Ce qui paraissait n'être qu'un terme de comparaison prend ainsi la quasi-autonomie d'un exemple, susceptible d'être développé pour son intérêt propre. De fait, dès les premières versions, le titre du chapitre désignait cet exemple comme véritable thème de la méditation; la position subordonnée que lui assignent la syntaxe et la ponctuation risquent d'en masquer l'importance, et de diminuer ainsi l'effet de la surprenante prétérition qui en abrège le développement;[7] en marquant son apparition par les demi-ruptures et le surcroît de vivacité dûs aux majuscules de scansion (combinées avec la simplification du système disjonctif, qui uniformise les lignes précédentes), Montaigne raffermit toute l'armature du discours.

C'est parfois la combinaison des signes de ponctuation avec les majuscules de scansion qui accuse, avec une précision remarquable, le schéma logique du texte. Dans les pages où Montaigne décrit ses attitudes successives à l'égard de l'argent et des dépenses, l'édition de 1588 présentait la phrase suivante:

Il ne m'est oncques advenu de trouver la bource de mes amis close: m'estant enjoint au delà de toute autre necessité, la necessité de ne faillir au terme que j'avoy prins, lequel ils m'ont mille fois estendu, voyant l'effort que je me faisoy pour leur satisfaire: en maniere que j'en rendoy une loyauté mesnagere & aucunement piperesse. (I, 14, 62-63; Ex. de B., f° 21)

Sur l'Exemplaire de Bordeaux, Montaigne remodèle le passage. Il se borne à inscrire en majuscules "*M*'estant enjoint . . ." et "*E*n maniere que . . . ," sans toucher aux deux-points précédents; mais il marque un point très appuyé après ". . . que j'avoy prins."—et le fait suivre naturellement d'une majuscule, "*L*equel . . ." (plus tard, il ajoute en interligne ". . . à m'acquiter.", en marquant encore le point, contre son habitude). Le propos se scinde ainsi en deux phrases bien distinctes, relatives aux emprunts: la première, pour faire état du crédit que Montaigne obtenait auprès de ses amis, et l'expliquer; la seconde, pour exposer avec quelque humour le bénéfice que lui procurait sa loyauté de débiteur scrupuleux.

Les lignes suivantes, remodelées par des procédés semblables, présentent en outre un détail significatif, de double correction. Rédaction primitive:

Je sens naturellement quelque volupté à payer, comme si je deschargeois mes espaules d'un ennuyeux poix, & de cette image de servitude. Aussi qu'il y a quelque contentement qui me chatouille à faire une action juste, & contenter autruy.

Premières retouches: Montaigne raccorde les deux phrases en remplaçant le point par un deux-points; selon l'usage, il biffe alors la majuscule de "Aussi" et inscrit, au-dessus et à droite, un *a* minuscule. Deuxième retouche: ayant résolu de faire prévaloir son système de scansion contre les conventions typographiques, il rétablit une majuscule, par surcharge à l'initiale de "Aussi," et ajoute probablement alors une majuscule à "Comme . . . ," sans transformer en point la virgule qui précède. Le résultat est un exposé clairement articulé, en

LIVRE PREMIER.   21
la neceffité, c'eft pluftoft l'abondance qui produiçt l'auarice.
Ie veux dire mõ expèrience autour de ce fubieçt.I'ay vefcu en
trois fortes de condition,depuis eftre forty de l'enfance. Le
premier téps,qui à duré pres de vingt années,ie le paffay,n'aiāt
autres moyés,que fortuites, & defpédant de l'ordonnance &
fecours d'autruy, fans eftat certain & fans prefcriptiõ. Ma def-
péce fe faifoit d'autāt plus allegremét & auec moins de foing,
qu'elle eftoit toute en la temerité de la fortune. Ie ne fu iamais
mieux. Il ne m'eft oncques aduenu de trouuer la bourçe de
mes amis clofe: m'eftant enioint au delà de toute autre neceffité,la neceffité de ne faillir au terme que i'auoy prins, lequel
ils m'ont mille fois attendu, voyant l'effort que ie me faifoy
pour leur fatisfaire : en maniere que i'en rendoy vne loyauté
mefnagere & aucunement piperefle. Ie fens naturellement
quelque volupté à payer, cõme fi ie defchargeois mes efpau-
les d'vn ennuyeux poix, & de cette image de feruitude: Auffi
qu'il y à quelque contentement qui me chatouille à faire vne
açtiõ iufte,& contenter autruy. I'excepte les payements où il
faut venir à marchander & conter, car fi ie ne trouue à qui en
commettre la charge , ie les efloingne honteufement & iniu-
rieufemét tāt que ie puis,de peur de cette altercatiõ,à laquelle
& mõ humeur & ma forme de parler eft du tout incõpatible.
Il n'eft rien que ie haiffe comme à marchander : c'eft vn pur
commerce de menterie & d'impudence: Apres vne heure de debat & de barquignage , l'vn & l'autre abandonne
fa parolle & fes fermens pour cinq fous d'amandement. Et
fi empruntois auec defaduentage: Car n'ayāt point le cœur
de requerir en prefence,i'en renuoyois le hazard fur le papier,
Qui ne faiçt guiere d'effort,& qui prefte grandement la main
au refufer. Ie me remettois de la conduitte de mon befoing
plus gayement aux aftres,& plus librement,que ie n'ay faiçt
depuis à ma prouidence & à mõ fens. La plus part des mefna-
F

dépit de sa brièveté, du plaisir que Montaigne éprouve à "payer," selon ses deux motifs: sentiment d'être quitte, donc libéré d'une obligation; conscience d'avoir agi avec rectitude et satisfait autrui. Quelques lignes plus loin sur la même page on trouve les traces d'une semblable hésitation, qui donne lieu au même type de solution: "Apres une heure de debat . . ." est corrigé en "*a*pres . . ." avec transformation du point précédent en deux-points, puis de nouveau corrigé en "Apres . . ." sans rétablissement du point. Grâce à ce remaniement, la parenthèse sur les marchandages garde à la fois sa structure discontinue et son unité (elle est encore interrompue par une ponctuation forte, après "incompatible," mais la brisure est compensée par le retour du verbe "marchander" qui associe thématiquement les deux parties). De ce fait, il est plus aisé de comprendre que la phrase suivante, "Et si empruntois avec desadvantage . . . " se raccorde, par-delà la parenthèse contiguë, à la formule qui régit l'ensemble du passage, "Il ne m'est oncques advenu de trouver la bource de mes amis close"—ce qui permet de donner à la locution conjonctive "Et si . . ." son sens strict, adversatif (= et cependant), au lieu de la gloser comme le fait Pierre Villey (qui ne tient pas compte de la scansion) par un "et aussi" dénué de signification.

De semblables exemples pourraient être présentés et analysés par dizaines. Interrompons leur série, qui deviendrait vite fastidieuse à l'excès, pour revenir sur les traces de Floyd Gray au sujet du "langage coupé" de Montaigne. Nous venons d'observer quelques effets de l'exploitation combinée de la ponctuation et des majuscules pour segmenter le texte. Ils n'ont rien d'insolite lorsque coïncident les coupures dues à ces deux procédés (et il s'agit alors assez rarement de retouches, l'imprimeur de 1588 ayant tout naturellement placé une majuscule après chaque point). En revanche, dans les très nombreux endroits où une majuscule détache un segment de phrase après un deux-points ou une simple virgule (ce dernier cas étant toujours l'effet d'une retouche autographe), l'énoncé est morcelé, par fragmentation visible des séquences syntaxiques, sans que soit compromise la continuité de son mouvement d'ensemble, puisque les ponctuations fortes qui l'interrompraient ne sont pas inscrites. Les deux tendances contraires, au "pointillisme" et à l'ampleur, ou encore à la vivacité de chaque élément dans un tempo lent, selon les descriptions de Floyd Gray, s'exercent donc simultanément. Même les hésitations de Montaigne en témoignent. A la note où il demande que l'imprimeur n'"espargne les pouincts & lettres majuscules," il ajoute: "Moimesme ai failli souvant à les oster & à mettre des comma où il faloit un poinct." Les corrections réitérées subies par le passage étudié ci-avant en dernier lieu autorisent quelques conjectures sur les motifs de ce revirement. Eprouvant le besoin de tracer plus fermement les grands linéaments de ses propos, il remplace par des "commas" les points qui les scindaient et risquaient d'en briser l'élan. Soucieux d'autre part de ne pas

ANDRÉ TOURNON 231

atténuer le morcellement caractéristique du "langage coupé," il se reproche d'avoir "failli," en affaiblissant la ponctuation. L'emploi des majuscules de scansion, imaginé tardivement, lui a permis de satisfaire à cette seconde exigence sans compromettre les effets recherchés en vertu de la première; il les multiplie donc, méthodiquement, lors des dernières révisions du livre, et pas seulement aux endroits où il avait "mis des commas où il fallait un point." Car le système, d'une extraordinaire souplesse, rend possibles les remodelages les plus fins, et la maîtrise parfaite d'un flux verbal dont la spontanéité n'est pas entravée, la segmentation se précisant après coup.

On entrevoit dès lors, dans ces détails de ponctuation et de graphie, un aspect au moins du problème philosophique du style, et plus généralement de l'*essai*: le projet difficile de coïncider exactement avec la pensée et l'expression "naïves," et en même temps de les contrôler par réflexion, d'affirmer leur sens par l'écriture sans les assujettir à ses schémas prédéterminés. Le schéma vient toujours après, et le contrôle qui donne forme, mais il faut que subsistent les traces du mouvement initial, pensée et parole à l'aventure charriant des matériaux à l'état brut. Cela requiert sans cesse des ajustements, des combinaisons et des superpositions de structures, en palimpsestes dont les strates se modifient mutuellement et se déchiffrent. Le résultat n'est pas des plus simples; l'écrivain a du moins multiplié les repères des infinis parcours qu'il propose à son lecteur et donne parfois à celui-ci le plaisir de rejoindre, par des voies de traverse que jalonnent des centaines d'infimes indices graphiques, les larges avenues du *Style de Montaigne*.

Notes

[1] Floyd Gray, *Le Style de Montaigne* (Paris: Nizet 1958) 29.

[2] Montaigne, *Essais* (Paris: PUF, 1965) III, 5, 873, cité par Gray 37.

[3] *Essais* III, 9, 965 (f° 425 de l'Exemplaire de Bordeaux).

[4] Aucune, semble-t-il, ne modifie ici les additions manuscrites; mais il est aventureux de se prononcer sur ce point. Une virgule—celle qui suit ". . . opinions humaines"—pourrait avoir été ajoutée; en tout cas, les points d'interrogation continuent à faire défaut, ainsi que la virgule ou le deux-points attendus après ". . . Académie."

[5] Reproduction phototypique de l'Exemplaire de Bordeaux (Paris: Hachette, 1912; réimpr. Slatkine 1988) planche 2. Ces consignes autographes de Montaigne à son imprimeur ne sont presque jamais retranscrites dans les éditions modernes des *Essais*. Faut-il s'en étonner? elles n'y sont jamais respectées.

[6] Plutarque blâme les interprétations malveillantes, dans le préambule de son traité "De la malignité d'Hérodote" où Montaigne a trouvé son avis sur Caton, mais il ne forme aucune conjecture sur leurs motifs; son but est d'esquisser une typologie sommaire des procédés de dénigrement qu'il dénoncera ensuite chez Hérodote.

[7] Voir sur ce point "Les Prétéritions marquées ou le sens de l'inachèvement," in *Montaigne et les Essais*, études réunies par Claude Blum (Paris: Champion, 1990).

FRENCH FORUM MONOGRAPHS

Karolyn Waterson. *Molière et l'autorité. Structures sociales, structures comiques.* 1976.

Donna Kuizenga. *Narrative Strategies in* La Princesse de Clèves. 1976.

Ian J. Winter. *Montaigne's Self-Portrait and Its Influence in France, 1580-1630.* 1976.

Judith G. Miller. *Theater and Revolution in France since 1968.* 1977.

Raymond C. La Charité, ed. *O un amy! Essays on Montaigne in Honor of Donald M. Frame.* 1977.

Rupert T. Pickens. *The Welsh Knight. Paradoxicality in Chrétien's* Erec et Enide. 1977.

Carol Clark. *The Web of Metaphor. Studies in the Imagery of Montaigne's* Essais. 1978.

Donald Maddox. *Structure and Sacring. The Systematic Kingdom in Chrétien's* Erec et Enide. 1978.

Betty J. Davis. *The Storytellers in Marguerite de Navare's* Heptaméron. 1978.

Laurence M. Porter. *The Renaissance of the Lyric in French Romanticism. Elegy, "Poëme" and Ode.* 1978.

Bruce R. Leslie. *Ronsard's Successful Epic Venture. The Epyllion.* 1979.

Michelle A. Freeman. *The Poetics of* Translatio Studii *and* Conjointure. *Chrétien de Troyes's* Cligés. 1979.

Robert T. Corum, Jr. *Other Worlds and Other Seas. Art and Vision in Saint-Amant's Nature Poetry.* 1979.

Marcel Muller. *Préfiguration et structure romanesque dans* A la recherche du temps perdu *(avec un inédit de Marcel Proust).* 1979.

Ross Chambers. *Meaning and Meaningfulness. Studies in the Analysis and Interpretation of Texts.* 1979.

Lois Oppenheim. *Intentionality and Intersubjectivity. A Phenomenological Study of Butor's* La Modification. 1980.

Matilda T. Bruckner. *Narrative Invention in Twelfth-Century French Romance. The Convention of Hospitality (1160-1200).* 1980.

Gérard Defaux. *Molière, ou les métamorphoses du comique. De la comédie morale au triomphe de la folie.* 1980.

Raymond C. La Charité. *Recreation, Reflection and Re-Creation. Perspectives on Rabelais's* Pantagruel. 1980.

Jules Brody. *Du style à la pensée. Trois études sur les* Caractères de La Bruyère. 1980.

Lawrence D. Kritzman. *Destruction/Découverte. Le fonctionnement de la rhétorique dans les Essais de Montaigne*. 1980.

Minnette Grunmann-Gaudet and Robin F. Jones, eds. *The Nature of Medieval Narrative*. 1980.

J.A. Hiddleston. *Essai sur Laforgue et les Derniers Vers suivi de Laforgue et Baudelaire*. 1980.

Michael S. Koppisch. *The Dissolution of Character. Changing Perspectives in La Bruyère's Caractères*. 1981.

Hope H. Glidden. *The Storyteller as Humanist. The Serées of Guillaume Bouchet*. 1981.

Mary B. McKinley. *Words in a Corner. Studies in Montaigne's Latin Quotations*. 1981.

Donald M. Frame and Mary B. McKinley, eds. *Columbia Montaigne Conference Papers*. 1981.

Jean-Pierre Dens. *L'Honnête Homme et la critique du goût. Esthétique et société au XVIIᵉ siècle*. 1981.

Vivian Kogan. *The Flowers of Fiction. Time and Space in Raymond Queneau's Les Fleurs bleues*. 1982.

Michael Issacharoff and Jean-Claude Vilquin, eds. *Sartre et la mise en signe*. 1982.

James W. Mileham. *The Conspiracy Novel. Structure and Metaphor in Balzac's Comédie humaine*. 1982.

Andrew G. Suozzo. *The Comic Novels of Charles Sorel. A Study of Structure, Characterization and Disguise*. 1982.

Margaret Whitford. *Merleau-Ponty's Critique of Sartre's Philosophy*. 1982.

Gérard Defaux. *Le Curieux, le glorieux et la sagesse du monde dans la première moitié du XVIᵉ siècle. L'exemple de Panurge (Ulysse, Démosthène, Empédocle)*. 1982.

Doranne Fenoaltea. *"Si haulte Architecture." The Design of Scève's Délie*. 1982.

Peter Bayley and Dorothy Gabe Coleman, eds. *The Equilibrium of Wit. Essays for Odette de Mourgues*. 1982.

Carol J. Murphy. *Alienation and Absence in the Novels of Marguerite Duras*. 1982.

Mary Ellen Birkett. *Lamartine and the Poetics of Landscape*. 1982.

Jules Brody. *Lectures de Montaigne*. 1982.

John D. Lyons. *The Listening Voice. An Essay on the Rhetoric of Saint-Amant*. 1982.

Edward C. Knox. *Patterns of Person. Studies in Style and Form from Corneille to Laclos*. 1983.

Marshall C. Olds. *Desire Seeking Expression. Mallarmé's "Prose pour des Esseintes."* 1983.

Ceri Crossley. *Edgar Quinet (1803-1875). A Study in Romantic Thought.* 1983.

Rupert T. Pickens, ed. *The Sower and His Seed. Essays on Chrétien de Troyes.* 1983.

Barbara C. Bowen. *Words and the Man in French Renaissance Literature.* 1983.

Clifton Cherpack. *Logos in Mythos. Ideas and Early French Narrative.* 1983.

Donald Stone, Jr. *Mellin de Saint-Gelais and Literary History.* 1983.

Louisa E. Jones. *Sad Clowns and Pale Pierrots. Literature and the Popular Comic Arts in 19th-Century France.* 1984.

JoAnn DellaNeva. *Song and Counter-Song. Scève's* Délie *and Petrarch's* Rime. 1983.

John D. Lyons and Nancy J. Vickers, eds. *The Dialectic of Discovery. Essays on the Teaching and Interpretation of Literature Presented to Lawrence E. Harvey.* 1984.

Warren F. Motte, Jr. *The Poetics of Experiment. A Study of the Work of Georges Perec.* 1984.

Jean R. Joseph. *Crébillon fils. Économie érotique et narrative.* 1984.

Carol A. Mossman. *The Narrative Matrix. Stendhal's* Le Rouge et le Noir. 1984.

Ora Avni. *Tics, tics et tics. Figures, syllogismes, récit dans* Les Chants de Maldoror. 1984.

Robert J. Morrissey. *La Rêverie jusqu'à Rousseau. Recherches sur un topos littéraire.* 1984.

Pauline M. Smith and I.D. McFarlane, eds. *Literature and the Arts in the Reign of Francis I. Essays Presented to C.A. Mayer.* 1985.

Jerry Nash, ed. *Pre-Pléiade Poetry.* 1985.

Jack Undank and Herbert Josephs, eds. *Diderot: Digression and Dispersion. A Bicentennial Tribute.* 1984.

Daniel S. Russell. *The Emblem and Device in France.* 1985.

Joan Dargan. *Balzac and the Drama of Perspective. The Narrator in Selected Works of* La Comédie humaine. 1985.

Emile J. Talbot. *Stendhal and Romantic Esthetics.* 1985.

Raymond C. La Charité, ed. *Rabelais's Incomparable Book. Essays on His Art.* 1986.

John Porter Houston. *Patterns of Thought in Rimbaud and Mallarmé.* 1986.

Mary Donaldson-Evans. *A Woman's Revenge. The Chronology of Dispossession in Maupassant's Fiction.* 1986.

Michèle Praeger. *Les Romans de Robert Pinget. Une écriture des possibles.* 1986.

Kari Lokke. *Gérard de Nerval. The Poet as Social Visionary.* 1987.

Virginia A. La Charité. *The Dynamics of Space. Mallarmé's* Un Coup de dés jamais n'abolira le hasard. 1987.

Anthony Pugh. *The Birth of* A la recherche du temps perdu. 1987.

Alain Toumayan. *La Littérature et la hantise du mal. Lectures de Barbey d'Aurevilly, Huysmans et Baudelaire.* 1987.

Robert Griffin. *Rape of the Lock. Flaubert's Mythic Realism.* 1988.

Michel Dassonville, ed. *Ronsard et Montaigne. Écrivains engagés?* 1989.

Lawrence D. Kritzman, ed. *Le Signe et le Texte. Études sur l'écriture au XVIᵉ siècle en France.* 1990.

Martine Motard-Noar. *Les Fictions d'Hélène Cixous. Une autre langue de femme.* 1991.

Barbara C. Bowen and Jerry C. Nash, eds. *Lapidary Inscriptions. Renaissance Essays for Donald A. Stone, Jr.* 1991.

Charles Krance. *L.-F. Céline. The I of the Storm.* 1992.

Maryann De Julio. *Rhetorical Landscapes: The Poetry and Art Criticism of Jacques Dupin.* 1992.

Raymond C. La Charité, ed. *Writing the Renaissance. Essays on Sixteenth-Century French Literature in Honor of Floyd Gray.* 1992.